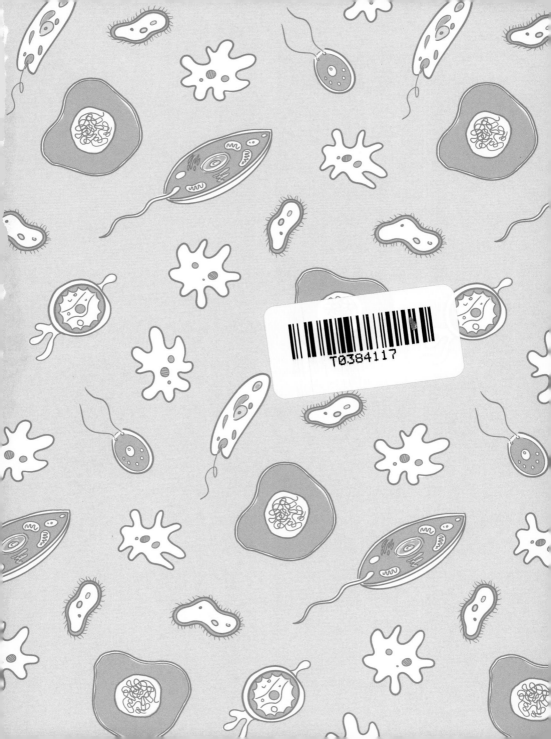

T0384117

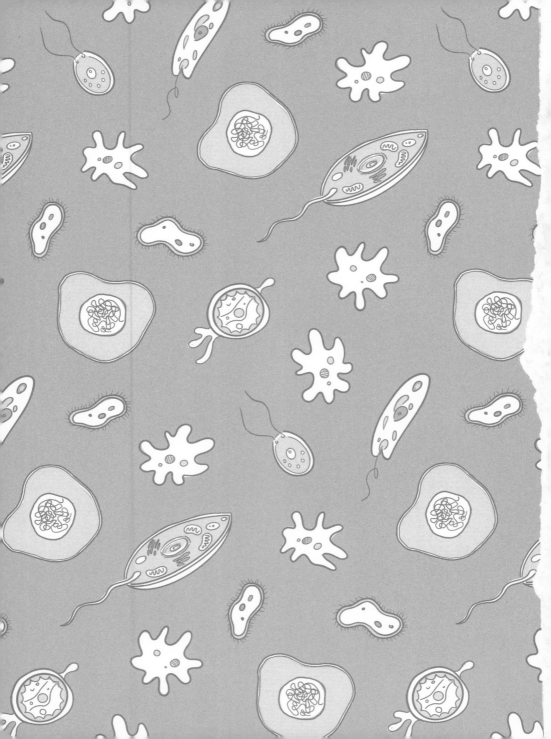

BIOLOGY

Library of Congress Cataloging-in-Publication Data is available.

ISBN: 978-1-5235-0436-7

Writer: Matthew Brown   Reviewer: Keyla Soto Hidalgo
Illustrator: Chris Pearce
Designer: Jessie Gang
Editor: Karen Edwards   Production Editor: Kim Daly
Production Manager: Julie Primavera

Workman books are available at special discounts when purchased in bulk for premiums, sales promotions, fundraising, catalogs, subscription boxes, and more. Workman also offers special discounts for schools and educators purchasing books in bulk. For more information, please email specialmarkets@workman.com.

Workman Publishing Co., Inc.
225 Varick Street
New York, NY 10014-4381

workman.com

WORKMAN, BRAIN QUEST, and BIG FAT NOTE-BOOK are registered trademarks of Workman Publishing Co., Inc.

Printed in Thailand

First printing March 2021

10 9 8 7 6 5 4 3

THE **COMPLETE** HIGH SCHOOL STUDY GUIDE

EVERYTHING YOU NEED TO ACE

BIOLOGY

IN ONE BIG FAT NOTEBOOK

WORKMAN PUBLISHING
NEW YORK

EVERYTHING YOU NEED TO ACE

BIOLOGY

Hi! Welcome to Biology!

This notebook is designed to support you as you work through the major areas of biology. Consider these the notes taken by the smartest person in your biology class—the one who seems to "get" everything and who takes clear, understandable, accurate notes.

Within these chapters you'll find important concepts presented in an accessible, relatable way. Cell theory, how bacteria and viruses work, the world of fungi, the animal kingdom, the human body systems, and more are all presented in a language you can easily understand.

Notes are presented in an organized way:

- Important vocabulary words are highlighted in **YELLOW**.
- All vocabulary words are clearly defined.
- Related terms and concepts are written in BLUE PEN.
- Key concepts are clearly explained and supported by diagrams, illustrations, and charts.

If you want a fun, easy-to-understand resource to use as a companion to your textbook, and you're not so great at taking notes in class, this notebook will help. It hits all the really important stuff you need to ace biology.

CONTENTS

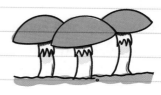

Unit 1

Basics of Biology

Chapter 1

INTRODUCTION TO BIOLOGY

WHAT IS BIOLOGY?

BIOLOGY is the study of life and living things. **BIOLOGISTS** refer to living things as **ORGANISMS**. Organisms, like humans, animals, and plants, all rely on one another to live.

Many organisms grow, change, reproduce, and die. The series of changes that an organism can go through are called the **LIFE CYCLE**.

> **BIOLOGY**
> The study of life and living things.

> **BIOLOGISTS**
> Scientists who study biology.

> **ORGANISM**
> A living thing.

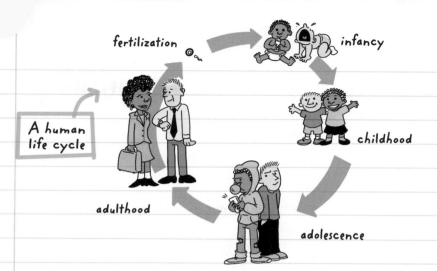

fertilization

infancy

A human
life cycle

childhood

adulthood

adolescence

An important part of biology is studying how organisms
interact and the laws that apply to their life cycles.

Biology is called a LIFE SCIENCE, or NATURAL
SCIENCE, because it is the study of life-forms in nature.

Biology comes from the Greek words *bios*, meaning
"life," and *logia*, meaning "the study of."

Biology translates to "the study of life."

Aristotle (384–322 BC) is said to be
the first biologist. He developed the first
organized study of the natural world.

3

TYPES OF BIOLOGY

Biology is divided into many branches, or **DISCIPLINES**.
The main disciplines are:

BRANCH	THE STUDY OF...
Anatomy	... the bodily structure of organisms.
Botany	... plants.
Ecology	... the relationships between various organisms.
Microbiology	... tiny organisms.
Pathology	... the causes and effects of diseases.
Pharmacology	... the uses and effects of drugs.
Physiology	... the functions of living organisms and their parts.
Taxonomy	... the classification of organisms.
Toxicology	... the nature and effects of poisons.
Zoology	... animals.

Biologists use their specialized knowledge in various ways. There are biologists who work as researchers on food products, medicines, or analyzing diseases. Others use their knowledge to advance agriculture or provide solutions to environmental issues.

THE TOOLS OF THE BIOLOGIST

Specialized tools are sometimes used to study organisms in specific branches of biology. For example, a botanist may need tools like a trowel and shears to collect specimens, while an anatomist might work with tweezers and scalpels.

Microscopes

Most biologists, regardless of their branch, rely on some type of imaging tool. The **MICROSCOPE** was the first imaging tool invented. A microscope is a tool that provides an enlarged image of an object. The most basic concept in biology—that organisms are made up of cells—would not have been discovered without microscopes.

There are two general types of microscopes:

- **COMPOUND** microscopes use visible light as a source of illumination and have multiple lenses (usually two) that can **MAGNIFY** specimens up to 1,500 times their actual size.

  make larger

  You can change the magnification by rotating to a different lens that is closer to the slide.

- ELECTRON microscopes use electron beams as a source of illumination and electron lenses to help magnify specimens up to 100,000 times their actual size.

All scientists begin their experiments with observation. A microscope helps scientists see tiny organisms and understand the fine details of cells, fibers, and other structures invisible to the naked eye. There are various types of compound and electron microscopes. These microscopes can be specialized to fit biologists' fields of study. However, they all have the same basic function: to show details in objects that cannot be seen by the naked human eye.

In a school lab, we usually use a **compound (light) microscope**. It has two lenses: the OCULAR LENS that we look through and the two OBJECTIVE LENSES that are closer to the **SLIDE**. The larger the magnification, the longer the objective lens is. Be careful not to crush the slide when you focus at a high magnification!

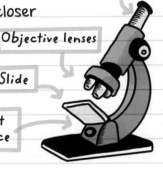

Ocular lens

Objective lenses

Slide

Light source

ELECTRON MICROSCOPES are similar to compound light microscopes, except they use really

SLIDE
A thin piece of glass used to hold a specimen.

6

tiny particles called ELECTRONS instead
of light to show the **SPECIMEN**.
There are two main types of electron
microscopes: TRANSMISSION
ELECTRON and SCANNING ELECTRON.

Other Imaging Tools

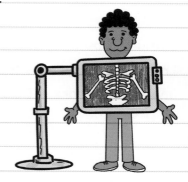

- X-RAY is another imaging
  tool used in biology. It's most
  commonly used in research
  and in the practice of
  medicine. X-rays are a type
  of **RADIATION** that are
  absorbed by various things.
  When a human, or animal,
  undergoes an X-ray, the image
  taken of their body reveals
  the structures that absorbed

RADIATION
The transmission of
energy in the form of
waves through an object.

the most radiation. In the picture, bones appear white
because the calcium in them absorbs the most radiation.
Everything else in the body absorbs less radiation, causing
the color of the organs to look gray or black.

There are many types of X-ray machines,
but they all work in the same way: by sending
X-ray radiation and displaying an image.

- MAGNETIC RESONANCE IMAGING SCANS (MRIs) are another form of imaging used in medicine. MRIs use a magnet and radio waves to produce detailed images of internal organs and muscles that might not show up in an X-ray.

Many microscopes and radiation-based imaging tools are linked to computer programs to create and visualize the images in a more efficient manner.

CHECK YOUR KNOWLEDGE

1. What is biology?

2. Biology is also known as a _____ science.

3. What is the life cycle? Name the stages of the human life cycle.

4. What is the purpose of having different disciplines of biology?

5. Anatomy is a discipline that studies _____ .

6. What is the function of tools for scientists?

7. What is the purpose of a microscope?

8. How can you magnify a specimen using a compound microscope?

9. Why do bones show up on an X-ray image?

10. What does magnetic resonance imaging show in a body?

ANSWERS

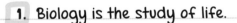

CHECK YOUR ANSWERS

1. Biology is the study of life.

2. natural or life

3. The life cycle is the changes that an organism goes through. The human life cycle includes infancy, childhood, adolescence, adulthood, and reproduction.

4. Disciplines help scientists focus on specific parts of biology.

5. the structure of the body

6. Tools help scientists study their discipline.

7. A microscope shows details that cannot be seen by ordinary human vision.

8. You can magnify a specimen by rotating to a lens that is closer to the slide.

9. Bones absorb the X-ray radiation.

10. Organs and muscles

Chapter 2

CRITICAL THINKING IN BIOLOGY

SCIENTIFIC INQUIRY

Scientists use evidence from observations and experiments to create an explanation of an event. This process is called **SCIENTIFIC INQUIRY**. Scientific inquiry begins with the observation of something unknown, which leads the scientist to ask questions. Scientists follow an organized system to conduct their research of this unknown factor. This system is called the **SCIENTIFIC METHOD**.

SCIENTIFIC METHOD
The use of a system of experimentation and analysis to explore observations and answer questions.

Scientists use the scientific method to help them find evidence, make observations, and organize new information. This system includes several steps that help scientists conduct their experiments.

The scientific method starts with a single question. The type of question asked creates the boundaries for the experiment. The more specific the question is, the more focused the experiment will be.

Using the scientific method is like building a house. The initial question could be thought of as the foundation of the house. Just as a shaky foundation can cause a house to fall apart, not having a clear, specific question can prevent an experiment from having a direction and then failing.

Once a question has been posed, scientists conduct background research to gather information about the experiment they need to perform.

Scientists use the information they've found to make an assumption about the answer to their question.

A **HYPOTHESIS** is a possible explanation for an observation or problem that can further be tested by experimentation. There can be many various hypotheses proposed to answer a single question; however, there should be only one experiment for each hypothesis.

HYPOTHESIS
The proposed answer to a scientific question.

← plural: *hypotheses*

Biologists use **EXPERIMENTS** to test hypotheses. During the experiments, they study VARIABLES, factors that can change an experiment's results. There are two different variables: An **INDEPENDENT VARIABLE** is a condition that has been changed before an experiment. A **DEPENDENT VARIABLE** is the factor that is influenced by the independent variable. It is what is affected during the experiment.

EXPERIMENT
A procedure used to test a hypothesis.

Independent variable
A change is made to a condition.

Dependent variable
The result showing the effect of the change made.

Any data from the experiment, even if that data proves the hypothesis wrong, is collected and analyzed in a RESULTS step. This analysis can be done by the team performing the experiment or by other scientists. After results are gathered and analyzed, conclusions can be made. These conclusions are important, and may result in the need for a brand-new experiment, which is why collecting all the results is important.

After the analysis scientists compare the conclusion and the original hypothesis. They ask: *Does the conclusion confirm or support the hypothesis?* If it does, then the experiment is complete and the results are considered the answer to the question.

When a hypothesis is supported by the results of an experiment, the hypothesis becomes a THEORY. If the hypothesis is not supported, a new hypothesis must be made and tested. In these cases, the scientific method begins the cycle again; from the conclusion that proved the hypothesis wrong, to a new hypothesis, to more experimentation.

Does the conclusion support the hypothesis?

YES

You have a theory!

NO

Back to the drawing board with a new hypothesis!

The final step in the scientific method is the SHARING OF RESULTS. Publishing results enables the scientific and medical communities to evaluate the findings themselves. It also provides instructions so that other researchers can repeat the experiment, build on it, and verify and/or confirm the results. Results should also be shared with other scientists who may be able to use those results in their own experiments in the future.

Results are often shared in scientific journals, which are written by the scientists who performed the experiment. In the case of clinical studies, published results can help make informed decisions about a person's health or behaviors.

Scientific Method

CHECK YOUR KNOWLEDGE

1. What is the purpose of the scientific method?

2. A(n) _____ must be created before the scientific method can be used.

3. What helps with focusing the scope of the experiment?

4. What is the purpose of doing background research?

5. How do scientists conduct experimentation?

6. What happens to the dependent variable when a change is made to the independent variable?

7. What is the purpose of the sharing results step?

8. What is the purpose of the analysis step?

9. If the conclusion proved the hypothesis wrong, what is the next step?

10. The process of scientific inquiry can be a _____.

ANSWERS

CHECK YOUR ANSWERS

1. The scientific method helps scientists structure their research.

2. inquiry/question

3. A specific question

4. Background research is used to make an assumption about the answer to the question.

5. By using scientific tools and observation

6. The dependent variable will also change.

7. The sharing results step exists for scientists to share their results with the public and with fellow scientists.

8. The analysis step allows you to examine your results to see if your hypothesis is supported.

9. The next step would be to restart the scientific method with a new hypothesis.

10. cycle

Chapter 3

CHARACTERISTICS OF LIFE

All living things share the same characteristics of life:

- They are made up of one or more **CELLS**.

> **CELLS**
> The basic units of life.

- They need energy to live.

- They respond to **STIMULI**—they react to their environment (for instance, light, temperature, and touch).

> **STIMULUS**
> (pl. stimuli)
> Anything that causes a response.

LIFE FUNCTIONS

All ORGANISMS (living things) must have the potential to carry out certain behaviors, known as **LIFE FUNCTIONS**. Life functions are processes that an organism takes on to help it survive. The life functions are:

1. Growth: an increase in the number of cells.

Some organisms, in order to live better in an environment, need more cells. As more cells are made, the organism goes through the process of growth.

> Adults are larger in size than babies because they have more cells. The growth in cells helps them live better in their environment.

2. Reproduction: the creation of a new organism with its own cells.

parent

offspring

A new organism is created from parent organisms. The new organism is referred to as OFFSPRING. Some offspring are born looking like their parents (for example, human babies); other offspring are born in one form and then change as they grow to another (like tadpoles changing into frogs).

Reproduction can happen with either one- or two-parent organisms.

- When one parent organism reproduces by itself, the process is called ASEXUAL REPRODUCTION. The offspring looks like the parent. Bacteria usually reproduce asexually.

- When two parents reproduce, it's called SEXUAL REPRODUCTION. Many plants and animals are sexual reproducers.

3. **Nutrition**: the taking in of food (nutrients).

SLURP!

All living things need **NUTRIENTS** to survive. Nutrients keep an organism healthy.

NUTRIENT
Any substance that promotes life and provides energy.

Organisms can be categorized according to how they get their nutrition:

- **AUTOTROPHS**, organisms that can make their own food, such as plants.

- **HETEROTROPHS**, organisms that cannot make their own food, such as animals.

Auto comes from the Greek word *autos*, meaning "self." *Hetero* comes from the Greek word *heteros*, meaning "other." *-troph* comes from the Greek word *trophos*, meaning "one who is nourished."

Autotrophs are nourished by themselves, and heterotrophs are nourished by others.

4. Respiration: the breakdown of nutrients to get energy.

After nutrients are ingested, **METABOLISM** begins. There are two metabolic processes:

- **DIGESTION**, where nutrients are broken down into simpler forms that are easier for the organism to use.

METABOLISM
The set of chemical reactions that maintain the life of an organism.

- **CELLULAR RESPIRATION**, using glucose and oxygen along with chemical reactions to produce energy from nutrients.

5. Transport: In humans, it involves, for example, the movement of nutrients from the stomach to the cells.

Before simple nutrients can be used by cells, they must first be transported from the stomach throughout the body in a process called **CIRCULATION**. Once the nutrients reach the cell, they are absorbed and become part of the process of respiration.

CIRCULATION
The movement of something through the body of an organism.

6. Synthesis: the use of energy to build more complex chemicals within the body, such as carbohydrates and proteins.

When an organism gets the energy it needs, it can create complex chemicals that perform various tasks. For example, it can create proteins, which help support the structure and function of the body.

7. **Excretion**: Removes waste products from the body.

Not all substances ingested are nutrients. Some of these substances are not useful to an organism. In these cases, the organism excretes the substance. There are some substances that act as both a nutrient and a waste product. After the organism excretes it, they must replace the product by ingesting or creating more of it.

> Water is an example of a material that humans ingest that is also a waste product. We drink it, and also excrete it, for example, as sweat.

8. **Regulation**: Organisms survive in changing environments by changing the conditions within their bodies.

Organisms sense what is happening in their environment and adapt to any changes in order to maintain **HOMEOSTASIS**.

HOMEOSTASIS
A state of steady internal physical and chemical conditions set by the body. Homeostasis keeps an organism alive despite a changing external environment.

Homeostasis comes from the Greek words *homeo*, meaning "same," and *stasis*, meaning "state." Homeostasis describes a state in which something remains the same.

An example of homeostasis in humans: When it's hot, we sweat to cool down our bodies. When it's cold, we shiver, which helps warm up our bodies.

An organism's body can also change over time to better fit a new environment. This process is called **ADAPTION**. Some evolving creatures may gain new traits that help them survive in their environment.

ADAPTION
A behavior or physical characteristic that allows an organism to survive or reproduce in its environment.

Adaptations are changes in a species that occur over many generations due to environmental pressures. The organisms do not make a conscious choice to adapt. Adaptations can be behavioral or physiological.

Camels have adapted to living in the desert. They are known to be able to survive without drinking water for six or seven months.

NO THANKS, I'M FINE.

CHECK YOUR KNOWLEDGE

1. What are three characteristics of all living things?

2. What are life functions?

3. Growth is the increase in the amount of _____ within an organism.

4. What is the outcome of reproduction?

5. What form of reproduction do bacteria usually undergo?

6. Why are nutrients important?

7. What are the methods by which nutrients can be gained?

8. When a substance is not useful to the body, it is _____.

9. What is the purpose of homeostasis?

10. How does adaption impact an organism's ability to survive in their environment?

ANSWERS

CHECK YOUR ANSWERS

1. They are made of cells, need energy to survive, and respond to stimuli.

2. The processes that an organism takes on that help it survive

3. cells

4. The creation of a new organism

5. Asexual reproduction

6. Nutrients are substances that promote life and provide energy.

7. Nutrients can either be created by the organism or ingested.

8. excreted

9. Homeostasis maintains the stability of the body's internal environment.

10. An organism may gain new traits that can either help it survive in its environment or prevent its survival.

Chapter 4

BIOLOGICAL CLASSIFICATION

CLASSIFICATION

The process of organizing living things is called
CLASSIFICATION. Scientists classify organisms by their
structure and how closely related they are. They arrange
them into groups and categories based on the features they
have in common.

Classification Hierarchy

TAXONOMISTS, scientists who classify organisms, developed
categories to organize every discovered organism. The
categories are DOMAIN, KINGDOM, PHYLUM, CLASS, ORDER,
FAMILY, GENUS, and SPECIES.

The order of categories from the broadest (at the top) to the most specific (at the bottom):

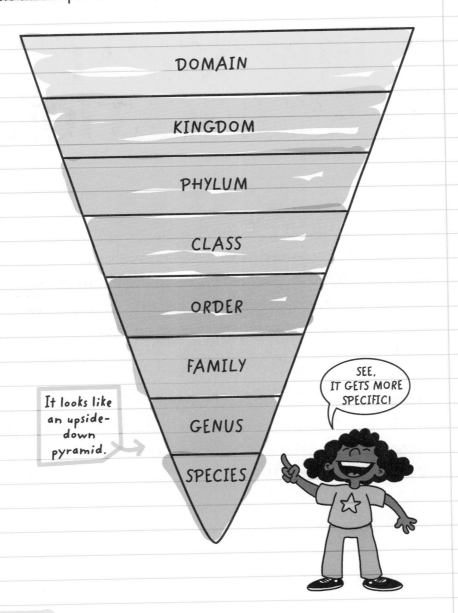

DOMAIN

KINGDOM

PHYLUM

CLASS

ORDER

FAMILY

GENUS

SPECIES

It looks like an upside-down pyramid.

SEE, IT GETS MORE SPECIFIC!

Use this mnemonic to recall the classification system:

Demanding Kids Prefer Cheese
Over Fried Green Spinach!

PUSH!

Domain, Kingdom, Phylum, Class,
Order, Family, Genus, Species

There are fewer and fewer organisms as you get to the more specific categories. So, a kingdom has many more organisms than a genus.

DOMAIN

The domain is the highest rank in the classification system. It is the broadest of all categories. Domain divides life-forms into three categories. All organisms fall under these three groups.

- Eukarya

- Bacteria

- Archaea

KINGDOM

Kingdom has the second-highest rank in the classification system. It is divided into six groups: Archaebacteria, Eubacteria, Protista, Fungi, Plantae, and Animalia. Organisms within each kingdom have different characteristics from organisms in the other kingdoms.

Latin names

ARCHAEBACTERIA
- From the Archaea domain
- Single-celled organisms
- Live in extreme environments: hot, toxic, acidic, or salty

EUBACTERIA
- From the Bacteria domain
- Single-celled organisms
- Live everywhere that archaebacteria don't

There are more eubacteria living in your mouth than there are humans living on Earth! But most of them are harmless.

PROTISTA
- From the Eukarya domain
- Single-celled or multicellular organisms
- Can be similar to Fungi, Plantae, or Animalia kingdoms in behavior and structure

FUNGI
- From the Eukarya domain
- Single-celled or multicellular organisms
- Are **decomposers** ← break down and recycle nutrients back into the environment
- Mainly live in soil

PLANTAE

YEP!

- Also known as the PLANT KINGDOM
- From the Eukarya domain
- Multicellular organisms
- Earth's primary producers of oxygen. Plants are crucial to the life of almost every other organism.

ANIMALIA
- Also known as the ANIMAL KINGDOM
- From the Eukarya domain
- Multicellular organisms
- Breathe oxygen during the process of metabolism

PHYLUM

Organisms in different phyla (plural of phylum) have different traits from one another.

In the **Animalia Kingdom**, there are many phyla. These phyla are divided into two categories:

- VERTEBRATES—**have a backbone** (for protection and mobility); make up 3 percent of all phyla in the Animalia kingdom.

  Examples: mammals, fish, amphibians, birds, reptiles

- INVERTEBRATES—**have no backbone**; make up 97 percent of all phyla in the Animalia kingdom.

  Examples: anthropods (lobsters, crabs, insects, spiders), mollusks, worms

Because vertebrates have so few organisms in comparison to invertebrates, they have their own phylum: CHORDATA.

All **CHORDATES** (organisms in the Chordata group) have these features at some point in their lives:

■ **pharyngeal slits**—openings that connect the inside of the throat to the outside, the neck; sometimes develop into gills.

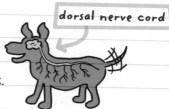

dorsal nerve cord

■ **dorsal nerve cord**—runs down the back of the animal, connecting the brain with muscles and other organs.

■ **notochord**—a rod running beneath the nerve cord and supporting it.

■ **post-anal tail**—a section of the body that extends beyond the anus, used for movement.

In many vertebrates (like humans) some of these features appear only during the embryonic stage (before the organism is born).

post-anal tail

CLASS

Organisms classified as Chordata are separated further into groups, called CLASSES.

There are seven classes in all. Three fish classes: agnatha (jawless), chondrichthyes (cartilaginous), and osteichthyes (bony); and:

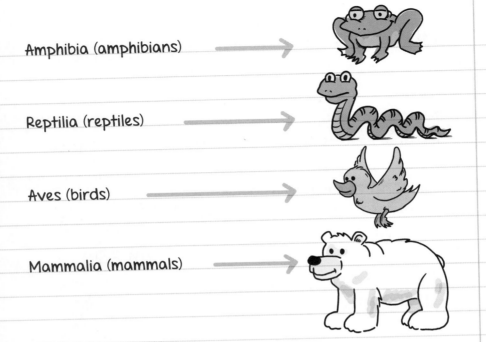

Amphibia (amphibians)

Reptilia (reptiles)

Aves (birds)

Mammalia (mammals)

Even though these organisms are of various classes, they are related because they are all vertebrates.

ORDER

There are different groups of animals in each class. These groups are called ORDERS. For example, Primates are an order within the Mammalia class. Animals in the Primate order are known for having large brains compared to their body weight, flat nails on their fingers instead of claws, and demonstrate social organization.

Primates include apes, gorillas, orangutans, lemurs, and baboons.

FAMILY

FAMILY is the subgroup of order. For example, there are 16 families within the Primates group. One of the Primate families is the HOMINIDAE, also known as the "great apes." Great apes are known to have a large body size, no tail, and eat both plants and other animals.

Gorillas and orangutans are part of the Hominidae family. All members of this family can recognize themselves in mirrors. This type of self-awareness is only possible in complex brains.

GENUS

There are four genera (plural of genus) in the Hominidae family:

- *Homo*—humans

- *Pongo*—orangutans

- gorilla (genus name is *Gorilla*)

- *Pan*—chimpanzees and bonobos

The *Homo* genus is composed of organisms that walk primarily on two legs, can make tools to solve problems, and have well-developed opposable thumbs.

thumbs that can touch the other fingers, giving the ability to grip objects

Homo comes from the Latin word *homonis*, which means "human being." Only humans exist in this genus.

SPECIES

The smallest and most specific unit of classification is the SPECIES. **Species are groups of organisms with similar characteristics that are able to reproduce only with one another.** For example, humans can reproduce only with other humans.

There were once three species within the *Homo* genus: the *habilis*, the *erectus*, and the *sapiens*. Now there is only one—the *sapiens*. The other two species have no living members.

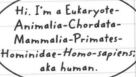

Hi. I'm a Eukaryote-Animalia-Chordata-Mammalia-Primates-Hominidae-Homo-sapiens; aka human.

Modern humans fall under the *sapiens* species. This species is separated from the other species by the size of its skull, which developed to protect its large brain. *Sapiens* are capable of making advanced tools for both survivability and entertainment.

Example of a species classification: a domestic cat.

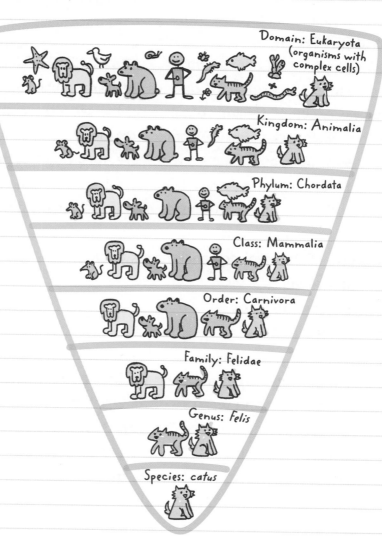

Domain: Eukaryota (organisms with complex cells)

Kingdom: Animalia

Phylum: Chordata

Class: Mammalia

Order: Carnivora

Family: Felidae

Genus: *Felis*

Species: *catus*

Binomial Nomenclature

Biologists use CAROLUS LINNAEUS's system of classification when referring to an organism. Linnaeus's system, which entails naming species using two terms, is called BINOMIAL NOMENCLATURE. This just means "a name with

Carolus Linnaeus
(1707–1778)
is known as the father of taxonomy because his system of classification, created in the 1700s, is still used today.

two terms." The first word defines the **genus**, which is the smallest group of similar species, and the second word defines the **species** itself. Binomial nomenclature is sort of like a first and last name—one is more specific than the other. Binomial nomenclature helps scientists from all over the world know which organisms have which characteristics.

Examples of binomial nomenclature system:

humans = *Homo sapiens*

dogs = *Canis familiaris*

cats = *Felis catus*

Binomial comes from the Latin prefix *bi-*, which means "two," and the Latin word *nomia*, which means "term." *Nomenclature* comes from the Latin words *nomen*, meaning "name," and *clatura*, meaning "calling." Binomial nomenclature translates to "two-term naming."

CHECK YOUR KNOWLEDGE

1. What is the purpose of classification?

2. What are the highest and lowest levels of classification?

3. How are eubacteria and archaebacteria different?

4. Which of the kingdoms survives best in hot and acidic environments?

5. What is a special characteristic of fungi?

6. The phylum of organisms with a backbone is called _____ .

7. How are fish, amphibians, reptiles, birds, and mammals related?

8. What species do human beings belong to?

9. A two-term name is called a _____ .

10. What two groups make up the two-term naming system?

ANSWERS

41

CHECK YOUR ANSWERS

1. To organize the organisms that have been and will be discovered

2. Domain is the highest classification; species is the lowest.

3. Archaebacteria live in extreme environments. Eubacteria live in all other places that are not extreme.

4. Archaebacteria

5. Fungi are decomposers. Their function is to help break down and recycle nutrients into the environment.

6. Chordata

7. They all have a backbone.

8. *Homo sapiens*

9. binomial

10. The genus and the species

Unit 2

The Chemistry of Life

Chapter 5

ATOMS AND MOLECULES

MATTER describes everything that we can touch, taste, see, smell, or feel. Matter is anything that has mass (takes up space). The smallest unit of matter is the **ATOM**. Atoms are so small that they cannot be seen by the human eye or by a compound microscope.

> **MATTER**
> Anything that has mass and takes up space.

> **ATOM**
> The smallest unit of matter.

> From the Greek word that means "cannot be divided."

As an atom absorbs energy (in the form of heat, light, sound), it vibrates and then releases that energy. This is

> Energy comes in the form of light, sound, and heat.

because atoms prefer to have as little energy as possible. For example, when the sun's bright light shines on Earth, it excites the atoms in the atmosphere, causing them to release energy, mostly in the form of heat.

Because the sun is out in the morning and not in the night, mornings are usually warmer than nights.

Atoms are more stable the less energy they have. All atoms try to release energy to be as stable as possible.

In science, cold temperature is defined as an absence of heat. This is why outer space, an environment with few to no atoms, has temperatures that can be as low as -455 degrees Fahrenheit.

ELEMENTS

Scientists have determined that there are around 118 different kinds of atoms that exist in nature. Different types of atoms are called ELEMENTS, and each has been listed in a PERIODIC TABLE of elements.

ELEMENT
Any substance that cannot be broken down into any simpler chemical substance. There are 118 elements.

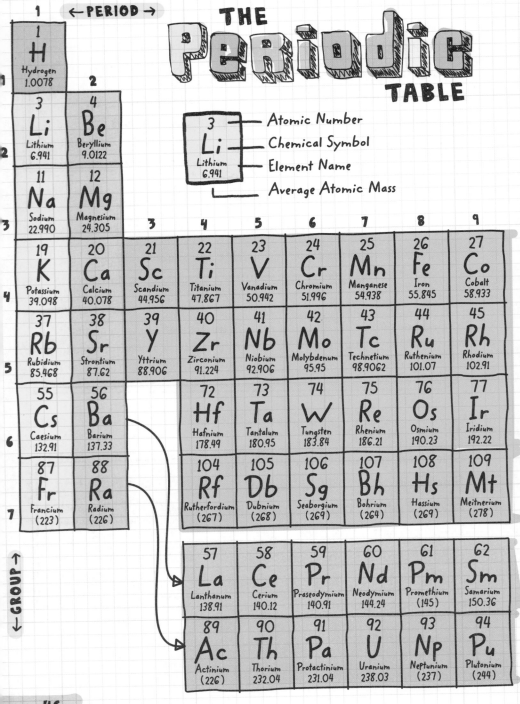

THE PERIODIC TABLE

← PERIOD →

Legend:
- 3 — Atomic Number
- Li — Chemical Symbol
- Lithium — Element Name
- 6.941 — Average Atomic Mass

1								
1 H Hydrogen 1.0078	2							
3 Li Lithium 6.941	4 Be Beryllium 9.0122							
11 Na Sodium 22.990	12 Mg Magnesium 24.305	3	4	5	6	7	8	9
19 K Potassium 39.098	20 Ca Calcium 40.078	21 Sc Scandium 44.956	22 Ti Titanium 47.867	23 V Vanadium 50.942	24 Cr Chromium 51.996	25 Mn Manganese 54.938	26 Fe Iron 55.845	27 Co Cobalt 58.933
37 Rb Rubidium 85.468	38 Sr Strontium 87.62	39 Y Yttrium 88.906	40 Zr Zirconium 91.224	41 Nb Niobium 92.906	42 Mo Molybdenum 95.95	43 Tc Technetium 98.9062	44 Ru Ruthenium 101.07	45 Rh Rhodium 102.91
55 Cs Caesium 132.91	56 Ba Barium 137.33		72 Hf Hafnium 178.49	73 Ta Tantalum 180.95	74 W Tungsten 183.84	75 Re Rhenium 186.21	76 Os Osmium 190.23	77 Ir Iridium 192.22
87 Fr Francium (223)	88 Ra Radium (226)		104 Rf Rutherfordium (267)	105 Db Dubnium (268)	106 Sg Seaborgium (269)	107 Bh Bohrium (264)	108 Hs Hassium (269)	109 Mt Meitnerium (278)

← GROUP ↓

57 La Lanthanum 138.91	58 Ce Cerium 140.12	59 Pr Praseodymium 140.91	60 Nd Neodymium 144.24	61 Pm Promethium (145)	62 Sm Samarium 150.36
89 Ac Actinium (226)	90 Th Thorium 232.04	91 Pa Protactinium 231.04	92 U Uranium 238.03	93 Np Neptunium (237)	94 Pu Plutonium (244)

→ ALKALI METALS
→ ALKALINE EARTH METALS
→ LANTHANIDES
→ ACTINIDES
→ TRANSITION METALS
→ UNKNOWN PROPERTIES
→ POST-TRANSITION METALS
→ METALLOIDS
→ OTHER NONMETALS

→ HALOGENS
→ NOBLE GASES
→ NEW AND PENDING DISCOVERIES

13	14	15	16	17	18
					2 He Helium 4.0026
5 B Boron 10.806	6 C Carbon 12.009	7 N Nitrogen 14.006	8 O Oxygen 15.999	9 F Fluorine 18.998	10 Ne Neon 20.180
13 Al Aluminum 26.982	14 Si Silicon 28.084	15 P Phosphorus 30.974	16 S Sulfur 32.059	17 Cl Chlorine 35.446	18 Ar Argon 39.948

10	11	12	13	14	15	16	17	18
28 Ni Nickel 58.693	29 Cu Copper 63.546	30 Zn Zinc 65.38	31 Ga Gallium 69.723	32 Ge Germanium 72.63	33 As Arsenic 74.922	34 Se Selenium 78.96	35 Br Bromine 79.904	36 Kr Krypton 83.798
46 Pd Palladium 106.42	47 Ag Silver 107.87	48 Cd Cadmium 112.41	49 In Indium 114.82	50 Sn Tin 118.71	51 Sb Antimony 121.76	52 Te Tellurium 127.60	53 I Iodine 126.90	54 Xe Xenon 131.29
78 Pt Platinum 195.08	79 Au Gold 196.97	80 Hg Mercury 200.59	81 Tl Thallium 204.38	82 Pb Lead 207.2	83 Bi Bismuth 208.98	84 Po Polonium (209)	85 At Astatine (210)	86 Rn Radon (222)
110 Ds Darmstadtium (281)	111 Rg Roentgenium (281)	112 Cn Copernicium (285)	113 Nh Nihonium (286)	114 Fl Flerovium (289)	115 Mc Moscovium (289)	116 Lv Livermorium (293)	117 Tn Tennessine (294)	118 Og Oganesson (294)

63 Eu Europium 151.96	64 Gd Gadolinium 157.25	65 Tb Terbium 158.93	66 Dy Dysprosium 162.50	67 Ho Holmium 164.93	68 Er Erbium 167.26	69 Tm Thulium 168.93	70 Yb Ytterbium 173.04	71 Lu Lutetium 174.97
95 Am Americium (243)	96 Cm Curium (247)	97 Bk Berkelium (247)	98 Cf Californium (251)	99 Es Einsteinium (252)	100 Fm Fermium (257)	101 Md Mendelevium (258)	102 No Nobelium (259)	103 Lr Lawrencium (262)

47

Dmitry Ivanovich Mendeleyev, a Russian scientist, invented the periodic table in 1869.

The periodic table is like a huge grid in which all the elements are organized. Each element sits in a specific place in the grid, according to its **ATOMIC NUMBER**. The number of protons in an element define its position in the table according to MODERN PERIODIC LAW.

SYMBOLS, NUMBERS, AND NAMES OF THE PERIODIC TABLE

Each element on the periodic table is assigned a **CHEMICAL SYMBOL**, which is one or two letters. The first letter is always uppercase and the second letter (if there is one) is lowercase.

For example:

Sodium is Na   Magnesium is Mg   Sulfur is S

> **Element**—composed of one type of atom
> **Periodic table**—a table of all the elements
> **Chemical symbol**—one or two letters that represent each element

Each square on the periodic table has the same information:
the atomic number, the chemical symbol, the element name,
and the average atomic mass.

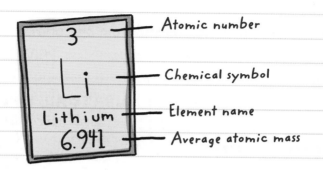

- Atomic number
- Chemical symbol
- Element name
- Average atomic mass

The **atomic number** is the number of protons an atom
contains. Each element has a different number of protons
that makes it unique.

The **atomic mass** is the average mass of a typical atom
of that element.

The periodic table is organized by rows and columns.
A horizontal row is called a **PERIOD**. A vertical column is
called a **GROUP** or **FAMILY**. The elements are arranged
from left to right by increasing **ATOMIC NUMBER**. As you
go across from left to right, each element has one more
electron and one more proton than the element to the left
of it.

For example, Hydrogen (H) has one proton, Helium (He) has two protons, and so on. Elements in the same column have similar physical and chemical properties.

Despite elements being different from one another, they are all made up of the same three particles: PROTONS, NEUTRONS, and ELECTRONS. All three of these elements are referred to as **SUBATOMIC PARTICLES**.

SUBATOMIC PARTICLE
A substance that is smaller than an atom.

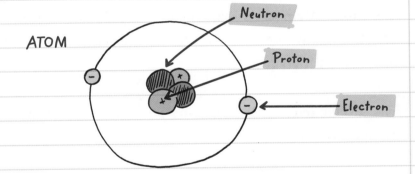

ATOM

Neutron

Proton

Electron

Sub is a prefix meaning "under" or "below"; *subatomic* means "below an atom." Subatomic particles refer to particles that are below an atom in size.

All three particles have different qualities. Both protons and electrons contain **ELECTRICAL CHARGES**, or quantities of electricity that can be either positive or negative. Protons hold a positive electrical charge. Electrons hold a negative charge.

Particles with the same electrical charge tend to **REPEL** one another, while those with opposite charges **ATTRACT** one another.

REPEL
To push away from.

ATTRACT
To bring closer to.

Neutrons do not have a charge. Neutrons play a key role in the structure of the atom. The center of an atom is its **NUCLEUS**, which is made of both protons and neutrons.

The protons within the nucleus give it a positive charge, which attracts the negatively charged electrons, causing the electrons to orbit (move around) the nucleus.

Atoms that have the same number of protons, but different numbers of neutrons, are called *isotopes*.

Because atoms are so small, scientists need to use **models** to represent them. However, because the atom cannot be seen by humans, the model of the atom has changed many times as scientists have learned more about it.

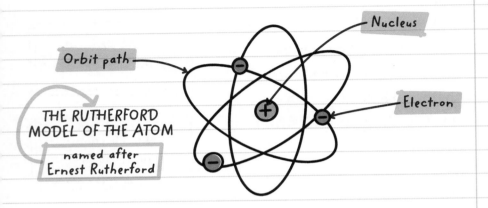

Nucleus

Orbit path

THE RUTHERFORD
MODEL OF THE ATOM

named after
Ernest Rutherford

Electron

The Rutherford model showed the atom as a tiny solar system with electrons orbiting around a nucleus.

ELECTRON SHELL

Electrons move outside the nucleus in various **SHELLS**, or energy levels. Think of shells as rings. The ring closer to the nucleus is numbered 1, followed by a ring around it numbered 2, which then has a ring around it numbered 3, and so on, as they extend outward. The greater the energy of the electron, the higher level shell it occupies (or the farther the outermost ring is from the nucleus).

The relationship between the nucleus and the electron shells is similar to the relationship between the planets and the sun within the solar system. Planets orbit at certain distances away from the sun. Some planets, such as Mercury, Venus, and Earth, have smaller orbits, while Mars, Jupiter, and Saturn have larger orbits. All the planets' orbits are affected by the gravity of the sun. The planets that are farthest from the sun feel less of its gravity.

An atom acts as its own solar system: The shells are the orbits taken by electrons, and the nucleus is the center that the electrons navigate around. The electrons in the shells closest to the nucleus (those that have the smallest orbits) are referred to as **CORE ELECTRONS**.

Core electrons have the strongest attractive force to the positively charged nucleus, and so they are the most stable. Stable subatomic particles have the lowest energy within their atom.

CORE ELECTRONS
The electrons in the shells closest to the nucleus.

The electrons in the shells farthest from the nucleus (those that have the largest orbits) are called **VALENCE ELECTRONS**. Valence electrons are more unstable than core electrons and have the highest energy levels. Because of this they are more likely to break away from the influence of the nucleus.

VALENCE ELECTRONS
Electrons in the shells that are farthest away from the nucleus.

There can be more than one valence electron within a shell. The maximum number of valence electrons in any orbit is dependent on how small the orbit is. The closer the shell is to the nucleus, the fewer electrons there are.

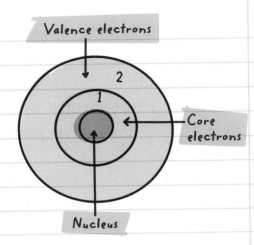

Valence electrons

2

1

Core electrons

Nucleus

This is due to the negative charge of each electron. If there were too many electrons in a small orbit, they would repel one another. This would cause the energy of the whole atom to increase, leading to a more unstable atom. The larger the orbit becomes, the more electrons can fit in it without influencing one another.

The shell closest to the nucleus holds a maximum of 2 electrons, the next shell holds a maximum of 8, and the third holds a maximum of 18.

Because of an atom's preference for stability, electrons will always occupy the shells closest to the nucleus—the core shells—before occupying the shells farthest away.

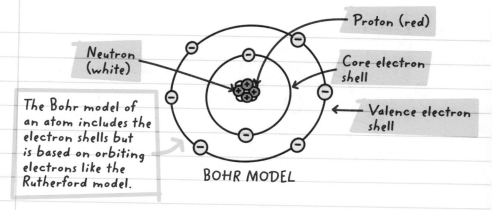

Proton (red)

Neutron (white)

Core electron shell

The Bohr model of an atom includes the electron shells but is based on orbiting electrons like the Rutherford model.

Valence electron shell

BOHR MODEL

The Bohr model shows 8 protons and neutrons in the nucleus of the atom, and 2 energy levels with 8 electrons.

ATOMIC BONDING

An atom usually seeks to be at its lowest energy state so that it can remain stable. There are two exceptions:

- Energy is added to it.
- An atom's valence electron shell is not completely filled.

Valence electrons contain a higher energy than other electrons in an atom. When an electron shell is filled, all electrons in that shell behave similarly to core electrons, increasing the atom's stability and lowering its energy.

An incomplete valence shell causes attractive forces from the positively charged nucleus to spill out of the atom. Electrons that are nearby will move toward the nucleus and plug those leaks, completing the valence shell in the process.

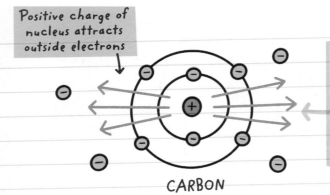

Positive charge of nucleus attracts outside electrons

The atom with an incomplete valence shell is like a leaky cup of water. Electrons plug the leaks and complete the valence shell.

CARBON

There are many atoms that have incomplete valence shells. These atoms participate in **ATOMIC BONDING**, the process where atoms interact with other atoms to lower their energy.

There are different types of atomic bonding. One of the most prevalent is **COVALENT BONDING**. During this process atoms share pairs of electrons. The shared pairs of electrons fill the outermost energy levels of the bonded atom.

A carbon atom needs 4 electrons to fill its outer energy shell. It bonds with 4 hydrogen atoms to share 1 electron from each atom.

Electrons shared between carbon + hydrogen

COVALENT BOND BETWEEN
CARBON + 4 HYDROGEN

Atoms will bond with as many other atoms as necessary to complete their shells. These groupings are called **MOLECULES**. If a molecule is made of two or more different elements, it is called a **COMPOUND**.

MOLECULES
A group of atoms bonded together.

Some elements are **DIATOMIC**, meaning that they exist as molecules composed of two of the same atom. Diatomic molecules include oxygen, hydrogen, nitrogen, bromine, iodine, fluorine, and chlorine.

COMPOUND
Combinations of two or more different atoms.

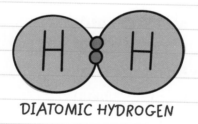

DIATOMIC HYDROGEN

MATTER

Scientists define anything that takes up space as matter. Matter is created by the various ways that atoms bond. Matter can appear in different states–solid, liquid, or gas. The arrangement of the molecules or atoms (generally called "particles") and how they behave determine the characteristics of substances. The amount of movement of the molecules and the distance between them determine its state.

STATE OF MATTER	DEFINITION	EXAMPLE
Solid atom	• Tightly packed atoms • Rigid	• Rocks • Ice • Wood
Liquid atom	• Atoms are close to one another, but not tightly packed together. • Atoms slide past one another, so it does not have a defined shape.	• Water • Blood • Gasoline
Gas atom	• Atoms are relatively distant from one another.	• Air • Water Vapor • Carbon Dioxide

CHECK YOUR KNOWLEDGE

1. How many elements have been cataloged in the periodic table of elements?

2. What three particles are atoms made of?

3. What does it mean to say that a particle is "subatomic"?

4. What do protons and electrons contain that a neutron does not?

5. _____ electrons are electrons with shells close to the nucleus.

6. What is the reason for the small number of electrons in the shell closest to the nucleus?

7. Why does an atom bond?

8. What occurs in a covalent bond?

9. What is the difference between an atom and a molecule?

10. What is the difference between a solid and a gas?

ANSWERS

CHECK YOUR ANSWERS

1. 118 elements

2. Protons, electrons, and neutrons

3. A subatomic particle is a particle that is smaller than an atom.

4. An electrical charge

5. Core

6. The shell closest to the nucleus has a small orbit. A small number of electrons ensures that they don't interfere with one another.

7. It bonds to lower its energy and increase its stability.

8. Atoms "share" their electrons with one another.

9. An atom is the smallest unit of an element which may or may not exist independently. A molecule is a group of atoms bonded together.

10. In solids, atoms are tightly packed together. In gases, atoms are farther apart.

Chapter 6

THE IMPORTANCE OF WATER

PROPERTIES OF WATER

Water is one of the molecules that is crucial to all living things. It is also one of the most abundant molecules on Earth. Water is made through the covalent bonding of two hydrogen atoms and one oxygen atom.

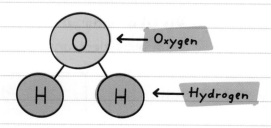

$\leftarrow$ Oxygen

$\leftarrow$ Hydrogen

WATER MOLECULE

Water is unique because of the kinds of atomic bonds that it can form. Water utilizes HYDROGEN BONDING, a type of chemical bond between hydrogen and one or more atoms such as fluorine, oxygen, or nitrogen. Fluorine, oxygen, and nitrogen are different from other atoms because of their high **ELECTRONEGATIVITY**. Atoms that are very electronegative, like oxygen, attract the electrons in the bond closer to its nucleus.

ELECTRONEGATIVITY
The ability to attract electrons.

Remember the three electronegative atoms by the acronym **FON** (sounds like *fun*): **F**luorine, **O**xygen, **N**itrogen.

Woo!

HYDROGEN BONDS ARE FON!

YEAH!

Electronegativity causes the creation of a positive and a negative **DIPOLE** within a molecule. When an electronegative atom pulls electrons toward it, that atom becomes more negatively charged and the other atoms in the bond become more positively charged.

DIPOLE
Occurs due to unequal sharing of electrons between atoms in a molecule.

In water, oxygen is more electronegative than hydrogen. This means that the oxygen atom acts as a negative dipole, while both hydrogen atoms act as positive dipoles.

Dipole comes from the prefix *di-*, which means "two," and the word *pole*, which refers to a point or position. A dipole refers to two positions within a molecule: a negative and a positive position.

Electrons, represented by the dots, are drawn to the more electronegative oxygen, which makes the oxygen atom more negative and the hydrogen atoms more positive.

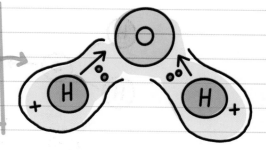

Molecules like water, which have these dipoles, are called POLAR MOLECULES.

Just as opposite electrical charges attract, so do opposite electrical dipoles. The negative dipole created by the oxygen atom in one water molecule is attracted to the positive dipoles created by the hydrogen atoms in another water molecule, resulting in the hydrogen bond between two molecules.

Hydrogen bonds are weak bonds; they tend to break and re-form between many different water molecules. Although these bonds are weak, they are formed just as fast as they are broken. This breaking and re-forming of bonds are what makes the surface of water flexible and strong. Hydrogen bonds increase water's **SURFACE TENSION**.

SURFACE TENSION
The rigidity of a liquid caused by the bonds created in its surface.

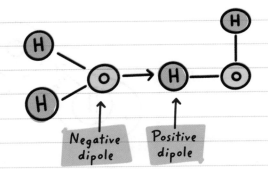

Negative dipole

Positive dipole

Having a high surface tension makes water incredibly stable. **As the stability of a liquid increases, it is less likely to change its state.** As a result, it is more difficult to boil water into a gas or to freeze it into a solid than other liquids.

Water's boiling point is 100 degrees Celsius, and its freezing point is 0 degrees Celsius. On Earth, air temperatures never get hot enough for water to boil, and only get cold enough for it to freeze on some days in winter.

WATER IN BIOLOGY

Biologists have traced the history of living things back nearly four billion years. Many scientists believe that the first living organisms originated in the depths of the seas, near volcano-like vents that provided valuable heat. Since then, all organisms have relied on water to survive. For example, plants need water to begin their food-making process (photosynthesis) and fish need water to breathe.

Humans are made of more than 60 percent water. Our lungs, skin, kidneys, muscles, and brains are all more liquid than solid. The primary reason that humans breathe is to create both energy and water through the process of cellular respiration. Because water is so important, humans need to consume a lot of it just to maintain homeostasis.

The most abundant element in humans is oxygen, which not only helps us breathe but also helps us create our own water.

Human brains, hearts, and lungs are more than 60 percent water. So are most muscles in the body.

Water also has biological importance because of its ability to dissolve many other molecules. For example, blood is composed of a liquid part, called **PLASMA**, and a solid part, which contains various types of cells. The blood's plasma is a mixture of solids, proteins, and salt, dissolved in water.

CHECK YOUR KNOWLEDGE

1. What is water composed of?

2. What atoms are necessary for hydrogen bonding?

3. What is electronegativity?

4. How are dipoles related to electronegativity?

5. What is a hydrogen bond in terms of dipoles?

6. What is the function of hydrogen bonds in water?

7. Having a high _____ makes water stable.

8. As the stability of a liquid increases, it's less likely to change _____.

9. What is blood plasma composed of?

ANSWERS

1. Two hydrogen atoms and one oxygen atom

2. Hydrogen and one or more atoms of either oxygen, fluorine, or nitrogen

3. Electronegativity is an atom's ability to attract electrons.

4. Electronegative atoms create dipoles when bonding.

5. Hydrogen bonds are the bonds between negative and positive dipoles.

6. Hydrogen bonds increase the surface tension of water.

7. surface tension

8. state

9. Blood plasma is composed of solids, salt, and proteins dissolved in water.

Chapter 7

ORGANIC COMPOUNDS

Water is one of the most important molecules for life because of its stability and ability to bond with other water molecules. Its components, hydrogen and oxygen, are two of the most abundant elements on Earth and within living organisms. However, life requires more than just hydrogen and oxygen to exist. Life also depends on the element CARBON.

Carbon and hydrogen are called **ORGANIC ELEMENTS** because they make up more than 90 percent of every living organism. Any molecules created by the bonding of carbon and hydrogen with other elements are called **ORGANIC COMPOUNDS**.

Organic means "related to 'organisms.'" Anything organic is related to living things. Organic chemistry is a discipline in chemistry that studies organic compounds.

CARBON

Carbon is an incredibly stable substance that can bond with itself. Because carbon contains four valence electrons and space for

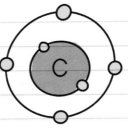

four more electrons in its valence shell, it is capable of covalently bonding with four different atoms. Carbon is capable of bonding with other carbon atoms, and often forms a long chain composed only of itself, called a CARBON CHAIN, on which multiple elements bond.

Hydrogen is the element that most commonly binds to carbon in organisms, forming the simplest kind of organic compound, referred to as a **HYDROCARBON**. Multiple hydrocarbons bonded together form a HYDROCARBON CHAIN.

Carbon + Carbon = Carbon Chain
Hydrogen + Carbon = Hydrocarbon Chain
Hydrocarbon + Hydrocarbon = Hydrocarbon Chain

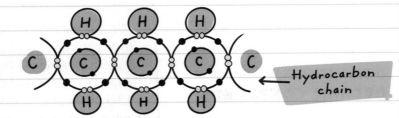

Hydrocarbon chain

Long hydrocarbon chains are common in the human body.

ESSENTIAL ORGANIC COMPOUNDS

Depending on the elements added to a hydrocarbon chain, an organic compound can change in complexity and function. There are four such organic compounds.

When oxygen is added onto the hydrocarbon chain, it forms a complex group of molecules called **CARBOHYDRATES**. Carbohydrates provide an organism with energy. In humans and plants, the most valuable carbohydrate is a sugar called **GLUCOSE**, which is broken down to produce energy.

> All sugars are carbohydrates.

LIPIDS have a larger amount of carbon and hydrogen than oxygen. Lipids assist in the storage of energy. The human body often converts carbohydrates into lipids and vice versa depending on whether energy is needed or not.

PROTEINS contain oxygen, nitrogen, and, in some cases, sulfur on the hydrocarbon chain. Proteins are required for the function of the body, including its structure and regulation.

In **NUCLEIC ACIDS**, oxygen, nitrogen, and phosphorus are bonded to the hydrocarbon. Nucleic acids are responsible for storing the information that allows the body to make proteins. These organic compounds are necessary for reproduction. Each organism's DNA is made of nucleic acids.

FOUR ESSENTIAL ORGANIC COMPOUNDS

ORGANIC COMPOUND	ATOMS INVOLVED	FUNCTION
Carbohydrates	Carbon, Hydrogen, Oxygen	Provides energy for an organism
Lipids	Carbon, Hydrogen, Oxygen (in small concentrations)	Stores energy for an organism
Proteins	Carbon, Hydrogen, Oxygen, Nitrogen (and Sulfur, in some cases)	Helps with the function of the body, including structure and regulation
Nucleic Acids	Carbon, Hydrogen, Oxygen, Nitrogen, Phosphorus	Stores information that the body uses to make proteins

1. What three elements are most necessary for life?

2. What percentage of living organisms are hydrocarbons?

3. Carbon and hydrogen are referred to as _____ elements.

4. What makes carbon similar to water?

5. How many other atoms can carbon bond with?

6. What is the most common element that binds with carbon in organisms?

7. What is the basis for all complex organic compounds?

8. What atoms are carbohydrates and lipids made of?

9. What atoms are proteins made of?

10. What is the function of nucleic acids?

ANSWERS

CHECK YOUR ANSWERS

1. Carbon, hydrogen, and oxygen

2. More than 90 percent

3. organic

4. Like water, carbon is a very stable substance, because it is capable of bonding with other carbon atoms.

5. Four

6. Hydrogen

7. Hydrocarbons

8. Carbon, hydrogen, and oxygen

9. Carbon, hydrogen, oxygen, nitrogen—and sulfur in some cases

10. Nucleic acids store the information that allows the body to make proteins.

Chapter 8

CHEMICAL REACTIONS AND ENZYMES

Atoms and molecules try to lower their energy level to the lowest possible state. In order to do so, they will often form CHEMICAL BONDS. Each chemical bond also changes the identity of the original substances that were combined. For example, when two hydrogen atoms and one oxygen atom bond, it creates water, which is a different substance from either hydrogen or oxygen alone.

Whenever chemical bonds are formed or broken, a CHEMICAL REACTION takes place. In all chemical reactions, there are REACTANTS, which are the substances that interact with one another, and PRODUCTS, the result of the reaction.

> Water is the product of its reactants: hydrogen and oxygen.

ENZYMES
Molecules that affect the rate of chemical reactions.

CHEMICAL REACTIONS

There are four different types of chemical reactions.

TYPES OF CHEMICAL REACTIONS

COMBINATION REACTION

Two or more reactants (atoms) form a product (molecule).

A + B → AB

DECOMPOSITION REACTION

A molecule (reactant) becomes two or more simpler molecules or atoms (products).

AB → A + B

COMBUSTION REACTION

Hydrocarbon + oxygen become carbon dioxide and water.

DISPLACEMENT REACTION

A reactant replaces an atom in another reactant.

Single-displacement:
AB + C → A + CB

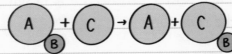

Double-displacement:
AB + CD → AD + CB

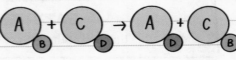

COMBINATION REACTIONS

The most common reaction is a combination reaction. This is where two or more reactants combine to form a molecule. If there are many reactants, then it is likely that more than one product will be created.

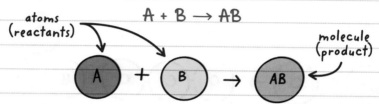

An example of combination reaction is the reaction that creates water: two hydrogen atoms and one oxygen atom reacting to form water.

DECOMPOSITION REACTIONS

Decomposition reactions are the opposite of combination reactions. These reactions occur when a complex molecule is broken down into simpler molecules or atoms.

In this case, the molecule is the reactant, and the atoms are the products.

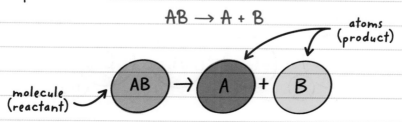

COMBUSTION REACTIONS

Combustion reactions are chemical reactions in which the reactants include a molecule and oxygen. If the reactant is a hydrocarbon, the products will always include carbon dioxide and water.

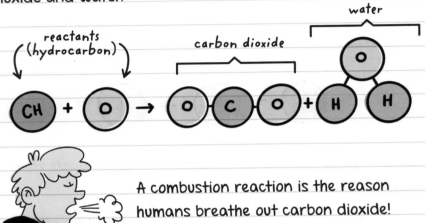

A combustion reaction is the reason humans breathe out carbon dioxide!

DISPLACEMENT REACTIONS

Displacement reactions are those in which one or more reactant element replaces another element within a compound.

This is a single-displacement reaction, in which one element replaces another.

$$AB + C \rightarrow A + CB$$

This is a double-displacement reaction, in which two elements replace each other.

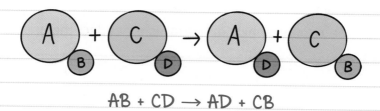

$$AB + CD \rightarrow AD + CB$$

ENZYME

Chemical reactions don't just happen randomly. Often, the reactants must have a certain level of energy for the reaction to take place. Otherwise, any atom that was near another atom would be able to bond with it, which could have bad consequences. The amount of energy needed to start a chemical reaction is referred to as **ACTIVATION ENERGY**.

A chemical reaction is like a hill that reactants need to climb. At the bottom of the hill there are two or more reactants. In order for the reactants to become a product, the reactants must climb the hill, reach the peak, and roll down the other side. That peak is the activation energy required.

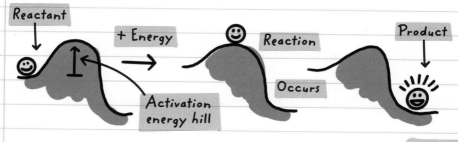

This energy requirement ensures that an organism can control when reactions take place. If they couldn't, then reactants would be used up at random times and they wouldn't be around when an organism needed them.

> If there was no activation energy, an organism would have to spend most, if not all, of its time taking in nutrients to replace reactants used in chemical reactions.

proteins that act as biological regulators

Organisms use **ENZYMES** to trigger chemical reactions. Enzymes provide reactants with an alternate pathway—one with lower activation energy—to become products. In other words, enzymes make the activation energy hill much lower.

Because enzymes control when chemical reactions happen, they are often referred to as the CATALYSTS or REGULATORS of the body.

Enzymes are necessary components for the functioning of organisms. However, they only function perfectly in the right environment. For example, temperature is one of the conditions that determine if an enzyme functions well. Cold-blooded animals, such as snakes, seek warmth in order for their bodies to function properly.

When an organism's enzymes cannot properly function, that organism will likely die.

1. Why do atoms bond?

2. What takes place when a bond forms or is broken?

3. What creates the products of a chemical reaction?

4. What kind of reaction takes place when two or more reactants combine to form a product?

5. What will always result from the combustion reaction of a hydrocarbon and oxygen?

6. The amount of energy needed for reactants to participate in a chemical reaction is called _____.

7. What is the benefit of a chemical reaction needing a certain amount of energy?

8. What do enzymes do?

9. Name two factors that can control whether an enzyme works.

10. What can occur if the conditions that enzymes need are not met?

ANSWERS

CHECK YOUR ANSWERS

1. Atoms bond to lower their energy level.

2. A chemical reaction

3. An interaction between reactants

4. Combination reaction

5. Both carbon dioxide and water

6. activation energy

7. It prevents chemical reactions from occurring when they're not necessary.

8. Enzymes provide reactants with an alternate pathway that requires lower activation energy.

9. Temperature and environment

10. The death of the organism

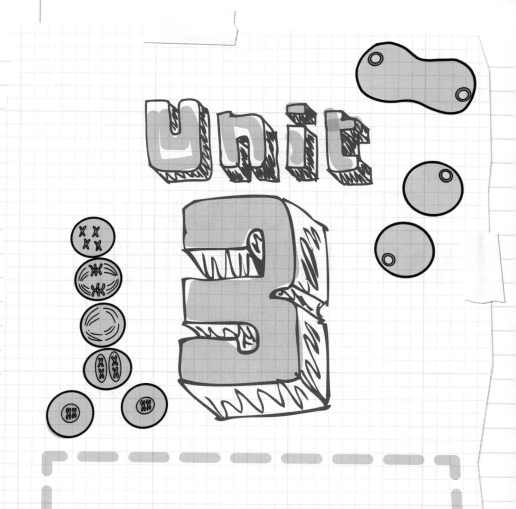

Unit 3

Cell Theory

Chapter 9

CELL STRUCTURE AND FUNCTION

For life to happen, there must be a place where organisms perform the functions crucial to life. This place is the **cell**. The cell is the foundation of all life. Cells perform most of the chemistry within an organism, and they also make up the structures within the body.

There are three principles that are true of all cells:

1. They make up all organisms (one or more cells).

2. The cell is the basic building block of the structure and function of life.

3. Every cell comes from another existing cell (cells divide to form new cells).

Cells work together in groups called TISSUES. These tissues work together to form ORGANS, like the heart and brain. Every organ works together within an organism, performing different functions to keep the organism alive.

> Many cells → tissues
> Many tissues → organs
> All organs → organism

Cells are able to perform different functions because of **ORGANELLES**. Organelles are parts of a cell, each having a different job. For example, organelles can:

> **ORGANELLES**
> The parts of a cell.

- produce energy
- make new proteins
- destroy and digest objects

> *Organelle* means "small organ." They are the small organs that help the cell function, just like the heart, brain, and lungs help the human body function.

ANIMAL CELL ORGANELLES

Animal cells are similar in the organelles that they contain:

A Typical Animal Cell

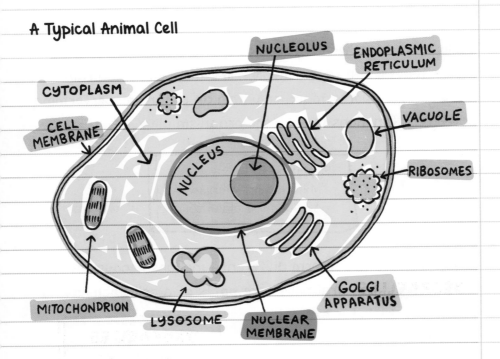

A typical animal cell is made up of these organelles:

1. Cell Membrane

The outer boundary of the cell in humans and animals is called the CELL MEMBRANE. The cell membrane is **SEMIPERMEABLE**. It is also flexible, giving the cell the ability to stretch and bend in many ways.

SEMIPERMEABLE
Allowing some things to selectively pass through.

Cells are similar to houses. In order to get into a house with a locked door, you need the key that fits the lock. Materials can get into cells only if they have the correct key to open the cell's door.

2. Cytoplasm

Within the cell membrane, a jellylike substance exists in which all the organelles float. This substance is the CYTOSOL. The cytosol is mostly made of water; however, the cytoplasm also contains a **CYTOSKELETON**, which is a network of protein fibers and tubes that maintain the structure of the cell and help move organelles within it.

The cytoplasm acts as cushions to the organelles and like a road system to transport proteins, metabolites, and other substances.

3. Ribosome

A RIBOSOME is a small organelle that produces proteins. The proteins are based on information given to the ribosomes by the organism's nucleic acids. Ribosomes are told which types of protein to make according to the cell that they reside in.

The suffix "-some" comes from the Greek *soma*, which means "body." "ribo-" refers to the carbohydrate ribose, which is an organic compound that forms the backbone of the ribosome.

4. Endoplasmic Reticulum

The ENDOPLASMIC RETICULUM (ER) is composed of flat sacs and tubes that package proteins, transport materials throughout the cytoplasm, and get rid of waste that builds up within the cell from other organelles.

Ribosomes can attach themselves to the walls of the cell's ER. This allows the cell to make protein and then immediately package it and send it off to where it needs to go inside or outside of the cell.

5. Golgi Apparatus

The GOLGI APPARATUS works closely with the endoplasmic reticulum. These organelles are flat sacs that temporarily store, package, and transport materials through and out of the cell.

6. Lysosome

A LYSOSOME is like a sac that contains enzymes that break down any kind of food, cell waste, or destroyed foreign organisms, such as bacteria or viruses. If waste products of the cell need to be disposed of, the Golgi apparatus will bring them to the lysosomes.

If a cell is injured or damaged, lysosomes release their enzymes into the cytoplasm, digesting the cell from within.

7. Vacuole

The cell doesn't always have to use everything the moment it creates it or takes it in. VACUOLES help by storing water and nutrients until the cell needs them. Vacuoles can also provide a space for waste.

8. Mitochondria

often referred to as the cell's powerhouses

The MITOCHONDRIA are some of the most critical organelles for the survival of an organism. In the mitochondria oxygen and sugars from food react in a series of chemical reactions to create energy. Just as ribosomes create different proteins according to which type of cell they're in, mitochondria show up in various amounts according to the type of cell.

Muscle cells, which require the most energy, have the most mitochondria of all cells. Some cells, such as red blood cells, have no mitochondria. This is because the only function of red blood cells is to carry oxygen from the lungs to the cells.

9. Nucleus

The NUCLEUS is called the "brain" of the cell because it holds the information needed to conduct most of the cell's functions. It is usually the largest and is the most important organelle in the animal cell. In healthy cells, the nucleus contains CHROMATIN, which are tightly wound strands of DNA (an acronym for deoxyribonucleic acid), the code for genetic traits like hair, skin, and eye color. This genetic information is passed down from cell to cell when they reproduce.

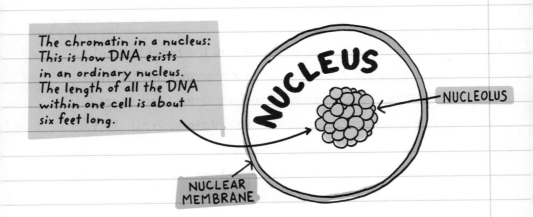

The chromatin in a nucleus: This is how DNA exists in an ordinary nucleus. The length of all the DNA within one cell is about six feet long.

NUCLEUS

NUCLEOLUS

NUCLEAR MEMBRANE

The nucleus has its own NUCLEAR MEMBRANE. This membrane is different from that of the other organelles; it's similar to the cell membrane. Other organelles have a single-layered membrane separating them from the cytoplasm, but the nuclear membrane has two layers offering it extra protection. The nuclear membrane also contains pores (small openings) so that materials can pass into and out of the nucleus.

The nucleus has a NUCLEOLUS, which creates RIBOSOMAL RNA (an acronym for ribonucleic acid). RNA exists to read and carry out the instructions given in DNA. Unlike DNA, which is trapped within the nucleus, RNA is able to leave through the openings in the nuclear membrane to deliver the instructions.

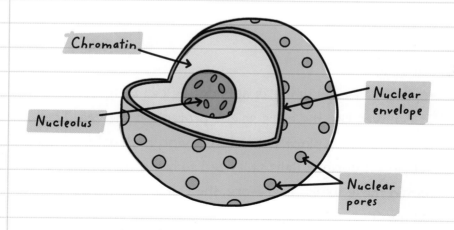

Chromatin

Nucleolus

Nuclear envelope

Nuclear pores

PLANT CELL ORGANELLES

Plant cells contain the same organelles that animal cells have. But they have two additional organelles.

A Typical Plant Cell

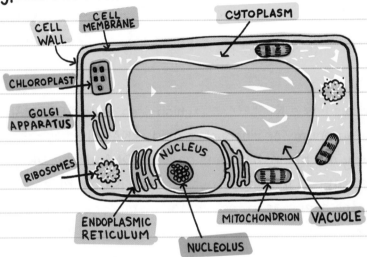

1. **Cell Wall**

   A plant cell's cell wall lies outside the cell membrane. It behaves like the cell's shield, protecting the cell. It also acts like a plant's skeleton, giving it structure and keeping it upright. Cells still need to bring materials within these walls. Therefore, the cell walls, like cell membranes, are semipermeable. Plant cell walls are made of a carbohydrate called **CELLULOSE**.

Plants do not have a skeleton like humans do, yet they push through the soil and can rise up to incredible heights, like the redwood tree, which can grow up to 380 feet tall.

Cellulose is the major component of cotton fiber and wood, and it is used in paper production. Cells in fungi, bacteria, algae, and some archaea also have cell walls. However, their cell walls are composed of different materials. Bacterial cell walls, for example, are composed of a sugar-and-amino-acid polymer called peptidoglycan.

2. Chloroplasts

Plants use light and carbon dioxide to generate glucose through photosynthesis. The process happens in the CHLOROPLASTS, which contain CHLOROPHYLL, the substance that powers synthesis. Chlorophyll is the pigment that gives green plants their color.

Chloroplasts are natural solar panels. Like solar panels on houses, chloroplasts use the light of the sun to create energy.

PLANT CELLS VS. ANIMAL CELLS

The main difference between animal cells and plant cells lies in their structure. Without a rigid cell wall, animal cells stretch and bend and are able to take on multiple shapes. There are more than 200 kinds of animal cells. There are far fewer plant cells. This is partially due to how much more complex animals are than plants, but it is also because the rigidity of the plant cell wall prevents the cell from taking various shapes.

The vacuoles of plant cells are also much larger than those of animal cells. This is because the plant has to store more water and generate its own food. Finally, plant cells have chloroplasts and animal cells do not.

1. All organisms are made of _____.

2. What is the function of an organelle?

3. What does it mean to say that a cell membrane is semipermeable?

4. What organelle do many ribosomes attach themselves to?

5. Which organelles transport waste outside the cell?

6. How do lysosomes break down various materials?

7. What is the function of the mitochondria?

8. What role does the nucleus play in the cell?

9. What substance reads the instructions that the DNA contains?

10. What organelle allows plants to create their glucose?

CHECK YOUR ANSWERS

1. cells

2. An organelle performs specific jobs within a cell.

3. Semipermeable means that a cell membrane allows some materials to pass through the cell.

4. The endoplasmic reticulum

5. The endoplasmic reticulum and the Golgi apparatus

6. Lysosomes break down materials with enzymes.

7. The mitochondria create the energy for the cell.

8. The nucleus provides the instructions for the other organelles within the cell.

9. Ribosomal RNA

10. Chloroplast

Chapter 10

CHEMICAL ENERGY AND ATP

In order for any living organism to function, its cells must have the energy to do so. Ingesting or creating **NUTRIENTS** is the first step to generating energy. Nutrients are complex organic compounds that can be broken down by organisms through the process of metabolism.

Nutrients include anything that nourishes the body and can be metabolized.

The simplest organic compound that is produced by organisms is the sugar glucose. Cells continue to break down glucose in the mitochondria to produce a majority of their energy.

Glucose contains six carbon atoms, six oxygen atoms, and twelve hydrogen atoms. When the bonds between the atoms are broken, the molecule provides the cell with energy.

Different organisms have different ways of getting glucose. Algae, plants, and some bacteria participate in a process called **PHOTOSYNTHESIS**. During this process, they create their own glucose and oxygen using light, water, and carbon dioxide. Such organisms are autotrophs.

AHHH!

PHOTOSYNTHESIS
The process in which plants, algae, and some bacteria create glucose using light, water, and carbon dioxide.

Animals, fungi, and most
bacteria, which can't produce
their own glucose, must get it
by eating autotrophs that make
glucose. These organisms are
heterotrophs.

Autotrophs are also often called producers, while
heterotrophs are commonly called consumers. Not every
consumer is an herbivore (an organisim that eat plants).

After the glucose is available,
the cells engage in CELLULAR
RESPIRATION to convert the
sugar into **ATP**, an energy-
rich organic molecule.

ATP
Adenosine triphosphate:
the molecule that cells
extract energy from.

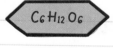

$C_6H_{12}O_6$	O_2	CO_2	H_2O	ATP
Glucose	Oxygen	Carbon dioxide	Water	Energy

CELLULAR RESPIRATION

Humans use more than their weight in ATP each day.

ATP is a molecule that is made up of a nucleic acid (adenine) and a carbohydrate (ribose) attached to three phosphate groups.

The bond between adenine and ribose creates the adenosine molecule. The word *triphosphate* represents the three (tri-) phosphate groups.

Adenosine is a building block of RNA, an essential molecule for all living things.

When energy is needed, one of the phosphate bonds is broken, giving off energy and turning the molecule into adenosine diphosphate (ADP). To store energy, a phosphate group is added.

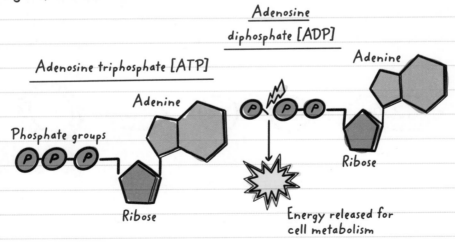

Adenosine diphosphate [ADP]

Adenosine triphosphate [ATP]

Adenine

Phosphate groups

Adenine

Ribose

Ribose

Energy released for cell metabolism

CHECK YOUR KNOWLEDGE

1. An organism's ability to function is tied to the amount of _____ it has.

2. Why are nutrients important?

3. What is metabolism?

4. What is the most important organic compound produced in an organism?

5. What is the process of photosynthesis?

6. What organisms undergo photosynthesis?

7. What are autotrophs?

8. What are heterotrophs?

9. What are a few organisms that are considered heterotrophs?

10. What is the process by which glucose is converted into energy?

ANSWERS

CHECK YOUR ANSWERS

1. energy

2. Nutrients are broken down to create energy.

3. Metabolism is the process in which nutrients are broken down.

4. Glucose

5. During photosynthesis, glucose and oxygen are produced using light, water, and carbon dioxide

6. Plants, algae, and some bacteria

7. Autotrophs are organisms that can make their own nutrients.

8. Heterotrophs are organisms that gain their nutrients through eating other organisms.

9. Animals, fungi, and most bacteria

10. Cellular respiration

Chapter 11

PHOTOSYNTHESIS

Photosynthesis is the process by which an organism uses carbon dioxide, water, and light to create oxygen and a simple carbohydrate called glucose. The energy-making process of photosynthesis is unique among organisms on Earth. Plant organisms that contain **CHLOROPLASTS** perform photosynthesis. Those organisms do not need to eat food to get their nutrients.

CHLOROPLAST
An organelle in plant cells where photosynthesis occurs.

There are some prokaryotes that do not have chloroplasts, but are able to photosynthesize.

The prefix *photo-* comes from a Greek word meaning "light." The root *synthesis* comes from another Greek word meaning "to put together." Through this process, plants use energy from light to put together a meal using water and carbon dioxide.

> Sunlight provides the energy for the reaction to happen. Without light, water and carbon dioxide will not have enough energy to interact.

SUNLIGHT

WATER + CARBON DIOXIDE → OXYGEN + GLUCOSE

The plant kingdom is the most effective kingdom at photosynthesis, because plants' leaves are designed to capture the most sunlight and carbon dioxide possible, and roots are designed to take in as much water as needed. Algae and bacteria don't have similar parts.

Plant Anatomy and Photosynthesis

1. The plant draws up water and minerals from the ground through the roots.

2. The leaves take in carbon dioxide from the air and release oxygen.

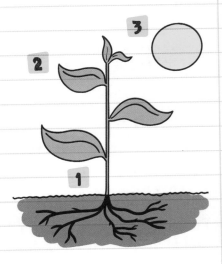

3. Sunlight gives chloroplasts energy to make sugar (food).

One of the two products of photosynthesis is oxygen. Because of this, plants are necessary to the survival of every oxygen-using organism. All organisms that breathe oxygen create carbon dioxide. This leads to a cycle where plants and animals both rely on and help one another to survive.

> Plants are the most important organism for removing the carbon dioxide created by human activity from the environment.

GLUCOSE STRUCTURE

The other product of photosynthesis, glucose, is more important for the plant itself than for the environment. Using some of the oxygen that the plant has stored, glucose is further broken down into adenosine triphosphate (ATP) in the process of cellular respiration for energy.

Not all of the glucose created by photosynthesis is needed for a plant or animal to function. Some of the glucose is stored in the form of a more complex carbohydrate called STARCH. Starch is created by chaining multiple glucose compounds together. It provides the organism with a backup if it is not able to create its own glucose through photosynthesis.

STARCH

A complex carbohydrate made by chaining glucose molecules together.

Photosynthesis mostly occurs in the day because it relies on light. However, ATP can be created from glucose at all times of the day and night.

STARCH STRUCTURE

CHECK YOUR KNOWLEDGE

1. What occurs during photosynthesis?

2. Where does photosynthesis happen in plant cells?

3. What is the function of leaves in plants?

4. What is the function of roots in plants?

5. How is photosynthesis crucial for kingdoms outside of the plant kingdom?

6. What happens to glucose after it's made?

7. ATP stands for _____.

8. What is starch made of?

9. When is starch useful?

1. Carbon dioxide and water are turned into glucose and oxygen.

2. Photosynthesis occurs in the chloroplasts.

3. Leaves capture sunlight for photosynthesis.

4. Roots gather water and minerals for the plants.

5. Photosynthesis generates oxygen, which organisms from other kingdoms use.

6. Glucose is broken down in the process of cellular respiration.

7. adenosine triphosphate

8. Starch is made of chains of glucose molecules.

9. When the organism cannot create its own glucose

Chapter 12

CELLULAR RESPIRATION

Regardless of how an organism receives its glucose, its cells must turn the glucose into adenosine triphosphate (ATP), the cell's energy. This is done through the process of cellular respiration.

Cellular respiration is broken into stages: **ANAEROBIC RESPIRATION** and **AEROBIC RESPIRATION**. Anaerobic respiration does not require oxygen, and it produces a very small amount of energy. Aerobic respiration requires oxygen and produces most of the energy.

The mitochondria is the organelle in which the aerobic stage of cellular respiration occurs, creating the majority of all the energy that the cell needs.

Anaerobic means "without oxygen," while *aerobic* means "with oxygen."

Think aerobic exercising.

THE MITOCHONDRION

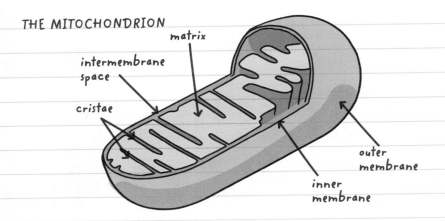

- The OUTER MEMBRANE separates the rest of the mitochondria from the cytoplasm, which is where anaerobic respiration takes place. Molecules are easily able to travel through the outer membrane from the cytoplasm.

- The INTERMEMBRANE space separates the outer and inner membranes.

- The INNER MEMBRANE separates the intermembrane space and the matrix, where chemical reactions happen. Molecules can only move through the inner membrane using transport proteins, which carry molecules through it.

- The CRISTAE are the spaces created by the folds of the inner membrane.

- The MATRIX is is the space within the inner membrane, where aerobic respiration takes place.

ANAEROBIC RESPIRATION

The first part of cellular respiration involves breaking glucose down into an even smaller molecule called PYRUVATE. The process of turning glucose into pyruvate is called GLYCOLYSIS. One glucose molecule produces two pyruvate molecules and a small amount of ATP.

> Pyruvate has three carbon, hydrogen, and oxygen atoms, while glucose has six carbon atoms, twelve hydrogen atoms, and six oxygen atoms. Only two pyruvate can be created from one glucose.

If oxygen is not present by the time the pyruvate is produced, anaerobic respiration continues into a step called **FERMENTATION** to create ATP and a **BYPRODUCT**. In animals the byproduct is LACTIC ACID, while in bacteria and yeast, the byproduct is ETHANOL.

FERMENTATION
The process by which pyruvate is broken down without oxygen, creating ATP and a byproduct.

BYPRODUCT
Additional products from chemical reactions that might be unintended and unable to be used.

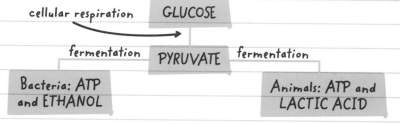

cellular respiration → GLUCOSE

fermentation ← PYRUVATE → fermentation

Bacteria: ATP and ETHANOL

Animals: ATP and LACTIC ACID

AEROBIC RESPIRATION

If oxygen is present after the creation of pyruvate, aerobic respiration occurs. During this process pyruvate moves into the mitochondrial matrix and enters into the **KREBS CYCLE**, where the molecule undergoes multiple changes in order to release its high-energy electrons.

KREBS CYCLE

A sequence of reactions that releases high-energy electrons from pyruvate.

Hans Krebs: German biologist, physician, and biochemist who demonstrated the "citric acid cycle"—now known as the Krebs cycle—in 1937, explaining aerobic respiration.

These high-energy electrons can't move on their own throughout the mitochondria. As the pyruvate moves through the cycle and transforms, molecules known as ELECTRON CARRIERS are also generated. Carriers take the electrons from the pyruvate molecules to the last step of aerobic respiration: the **ELECTRON TRANSPORT CHAIN (ETC)**.

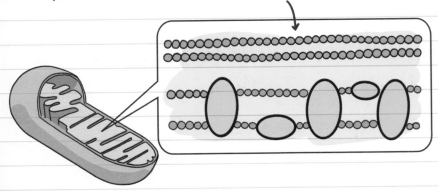

The electron carriers bring the high-energy electrons to the inner membrane of the mitochondria. Within the inner membrane of the mitochondria, there is a series of proteins that exist to transfer electrons across the mitochondria, like a conveyor belt. As electrons move through these proteins, the proteins absorb their energy. With that energy, the proteins pump hydrogen **IONS** from the matrix into the intermembrane space.

IONS
Atoms that contain either a positive
or negative charge.

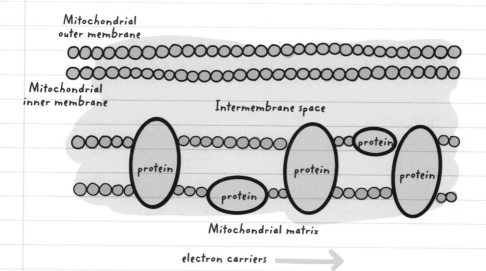

Mitochondrial
outer membrane

Mitochondrial
inner membrane

Intermembrane space

protein

protein

protein

protein

protein

Mitochondrial matrix

electron carriers

Electrons moving through the ETC create a difference in charge on both sides of the inner membrane. The mitochondrion in this state is like a battery. Batteries power devices by passing the energy of electrons held within it to the device. Electrons pass energy to the proteins in the membrane.

Having such a high concentration of ions in one area drives **DIFFUSION** in the mitochondria. Diffusion is the movement of anything from an area of high concentration to an area of low concentration. So, the hydrogen ions must find their way back into the matrix, which has a lower concentration of hydrogen atoms. They do this through the last complex protein in the ETC, **ATP SYNTHASE**.

ATP synthase is a gate for hydrogen ions to go through. As they pass through the gate, the ions power it, causing it to turn, just like a waterwheel. As ATP synthase turns, it creates ATP. This process is called **CHEMIOSMOSIS**.

CHEMIOSMOSIS
The movement of ions across a membrane from a high concentration to a low concentration through diffusion.

Lastly, oxygen, because it tends to attract electrons, accepts the low-energy electrons after they reach the last protein in the chain. Any remaining hydrogen atoms will bond with this oxygen to form water.

This generates 90 percent of the body's ATP.

The most important reason humans and other animals breathe in oxygen is to clean up hydrogen and low-energy electrons. The electron transport chain, the process of chemiosmosis, and the creation of water are called **OXIDATIVE PHOSPHORYLATION**.

Oxidative Phosphorylation

Electron Transport Chain + Chemiosmosis → Water

Without oxygen, the electrons would remain in the chain, clogging it and stopping any more electrons from moving. This would prevent all cells from creating energy.

Exercise

Cells cannot store large amounts of oxygen. Breathing provides only the amount of oxygen needed for regular activities. When you exercise, you tend to breathe more quickly because your body cannot produce enough oxygen for your cells. So, your muscles cells try to create the most energy possible through aerobic respiration. The rapid breathing is the body's response to the energy requirements of exercise. Over time, you may begin to feel pain in your muscles. The pain is because you are not taking in enough oxygen to keep the electron transport chain going. As a result, the process stops, forcing your body to go through fermentation and produce lactic acid. Lactic acid is sent through the blood to the liver, where it is turned back into glucose and processed during cellular respiration.

1. What happens in cellular respiration?

2. When does the anaerobic respiration phase occur?

3. What is the byproduct of fermentation in bacteria?

4. What is the most important product of the Krebs cycle?

5. Where is the electron transport chain located in the mitochondria?

6. What do the proteins in the electron transport chain do as electrons pass through them?

7. What is the function of ATP synthase?

8. What is chemiosmosis in the electron transport chain?

9. The electron transport chain, chemiosmosis, and the creation of water are together called _____.

10. How can exercise result in the production of lactic acid?

CHECK YOUR ANSWERS

1. Glucose is converted into energy.

2. When oxygen is not present after the creation of pyruvate

3. Bacteria produce ethanol as a byproduct in fermentation.

4. High-energy electrons from pyruvate in molecules called electron carriers

5. The inner membrane of the mitochondria

6. They pump hydrogen ions from the matrix to the intermembrane space.

7. ATP synthase creates ATP.

8. The movement of hydrogen ions across the inner membrane from a high to a low concentration

9. oxidative phosphorylation

10. When you exercise you are not taking in enough oxygen so the ETC stops, forcing the body to go through fermentation, which produces the byproduct lactic acid.

Chapter 13

MITOSIS

The cell's primary function is to maintain the stability of the entire organism by working together with other cells. However, as cells get older, many of their systems begin to fail, preventing the body from functioning at the level it needs to.

> Organisms are just like machines. Once parts get old, machines stop functioning the way they once did.

Cells can be replaced by new ones in a process called **REPRODUCTION**. Reproduction is the process of making a copy of something else. In this case, the cell makes a copy of itself. As a cell gets older it goes through the process of CELLULAR REPRODUCTION, splitting into two exact copies of itself. A constant supply of new cells ensures that the organism can continue to function before the machinery in the older generation of cells begins to malfunction.

Cellular reproduction happens in most cells. The older cell, the "parent," creates two copies, the "daughter" cells.

> **CELLULAR REPRODUCTION**
> The process of a cell splitting into exact copies of itself.

All organisms reproduce their genetic material. EUKARYOTES are organisms, like humans, that have a distinct nucleus containing the cell's genetic material, while PROKARYOTES are organisms, like bacteria, that do not have a nucleus and have free genetic material within the cell.

> If cells did not reproduce, all organisms would die. This reproduction is crucial for the life of every organism on Earth.

(Some eukaryotic organisms are unicellular as well.)

THE CELL CYCLE

Cellular reproduction is split into several phases that cover the **CELL CYCLE**. The growth of a cell takes up most of the cell's life, with the act of **CELL DIVISION** occurring later in the life cycle. Cells also divide so living things can grow. When organisms grow, it isn't because cells become larger. Organisms grow because cells divide and produce more and more cells.

> **CELL CYCLE**
> Life of a healthy cell.

> **CELL DIVISION**
> The act of one cell splitting into two cells.

Interphase

The cell cycle begins with INTERPHASE, the growth period of the cell. As a cell grows, it prepares itself for division. Interphase is broken down into three smaller phases: G1, S, and G2.

- **G1 (GAP 1):** In the first gap phase, the cell begins to grow and create proteins necessary for a rapid growth phase. Before the synthesis phase, the cell checks itself. In the G1 CHECKPOINT, the cell checks if:
  * there is any damage in the DNA.
  * it has grown to a large enough size.
  * the cell has enough ATP to divide.

- **S (SYNTHESIS):** At this time, the number of **CHROMOSOMES**, which contains the cell's genetic information in the nucleus, is doubled. The chromosomes are identical and attached at a point called the CENTROMERE.

  individual molecules of DNA

The number of chromosomes that a cell originally has and the amount that it doubles to varies depending on the organism.

The **CENTROSOME** is also duplicated during the synthesis phase. The centrosomes are major microtubule organizing centers. The microtubules, made up of protein tubes and fibers in the cytoplasm play an important part in the later phases of cell division.

● **G2 (GAP 2):** During this phase, the cell enters its last growth phase and prepares itself for division. In some organisms, the G2

> **CENTROSOME**
> A structure that organizes the cell's spindle fibers.

phase is skipped, but in many animals, the G2 phase marks the creation of more proteins as the cell continues to grow. Before mitosis actually begins, the cell checks itself again. In this G2 CHECKPOINT, the cell checks if:

✳ there is any damage in the DNA, or

✳ all of the chromatin has been replicated properly.

Mitosis

Mitosis describes the phases of cell division: prophase, metaphase, anaphase, and telophase.

> separates the chromosomes from the rest of the cell

● **Prophase**
The nuclear membrane dissolves, and the chromatin condenses into chromosomes. Each chromosome has a copy of itself due to the duplication of the chromatin during interphase. These copies are called "sister" **CHROMATIDS**. The joined sister chromatids form an X shape.

One chromatid is one chromosome, but sister chromatids joined by their centromere are considered one "duplicated" chromosome. Biologists do not consider the two sister chromatids **two** chromosomes when they are bound.

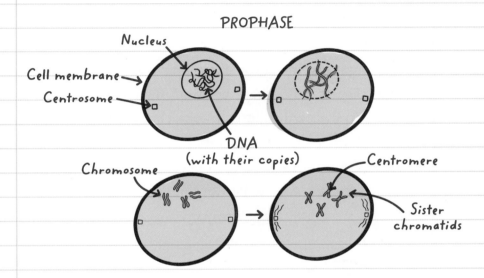

PROPHASE

Nucleus

Cell membrane

Centrosome

DNA
(with their copies)

Chromosome

Centromere

Sister chromatids

The centrosomes formed during interphase also produce **SPINDLE FIBERS** from the protein cytoskeleton, which will be responsible for pulling the two chromatids apart in anaphase.

Prophase is one of the most important phases of reproduction because in order for each daughter cell to function like the parent cell, it must have the same genetic material. The condensing of chromatin ensures that no genetic material is lost in the future phases.

Chromosomes are so thick that they can be counted with a strong light microscope. Generally, humans have 46 chromosomes, a typical snail has 24, sheep have 54, elephants have 56, and donkeys have 62.

Metaphase

During metaphase, the chromosomes line up at the center of the cell. The spindle fibers created in prophase attach themselves to the centromeres of the chromosomes.

At this point, the cell undergoes its last checkpoint, the M CHECKPOINT, where the cell pauses to check that all the chromosomes are attached to the spindle fibers.

METAPHASE

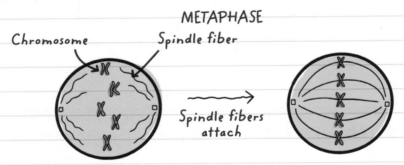

Chromosome   Spindle fiber

Spindle fibers
attach

Chromosomes line up
at center of cell

Anaphase

The centrosomes pull the chromosome pairs apart, separating the sister chromatids evenly and dragging them to the opposite sides of the cell. During this phase the cell begins to stretch.

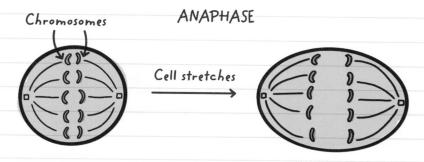

Chromosomes

ANAPHASE

Cell stretches

Telophase

In telophase, a new membrane forms around the
new nuclei, which are now at opposite ends of the
cell. Once the nuclear envelope and nucleolus form,
the chromosomes decondense
(unwind and relax). The spindle
fibers that pulled apart the
chromatid also begin to break
apart.

> Telophase can be
> thought of as the
> reverse of prophase.

At this point in mitosis, the cell continues to stretch,
preparing to separate the parent cell in two.

TELOPHASE

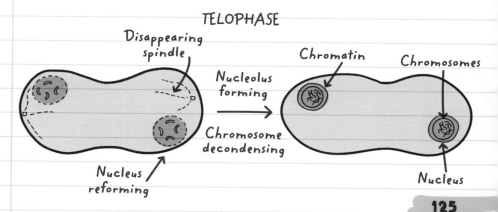

Disappearing
spindle

Chromatin

Chromosomes

Nucleolus
forming

Chromosome
decondensing

Nucleus
reforming

Nucleus

Use this mnemonic to remember the phases of the cell cycle.

IPMAT: I Poured My Aunt Tea:

Interphase, Prophase, Metaphase, Anaphase, Telophase

Cytokinesis

This is the final stage of cell division, where the parent cell pinches in the middle and separates to create two daughter cells. From here, both daughter cells enter interphase to start the cell cycle again.

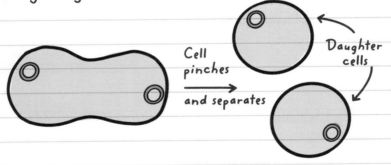

Cell pinches and separates

Daughter cells

Cyto- means "cell," and *-kinesis* means "motion." Cytokinesis is the motion of cells away from one another.

THE CELL CYCLE:

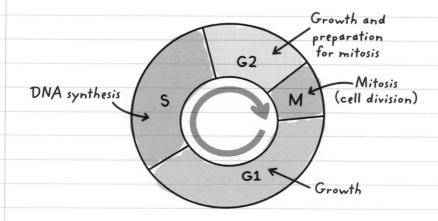

DNA synthesis → S

Growth and preparation for mitosis ← G2

Mitosis (cell division) ← M

G1 ← Growth

WHEN SIGNALS ARE IGNORED

The various checkpoints in mitosis produce signals within the cell to make sure that mitosis happens properly. However, cells also receive signals from nearby cells to share information about the body and help each other survive. Sometimes, a cell's DNA mutates, causing it to ignore signals from other cells that would normally tell them to stop growing and overcrowding their environment. These cells become CANCER CELLS, which continue to grow and can even spread to areas of the body where they are not supposed to be. Cells that grow abnormally are called TUMORS. Cancer cells *also* send signals, which is why they can survive anywhere in the body. The most important of these signals is one that encourages blood vessels to grow into those tumors. This gives them a supply of oxygen and a way to carry waste out of the cell.

PHASE	DESCRIPTION
Interphase	• G1: Cell grows. • S: Chromosomes are replicated (copied). Sister chromatids are created, attached at the centromere. • G2: Cell continues to grow.
Prophase	• Doubled chromatin condenses into chromosomes. Each copy of a chromosome is referred to as a sister chromatid. • Centrosomes produce spindle fibers.
Metaphase	• Chromosomes line up at center of the cell. • Spindle fibers attach to chromosomes at the centromere.
Anaphase	• Spindle fibers pull apart the sister chromatids. • Cell stretches.
Telophase	• Nuclear envelopes begin to form around each nuclei. • Chromosomes decondense. • Spindle fibers disassemble.
Cytokinesis	• Cells pinch and split down the middle.

CHECK YOUR KNOWLEDGE

1. Why do cells reproduce?

2. What is the cell cycle?

3. What happens during the S phase of interphase?

4. What is the function of centrosomes?

5. Why is it important that each daughter cell have the same genetic material?

6. What is the function of spindle fibers?

7. What do chromosomes do in metaphase?

8. In which phase does the cell begin to stretch?

9. In telophase, the _____ begin to form around the chromosomes.

10. In which phase do spindle fibers disassemble?

CHECK YOUR ANSWERS

1. To maintain the stability of the organism and to allow the organism to grow

2. The cell cycle is the life of an ordinary cell.

3. In the S phase, the chromatin and centrosomes are copied.

4. Centrosomes organize the cell's spindle fibers.

5. Each daughter cell must eventually become a parent cell, so each must have a complete set of the genetic material.

6. Spindle fibers exist to pull apart sister chromatids.

7. Chromosomes line up at the center of the cell.

8. Anaphase

9. Nuclear envelopes

10. Telophase

Chapter 14

MEIOSIS

ASEXUAL AND SEXUAL REPRODUCTION

Although mitosis occurs in every cell, the process of cellular reproduction can occur only a certain number of times before the last generation of daughter cells dies. In order to maintain the species, the **GENES** of that organism must be passed down to a new organism.

> **GENE**
> The sequences of DNA that code for individual proteins.

There are two ways that an organism can pass down their genetics: **ASEXUAL** and **SEXUAL REPRODUCTION**.

Asexual reproduction is when one parent organism reproduces alone, resulting in new organisms with the same genes as the parent. Mitosis is the only kind of cell division that asexually reproducing organisms require, because it results in new cells identical to the parent.

Asexual reproduction typically occurs within prokaryotes, like bacteria.

Mitosis:	Asexually Reproducing Organisms
Mitosis and Meiosis:	Sexually Reproducing Organisms

Sexual reproduction typically happens in multicellular organisms, like plants and animals.

Sexual reproduction occurs when a male and female organism combine their genetic material to create new offspring. Unlike in asexual reproduction, where the parent and its offspring are genetically similar, sexual reproduction results in an different organism.

GAMETE
A cell containing half the amount of chromosomes needed.

To create a new organism from two parents, both parents must each have a special kind of cell that contains half of the ordinary amount of chromosomes needed for that species. These cells would then be able to combine to create an organism with a full set of chromosomes. This cell is referred to as a **GAMETE**, which is created only during the process of **MEIOSIS**

HOMOLOGOUS CHROMOSOMES

In humans, who have 46 chromosomes, 23 chromosomes come from the mother and 23 come from the father. These two pairs of 23 chromosomes are known as **HOMOLOGOUS**. They have the same structure and features. Homologous chromosomes are those that, at certain positions on each chromosome, contain the gene for the same genetic trait, such as hair or eye color. That position is called a LOCUS.

Plural of locus is loci.

Homo- is from the ancient Greek *homos*, meaning "same," and *-logous* is from the Greek *logos*, meaning "relation." Homologous means that two things have the same relationship.

HOMOLOGOUS CHROMOSOMES

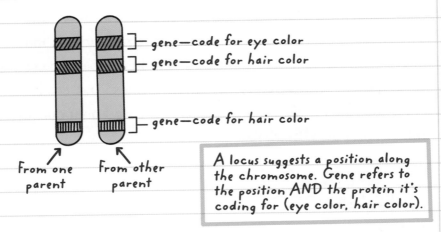

gene—code for eye color
gene—code for hair color

gene—code for hair color

From one parent

From other parent

A locus suggests a position along the chromosome. Gene refers to the position AND the protein it's coding for (eye color, hair color).

Even though homologous chromosomes have genes that encode for the same kind of protein, the genes themselves may take various forms. For example, the mother could have genes that encode for blue eye color, whereas the father's genes encode for brown eye color. These gene forms are called **ALLELES**, and they play an important role in maintaining the variety that exists within and among species.

The reason that humans look so different from one another, even if they're related (with the exception of identical twins), is because of how alleles interact with one another in sexual reproduction.

HEY, SIS!

MEIOSIS

Meiosis is the process by which gametes are created. The same phases of mitosis—interphase, prophase, metaphase, anaphase, and telophase (IPMAT)—occur in meiosis, because cell division is necessary to create gametes. However, to halve the number of chromosomes in a cell, cell division must occur twice. This results in four gametes from one original parent cell.

To account for each cell division, meiosis is broken up into two large categories: meiosis I and meiosis II.

MEIOSIS I

Meiosis I is the division of one parent cell into two daughter cells.

- **Interphase**
  The cell's chromosomes are doubled and centrosomes, which organize the cell's spindle fibers, are made.

After meiosis I, there is no interphase. The cell does not need a growth period before going to meiosis II.

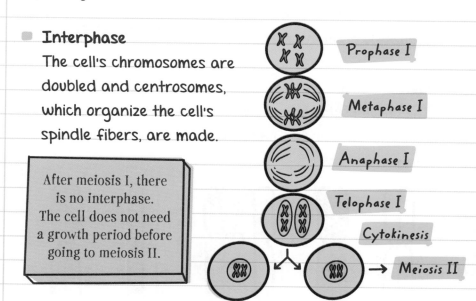

Prophase I

Metaphase I

Anaphase I

Telophase I

Cytokinesis

Meiosis II

● **Prophase I**

The doubled chromatin condenses into two copies of chromosomes, called **sister chromatids**. The two chromatids are bound by their centromere. The centrosomes produce spindle fibers.

The homologous chromosomes gained from both parents group and attach themselves together so that each chromosome perfectly matches its partner. Then, each chromosome exchanges bits of their DNA with each other in a process called crossing over, which results in **RECOMBINATION**. After this occurs, the nucleus dissolves, releasing the groups of chromosomes.

> **RECOMBINATION**
> The exchange of DNA between two homologous chromosomes.

● **Metaphase I**

The chromosome pairs line up at the center of the cell, and the spindle fibers attach themselves to the centromeres.

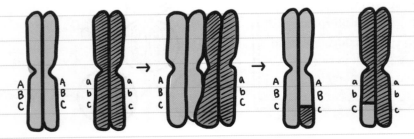

> Recombination is why human children can look so different from their parents. Children are a mixture of their parents' DNA.

Anaphase I

The attached homologous chromosomes are pulled apart by the spindle, dragging them to both sides of the cell. Each chromosome still has two chromatids, although, due to the recombination because of crossing over, they are no longer the same.

Telophase I

A nucleus and a nuclear membrane form around both sets of chromosomes on each side. The spindle fibers are disassembled. The cell continues to stretch.

> This is why there's a need for two cell divisions. The second is to separate the sister chromatids into individual chromosomes.

Cytokinesis

The cell pinches in the middle to form two daughter cells, each containing a chromosome with two bound chromatids.

MEIOSIS II

In meiosis II, both daughter cells have their bound chromatids separated. Because there is no need to replicate DNA or grow the cells, there is no interphase.

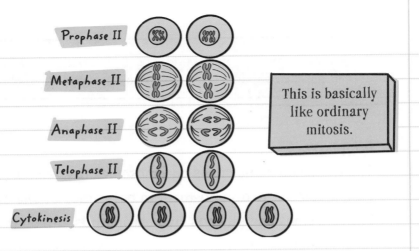

Prophase II

Metaphase II

Anaphase II

Telophase II

Cytokinesis

This is basically like ordinary mitosis.

- **Prophase II**
  The nuclear membrane and nucleus dissolve, freeing the chromosomes. New spindle fibers are created.
- **Metaphase II**
  The chromosomes line up at the center of each cell, and the spindle fibers attach themselves to the centromeres.
- **Anaphase II**
  The chromatids are pulled apart into individual chromosomes and dragged to opposite ends of each cell.
- **Telophase II**
  A nucleus forms around each set of chromosomes. The spindle fibers are disassembled. The cells stretch.

Cytokinesis

The two cells both pinch, resulting in four new daughter cells, each containing DNA that is different from the other cells. The cells have half the number of chromosomes the organism requires, making them gametes.

CHECK YOUR KNOWLEDGE

1. Why must the genes of any organism be passed down to a new organism?

2. What is asexual reproduction?

3. What is sexual reproduction?

4. What is the outcome of meiosis?

5. What are homologous chromosomes?

6. Various forms of genes on homologous chromosomes are known as _____.

7. What is the consequence of crossing over between homologous chromosomes?

8. Is there an interphase step before meiosis II? Why or why not?

9. In what phase do the chromatids bound in prophase I separate?

10. Meiosis II creates _____ daughter cells.

ANSWERS

139

CHECK YOUR ANSWERS

1. Cellular reproduction can occur only a few times.

2. Asexual reproduction is the reproduction of a new organism that contains the same genes as the parent.

3. Sexual reproduction is the reproduction of a new organism with a combination of genetic materials from two parents.

4. The process of meiosis creates gametes, cells that contain half a species's ordinary number of chromosomes.

5. Chromosomes that are homologous code for the same genetic traits at specific loci.

6. alleles

7. It creates recombination by exchanging DNA between two homologous chromosomes.

8. There is no interphase step before meiosis II because there is no need to replicate DNA or grow the cells before cell division.

9. Anaphase II   10. four

Unit 4

Bacteria, Viruses, Prions, and Viroids

Chapter 15

BACTERIA

BINARY FISSION

BACTERIA (singular: bacterium) are **MICROORGANISMS** that have only one cell. They are **PROKARYOTES**. Most bacteria also are surrounded by cell walls.

Bacteria reproduce through a process called **BINARY FISSION**. Binary fission has two steps:

1. The cell duplicates the genetic material and then elongates, causing the genetic material to split.

> **MICROORGANISM**
> A living thing that is smaller than can be seen by the human eye.
>
> **PROKARYOTES**
> Cells that do not have a nucleus or membrane-bound organelles.

parent cell

←DNA duplicates

2. The cell then pinches down the middle, producing two new daughter cells. The two cells are identical to the parent cell.

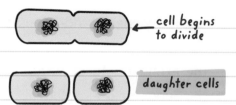

cell begins to divide

daughter cells

Some species of bacteria can grow and reproduce in as little as 20 minutes. Most human cells take about 24 hours before going through mitosis again. That means bacteria can reproduce around 72 times for every one time a human cell does!

Antonie van Leeuwenhoek
A Dutch scientist who discovered bacteria in the late 1600s. He first saw bacteria after scraping plaque from his own teeth and viewing it under a microscope. At that time, he called bacteria "animalcules," because they moved like animals.

Classification of bacteria has changed many times. Before, all types of bacteria were a part of a kingdom known as MONERA, because they all functioned in a similar way. Scientists then discovered that there are differences between several types of bacteria, such as how they get their energy and where they live.

Today, the Monera kingdom is split between two kingdoms:

- the Archaebacteria kingdom
- the Eubacteria kingdom

ARCHAEBACTERIA

ARCHAEBACTERIA (singular: archaebacterium) are a type of bacteria that can survive in harsh environments. Many are **ANAEROBES**, and their cell walls are made of a chemical called PSEUDOMUREIN, a complex carbohydrate.

ARCHAEBACTERIA
A type of bacteria that can survive in harsh environments.

ANAEROBE
Any organism that can survive without oxygen.

Because many archaebacteria don't need oxygen, they can thrive in a wide variety of environments, have different ways to create their energy, and can give off several byproducts.

Types of Archaebacteria

METHANOGENS: Archaebacteria that give off methane as they produce their energy. They live at the bottoms of lakes and marshes, where there is little to no oxygen, and even in the gut of humans and other animals.

Ordinary cells would be unable to create energy in an environment without oxygen, and they would die. Many methanogens use hydrogen instead of oxygen to create the energy they need.

Methanogen comes from *methane + -gen*. *Gen* means "that which is generated."

A methanogen is an organism that generates methane.

HALOPHILES: Archaebacteria that thrive in places with a high concentration of salt. Normally, salt causes cells to lose their water and shrink. Halophiles contain chemicals within their cell membranes that prevent them from losing that water, allowing them to stay stable.

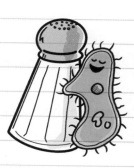

Halophile comes from *halo- + -phile*. *Halo* means "salt," and *-phile* means "loving."

Halophiles are salt-loving organisms.

THERMOPHILES: Archaebacteria that live in the
hottest places, such as volcanoes or hot springs.
Other types of cells living in the same
environments would be damaged,
stop functioning, and eventually
die. Thermophiles have enzymes
that work only at these high
temperatures.

AHH!

Thermophiles are said to be among the oldest bacteria
on Earth. This is because Earth in its earliest years was
extremely hot, often reaching several thousand degrees.

Thermophile comes from *thermo- + -phile.*
Thermo- means "heat," and *-phile* means "loving."

Thermophiles are heat-loving organisms.

EUBACTERIA

Eubacteria are the type of bacteria that live outside of
harsh environments. Because these bacteria live in more
normal conditions, they are often called the "true bacteria."
Eubacteria cell walls are made of PEPTIDOGLYCAN, which is
a carbohydrate that's similar to pseudomurein (the material
of the archaebacteria's cell walls).

The cell walls of eubacteria are much tougher and thicker than those of archaebacteria. The thicker cell walls can even prevent some of the cells from moving.

When you refer to *bacteria* in daily life, eubacteria are often the kind of bacteria that you're talking about.

Eubacteria can be **PATHOGENIC**, meaning that they can cause disease. Only eubacteria can cause an infection.

PATHOGEN
Any organism that can cause disease.

CLASSIFICATION OF BACTERIA

All bacteria, no matter the kingdom, have similar shapes. They are usually found in three shapes:

SPHERICAL   ROD-LIKE   SPIRAL
COCCI   BACILLI   SPIRILLA

Bacteria can also be found as

- an independent cell or attached in pairs called **diplo**:

- chains called **strepto**:

- CLUSTERS called **staphylo**, which are groups of bacteria that help one another to survive:

The combination of how the bacteria is grouped and its shape create its genus. For example, a rod-shaped bacteria that groups in colonies has the genus *Staphylobacillus*. ← staphylo + bacilli

Strep throat and staph infections are named after the genus of bacteria that causes them:

Streptococcus and **Staph**ylococcus.

IMPORTANCE OF BACTERIA

Bacteria are important to the life cycle of every organism. They can be either autotrophic or heterotrophic. Bacteria will usually live wherever they can gain the most nutrients.

AUTOTROPHIC BACTERIA are often found in sunny areas, where they participate in photosynthesis to gain nutrients.

HETEROTROPHIC BACTERIA are found wherever dead organic matter can be found, including the soil, water, and even inside living animals' digestive systems.

Bacteria that interact closely with living organisms are often **MUTUALISTIC**. This means that they help those organisms in exchange for receiving help for their effort. Humans, for example, have bacteria on their skin that is mostly harmless to us, but that bacteria can defend us from more dangerous bacteria. Some cows have bacteria that live in their digestive tracts. In return for helping the cow digest its food, the bacteria receives a constant food supply: all the food the cow eats.

> **MUTUALISTIC**
> The interaction between two living organisms in which both receive benefits.

Biologists use the mutualistic nature of bacteria to help people. For example, because some bacteria can create vitamins that are useful to humans, biologists learned how to gather live bacterial clusters for humans to ingest to help keep them healthy.

Bacteria are also used by researchers to test various ANTIBIOTICS, improve the growth of plants, and even break down nondegradable substances such as plastic.

ANTIBIOTIC
A type of medicine that kills bacteria.

1. What is a prokaryote?

2. What is the purpose of binary fission?

3. How did Antonie van Leeuwenhoek discover bacteria?

4. What two kingdoms make up the Monera kingdom?

5. Where do archaebacteria live?

6. What do biologists call archaebacteria that reside in places with a high salt concentration?

7. What shape are *diplobacilli* bacteria?

8. What kingdom(s) of bacteria can cause disease?

9. Where are autotrophic bacteria mostly found?

10. What does it mean when bacteria are described as mutualistic?

ANSWERS

CHECK YOUR ANSWERS

1. Prokaryotes are cells that do not have a nucleus or membrane-bound organelles like mitochondria or lysosomes.

2. Binary fission allows bacteria to reproduce identical copies of themselves.

3. Antonie van Leeuwenhoek scraped plaque from his own teeth and looked at the bacteria in it under a microscope.

4. The kingdoms Archaebacteria and Eubacteria

5. Archaebacteria live in harsh environments.

6. Halophiles

7. Rod-shaped bacteria that are attached in pairs

8. Only the Eubacteria kingdom

9. Sunny areas

10. When bacteria is described as mutualistic it means that they benefit an organism and receive benefits from that organism in return.

Chapter 16

VIRUSES

VIRUS CHARACTERISTICS

A VIRUS is a strand of nucleic acid (hereditary information) enclosed in a protein coat. It's like a simple package of DNA or RNA.

Viruses are unique. Scientists are unsure if they can be classified as organisms because they are not cells, nor do they exhibit many of life's characteristics. Unlike bacteria, viruses have no structure or membranes and don't have cells that need energy or oxygen. Viruses are not able to do anything themselves, from surviving to reproducing. In order to perform many tasks, they require a **HOST**.

Other organisms also benefit from hosts, including microorganisms like bacteria and larger organisms like insects. Sometimes these organisms

HOST
An organism that another organism lives within or on.

help their host, creating a mutualistic relationship. However, viruses are different. They are **PARASITES**, which means that they not only use a host to live, but they also cause that host harm.

> **PARASITE**
> An infectious agent that lives within or on an organism of another species.

> Viruses are not organisms because they do not exhibit the same characteristics as living things. Biologists call them "infectious agents."

VIRUS STRUCTURE

Viruses can have different structures. Their structures determine how they work (infect hosts). A virus fits its surface proteins into receptors in a host. Some virus structures are able to fit several hosts, while others can fit only one host.

Types of Virus Structures

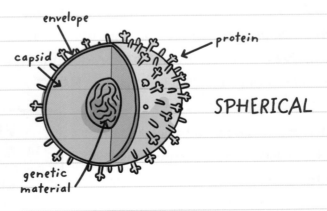

envelope

capsid

protein

genetic material

SPHERICAL

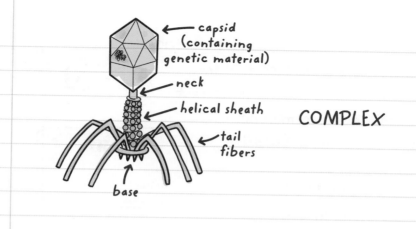

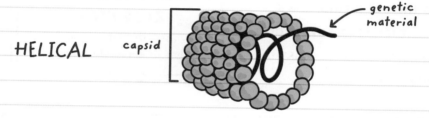

Proteins

One of the few similarities between living things and viruses is the goal of reproduction. However, viruses do not reproduce sexually or asexually. Instead, they **INFECT** other cells and pass their genetic information into a host, forcing them to reproduce copies of the virus. In order to get their genetic material inside the cell, viruses have to attach to and enter that cell.

> **INFECT**
> To invade an organism.

Viral proteins are attached to the outside of the virus. These proteins are one of two types:

KEY VIRAL PROTEINS: Viruses can trick cell membranes into thinking that they should be accepted by using the correct "key" to "unlock" the membrane. This key is known as a **LIGAND**. The cell membrane's "lock" is known as a **RECEPTOR**. The virus's ligand attaches to the cell membrane's receptor, unlocking it and beginning the process of infection.

> **LIGAND**
> Any molecule that binds to a protein.

> **RECEPTOR**
> Any protein that responds to another molecule binding to it.

> Only cells with specific receptors can be infected by specific viruses.

NUTRIENT VIRAL PROTEINS: In order to get into the cell membrane, a molecule can either have the right ligand for the cell's receptors or be the right kind of substance to pass through the cell membrane. Nutrients are one kind of substance that can get through cell membranes. Viruses can have proteins that are similar enough in molecular structure to nutrients that they can fool the cell membrane into taking them in.

> Viruses that don't have "key" proteins will usually use this method.

If the proteins look like a nutrient that the cell needs, the cell membrane will open its own "door" for the virus to enter.

Capsid

The outer covering of the virus is the **CAPSID**. It protects the genetic material inside. The capsid is made of simple proteins.

> **CAPSID**
> The outer covering of the virus, made of protein.

The different proteins that make up the capsid give viruses different shapes. Once a virus has entered the cell, the capsid degrades, releasing the virus's genetic material that was inside.

breaks down

Envelope

Some viruses have a protective **ENVELOPE**, which contains viral proteins and is similar in structure to a cell membrane. This similarity is important because it allows the envelope to combine with the cell

> **ENVELOPE**
> The protective layer of a virus, similar in structure to cell membranes.

membrane to let the virus inside, allowing the capsid to enter the cell without the cell knowing that it has been infected.

Genetic Material

The genetic material of a virus differs between **STRAINS**. Some viruses contain **DNA**, deoxyribonucleic acid, while others contain **RNA**, ribonucleic acid.

STRAIN
A subtype or certain form of a microorganism.

DNA
(DEOXYRIBONUCLEIC ACID)
Nucleic acids that code for the proteins the cell needs to live.

RNA
(RIBONUCLEIC ACID)
Nucleic acids that read DNA, allowing for the transmission of gentic information.

After a cell is infected, a molecule of RNA is created through the process of transcription via RNA polymerase. It is like the host cell's RNA "reads" the viral DNA (thinking that it's its own DNA) and creates a set of instructions for the cell's ribosomes to follow. Those ribosomes then make the virus's proteins. At the same time, the viral DNA moves to the cell's nucleus, where it undergoes the process of **REPLICATION**.

With the virus's proteins and the replicated DNA, an entire virus molecule can be re-created within the host cell.

REPLICATION
The process of copying something.

DNA viruses enter a cell, create multiple copies of all the components that make them up, and then create many more viruses through replication. Thousands of viruses can be reproduced from just one.

RNA viruses must first turn their RNA into DNA. This process is called **REVERSE TRANSCRIPTION**, because it is the opposite of the normal direction of transcription, which is from DNA to RNA. The virus usually carries the enzymes to perform this process. When the DNA created from a virus is complete, the host cell goes through the same processes that DNA viruses go through.

Transcription means "to write."

REVERSE TRANSCRIPTION
The creation of DNA from RNA—the reverse of the normal transcription of RNA created from DNA.

Transcription: **DNA → RNA**
Reverse Transcription: **RNA → DNA**

If the host cell's machinery is being used to make viruses, then it can't be used to make the vital proteins that the host cell needs to survive. The viruses eventually kill the host cell because the cell cannot properly function.

IMPORTANCE OF VIRUSES

Because viruses can insert their genetic material into cells, scientists can use viruses to put helpful genes into humans. This practice is called GENE THERAPY. In it, scientists use viruses to force cells to create the proteins that an unhealthy organism may need to survive. This type of therapy could result in treatments for a wide range of diseases, such as heart disease, diabetes, and cancer. Viruses are grouped according to their genetic material. Viruses such as HIV (human immunodeficiency virus), SARS-CoV-2 (severe acute respiratory syndrome coronavirus 2), and influenza are RNA-based. Other viruses, like the chicken pox or smallpox, are DNA-based.

CHECK YOUR KNOWLEDGE

1. Are viruses considered living organisms? Why or why not?

2. What does a virus need to reproduce?

3. How do viruses reproduce?

4. What are the two ways that a virus can enter a cell?

5. Why is the envelope able to combine with a cell membrane?

6. What happens to the virus's capsid when it enters the cell?

7. What genetic material can viruses contain?

8. What is the purpose of replication?

9. What additional step do RNA viruses have to go through?

10. What is gene therapy?

ANSWERS

161

CHECK YOUR ANSWERS

1. No, because they do not exhibit all of life's characteristics.

2. A host

3. Viruses reproduce by infecting other cells and forcing them to make more copies of the virus.

4. Viruses can enter the cell by having the correct ligand for the cell's membrane or by tricking the cell into thinking that it's a nutrient.

5. A virus's envelope has a structure similar to a cell membrane.

6. The virus's capsid degrades when it enters the cell.

7. DNA or RNA

8. Replication allows the viral DNA to be copied.

9. RNA viruses must go through reverse transcription, where the RNA is turned into DNA.

10. The use of viruses to insert helpful genes into humans

Chapter 17

PRIONS AND VIROIDS

PRIONS

Prions are a type of protein. They have no genetic material. This means that, like viruses, prions do not support ordinary living things. Also, prions are not able to move on their own. In order to find a host, prions attach themselves to organisms that they can't infect, like plants. These organisms then get eaten by other organisms that the prions can infect. Animals are the only organisms that are known to be susceptible to prion infection.

The prion is in the grass, but infects the animal, not the grass.

Protein Folding

Prions cause damage by interrupting how a host's proteins function. This is done by changing the protein's shape.

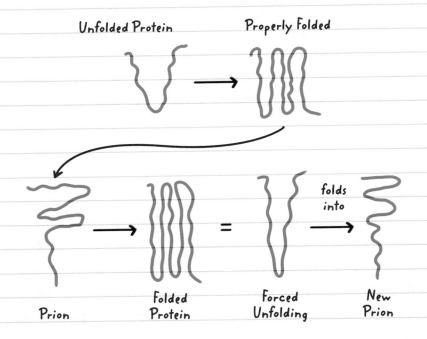

Unfolded Protein → Properly Folded

Prion → Folded Protein = Forced Unfolding → folds into → New Prion

A protein can function properly only if it has the correct shape. When a prion is near a protein, it can unfold and refold that protein. However, during the refolding, the protein folds in the same shape as the prion, creating a new prion. This protein folding process damages the cell—by stopping normal proteins from functioning properly. Folding is also the way that a prion reproduces (by creating a new, identical protein).

Prions usually affect the proteins in the brains of infected animals, destroying brain tissue.

VIROIDS

They're subviral.

VIROIDS are smaller than viruses. They are the smallest known pathogens and do not have a protein coat. Viroids behave in opposite ways to prions:

- Viroids are made of a single RNA molecule, with no proteins.

- Viroids infect only plants, causing diseases.

Viroids use an enzyme called RNA POLYMERASE to reproduce. This enzyme is responsible for making new RNA and exists within all host cells. RNA polymerase reads DNA. The viroid RNA strand tricks the host's RNA polymerase into believing that it is a DNA strand.

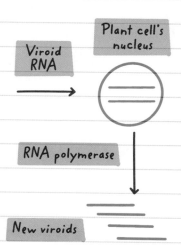

Viroid RNA

Plant cell's nucleus

RNA polymerase

New viroids

The RNA polymerase then copies the viroid RNA strands. This differs from the RNA virus, which uses a different enzyme to turn the RNA into DNA.

Viroids are often transmitted through farming, seeds, and contaminated equipment.

The first viroids were discovered in 1971 by DR. THEODOR O. DIENER, an American pathologist.

CHECK YOUR KNOWLEDGE

1. Why are prions considered nonliving?

2. What are prions made of?

3. How do prions find a host?

4. What organisms are not affected by prions?

5. How might an animal get infected by a prion?

6. What is the process of reproduction for a prion?

7. What does a viroid infect and how does that differ from prions?

8. What is a viroid made of?

9. How do viroids reproduce?

CHECK YOUR ANSWERS

1. Prions don't have any parts that support living things.

2. Prions are made of protein.

3. Prions are carried on organisms that they cannot infect and are eventually eaten.

4. Prions cannot infect plants.

5. Prions attach themselves to an organism, without infecting it. That organism is then eaten by an animal. The prion infects that animal.

6. Prions unfold a nearby protein and refold it to look like a prion. This turns the protein into a prion.

7. Viroids infect plants; prions infect animals.

8. Viroids are made of a single RNA molecule.

9. Viroids trick the RNA polymerase in a host into thinking that its RNA is DNA. The host cell then duplicates the viroid's RNA.

Chapter 18

DISEASE

PATHOGENS

When harmful bacteria, viruses, prions, or viroids infect another organism, they become PATHOGENS, infectious organisms that can cause **DISEASE**. Pathogens can be deadly. They exist everywhere on Earth in various forms.

> **DISEASE**
> Conditions within an organism that prevent it from functioning normally.

Pathogen comes from the Greek *pathos + -gen*. *Pathos* means "disease," and *-gen* means "that which is generated."

A pathogen is that which generates disease.

All living things have a reaction to being infected by a pathogen. In humans, the **IMMUNE SYSTEM** is responsible for protecting the body from foreign substances. If a pathogen enters the body, the immune system responds by trying to kill the pathogen and remove it from the body. If the immune system is unable to kill the pathogen immediately, or if it takes a while to kill that organism, then the body will become diseased.

IMMUNE SYSTEM
The body's defense mechanism, responsible for protecting the body from foreign substances and diseases.

Allergic reactions in humans are caused by the immune system treating a substance such as pollen, dust, or mold as a harmful, foreign substance.

ACHOO!

The SYMPTOMS of a disease are the side effects of the disease's progress. The type of symptoms depend on how the pathogen affects the organism. Fevers, for example, are a symptom of a bacterial or viral infection.

Symptoms eventually disappear if the immune system removes the pathogen from the body. If a pathogen isn't stopped, it reproduces, infects more cells, and makes the disease last longer. The longer an organism's normal functions are stopped by a disease, the more likely the organism is to die.

If a parasite is the cause of a disease, that parasite will die when the host dies. The most effective parasites evolve to keep their host alive as long as possible.

EXAMPLES OF DISEASES

PATHOGEN	DISEASE
Bacteria	(Humans) Tuberculosis **SYMPTOMS**: coughing that lasts for weeks
	(Animals) Bumblefoot **SYMPTOMS**: swelling on the pads of chicken feet
	(Plants) Gall **SYMPTOMS**: growths on the plants (similar to cancer)
Viruses	(Animals) West Nile Virus **SYMPTOMS**: high fever, headaches, muscle weakness
	(Humans) Influenza **SYMPTOMS**: high fever, headaches, sore throat, nasal congestion
	(Plants) Mosaic Viruses **SYMPTOMS**: yellow, light-green, or white spots on the leaves of plants
Prions	(Humans) Creutzfeldt-Jakob Disease **SYMPTOMS**: memory problems, behavior changes, vision changes
	(Animals) Mad Cow Disease **SYMPTOMS**: strange behavior, trouble walking
Viroids	(Plants) Tomato Chlorotic Dwarf Viroid **SYMPTOMS**: yellow and curling leaves on tomato plants

DISEASE RESISTANCE AND PREVENTION

PATHOLOGISTS have developed an understanding of diseases and their causes. Their research has also led to the creation of cures for various diseases.

> **PATHOLOGIST**
> A scientist who studies diseases and their causes.

Most bacterial and viral diseases result in the creation of **ANTIBIOTICS** and **ANTIVIRALS**. These are medicines that help the body fight bacteria or viruses along with the immune system.

against or opposite of

Public health efforts have also taught people the best ways to prevent infection. They recommend washing your hands regularly and taking regular showers. This is because both actions remove built-up bacteria from the skin, which lowers the possibility that you get infected. The removal of harmful bacteria from the skin is called **DISINFECTION**.

173

Different people have different sensitivities to strains of bacteria and viruses. For people with stronger sensitivities, removing only the harmful bacteria and viruses may not be enough. The process of **STERILIZATION** kills or removes all microorganisms from a surface. This could be useful when, for example, taking care of items that a baby uses, like a pacifier, because babies' immune systems are sometimes not developed enough to fight infection.

CHECK YOUR KNOWLEDGE

1. What is a pathogen?

2. What prevents disease in humans?

3. What happens when a foreign organism enters the body of a human?

4. What happens to the body the longer a pathogen is present?

5. What is a disease?

6. What determines the symptoms that an infected organism goes through?

7. What are the symptoms of bumblefoot?

8. What do pathologists study?

9. What medicine helps the body fight viruses?

10. What is the purpose of sterilization?

ANSWERS

CHECK YOUR ANSWERS

1. A pathogen is an agent that can cause disease.

2. The immune system

3. The immune system tries to kill the microorganism and remove it from the body.

4. The longer a pathogen is present, the more likely it is a disease will result.

5. A disease is any condition that prevents an organism from functioning normally.

6. The type of pathogen determines the symptoms.

7. Swelling on the pads of chicken feet

8. Pathologists study diseases and their causes.

9. An antiviral

10. The purpose of sterilization is the killing or removal of all microorganisms from a surface.

Unit 5

Protists

Chapter 19

THE PROTIST KINGDOM

THE SAME, BUT DIFFERENT

PROTISTS are mostly single-celled organisms. However, protists are eukaryotes that are not animals, plants, or fungi. Because they are eukaryotes,

> **PROTIST**
> Diverse, eukaryotic, usually single-celled organisms.

their organelles are bound by membranes. This means that they have a nucleus and organelles that carry out specific functions, making them more complex than bacteria.

Protists appear in a majority of scientists' classification systems, which makes the Protist kingdom one of the most diverse kingdoms of life.

For example:

- Protists include both heterotrophic and autotrophic organisms.

- Protists include both pathogens—disease causers—and symbiotes—organisms that help and receive help from other organisms.

- Protists can be sexual reproducers or asexual reproducers.

Due to their diversity, protists do not have defined shapes like bacteria. There are even a few protist species that are multicellular. Scientists are still learning about protists and are classifying new ones all the time.

> Many scientists define protists as eukaryotic organisms that don't fit into any of the other eukaryotic kingdoms. For example, algae. Most people would consider algae to be plants. However, most algae are single-celled, which is not a characteristic of a plant.

TYPES OF PROTISTS

Because protists fit into so many categories, scientists classify protists according to the kingdom that they behave most similarly to. There are three major categories of protist:

Animal-like Protists

Animal-like protists are called **PROTOZOA**. They are called this because they can move and are heterotrophic. All animal-like protists are single-celled; however, all animals are multicellular.

PROTOZOA
Animal-like protists.

Types of Protozoa

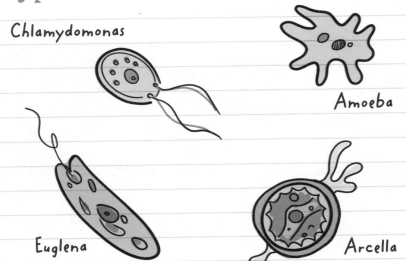

Chlamydomonas

Amoeba

Euglena

Arcella

Plant-like Protists

Plant-like protists are mostly autotrophic; they have cells that contain chloroplasts. Chloroplasts are the organelles in which photosynthesis takes place. Plant-like protists are called **ALGAE**.

ALGAE
Plant-like protists.

The floating green substance on the surface of a pond is algae. They grow there because the water provides a variety of nutrients for them to use.

Multicellular algae like seaweed don't have stems, roots, or leaves to take in nutrients that are long distances away from their bodies. This means that they are able to live only where nutrients already exist, such as lakes, moist soils, and oceans. These sources also expose the algae to sunlight and provide a constant source of water.

Fungus-like Protists

Fungus-like protists are protists that obtain most of their nutrients the way organisms of the Fungi kingdom do—from dead organic matter. Depending on the species, these organisms are capable of either sexual or asexual reproduction. Fungus-like protists are referred to as SLIME MOLDS.

NO THANK YOU!

Some fungus-like protists cannot move. But a few are able to move when they are fully developed. They can live freely as single cells, but can aggregate together to form multicellular reproductive structures.

CHECK YOUR KNOWLEDGE

1. How many cells do most protists have?

2. What is a eukaryote?

3. Why do protists not have defined shapes like bacteria?

4. For what two reasons are animal-like protists compared to organisms of the animal kingdom?

5. What are animal-like protists called?

6. What kind of protists are mostly autotrophs?

7. What organelle allows plant-like protists to engage in photosynthesis?

8. Where do plant-like protists live?

9. How do fungus-like protists obtain their nutrients?

10. What are fungus-like protists called?

CHECK YOUR ANSWERS

1. One cell

2. A eukaryote is an organism that has organelles and a nucleus bound by membranes.

3. Because of their diversity, there is no single feature common to all these organisms.

4. Animal-like protists move and gain their nutrients through ingesting, like organisms from the animal kingdom.

5. Protozoa

6. Plant-like protists/algae

7. Chloroplast

8. Plant-like protists live in places where nutrients surround them. They don't have roots, stems, or leaves to take in nutrients from farther away.

9. Fungus-like protists obtain their nutrients from other organic matter.

10. Slime molds

Chapter 20

PROTOZOA

THE WAY THEY MOVE

PROTOZOA are species within the Protist kingdom that behave most similarly to animals. They are mostly heterotrophic.

they eat other things

There are four major groups of protozoa, based on locomotion (or lack of).

Amoeboids

Amoeboids (**AMOEBAS**) are protists that constantly change shape in order to move. Amoebas extend their cytoplasm outward and use **PSEUDOPODS** to grip and pull themselves in the direction they want to move. This changes the shape of the organism. When the amoeba wants to move in another direction, it extends another part of its body to grip and pull.

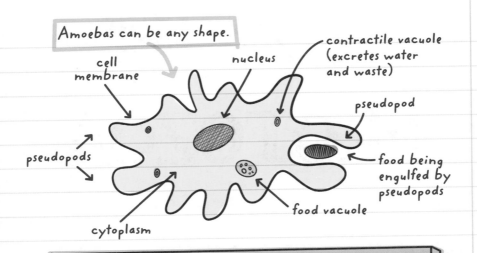

Amoebas can be any shape.

cell membrane

nucleus

contractile vacuole (excretes water and waste)

pseudopod

pseudopods

food being engulfed by pseudopods

food vacuole

cytoplasm

AMOEBA
A type of protozoa that has the ability to move by temporarily extending its body to grip and pull it toward surfaces.

PSEUDOPOD
A part of the amoeba's cytoplasm temporarily used as a foot.

Pseudopod comes from the Greek words *pseudos*, meaning "false," and *pous*, meaning "feet."

Pseudopods are "false feet," referring to the temporary extensions of the amoeba's body that it uses to move.

Amoebas also use their pseudopods to eat. This is known as **PHAGOCYTOSIS**. In this process, an amoeba surrounds a substance using its pseudopods and drags the substance into its body. That substance is then broken down in a special vacuole that exists only to digest food. Any waste created is removed from the cell. Because pseudopods can grow from any part of the amoeba, an amoeba is also capable of eating with any part of its body.

Flagellates

Flagellate protozoa are protozoa that use long, hairlike body parts, or **FLAGELLA**, to move. Flagellates whip their flagella around to "swim" on surfaces. Certain flagellates will have more than one flagellum, which gives them greater ability to control their movements.

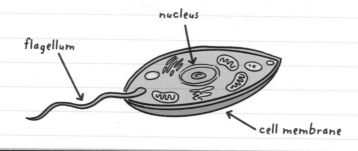

nucleus

flagellum

cell membrane

> Several kinds of bacteria also use flagella to move.

Flagellates can be either heterotrophic or autotrophic.

- Heterotrophic flagellates are called **ZOOFLAGELLATES**. They eat using phagocytosis, just like amoebas.

- Autotrophic flagellates are called **PHYTOFLAGELLATES**. Phytoflagellates contain chlorophyll, which allows them to obtain nutrients through photosynthesis.

Ciliates

Ciliates are protozoa that use **CILIA**, the small hairs all around their bodies, to move. Cilia sway back and forth, using a motion that's like someone rowing a boat. This movement allows them to push themselves along a surface.

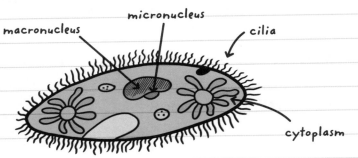

Ciliates contain two kinds of nuclei: ← plural of nucleus

- The MACRONUCLEUS, which is the larger of the two nuclei, handles all functions of the cell except those that deal with reproduction.

- The MICRONUCLEUS handles reproduction. When the cell reproduces, only the genes contained in the micronucleus pass to the offspring. A new macronucleus is created from the genes of the micronucleus.

Ciliates are the only eukaryotes to have two different kinds of nuclei.

The Immobile Protozoa: Apicomplexa

The last form of protozoa are the apicomplexa, also known as **SPOROZOA**, because of their ability to form sporelike cells. Sporozoa are immobile; they cannot move on their own. They do not have flagella or cilia or make pseudopods. Sporozoa "move" by hitching a ride on other organisms. Most sporozoa are parasitic; they use other organisms not only to move but also for nutrients.

nucleus

rhoptries

apical cap

SPOROZOA
Parasitic, sporelike protozoa that are unable to move on their own.

Sporozoa enter their host cells through a special set of organelles called the **APICAL COMPLEX**.

Sporozoa can even live inside other sporozoa!

This complex is made up of the APICAL CAP—the tip of the sporozoa—and the RHOPTRIES, which produce enzymes to make it easier to invade host cells.

More complex organisms, like humans, have cells that move using one or more of these methods. For example, the human ear and throat have cells with cilia, while the white blood cells use pseudopods and the male sex cells, spermatozoa, use flagella.

Sporozoa are similar to viruses in that they use their apical complex to trick the cell into thinking that they're safe to take in.

The most known sporozoan genus, PLASMODIUM, is taken in by mosquitoes when they feed on an infected animal. The mosquito is unaffected by the plasmodium, even when the protists multiply. When the mosquito goes to feed again, it transfers the plasmodium to another animal host. The plasmodium does have an effect on this animal, causing an infection and, eventually, disease.

In humans, plasmodium is the cause of malaria, a disease in which the parasite enters blood cells, rapidly reproduces, and destroys the blood cells in the process. Without healthy blood cells, humans can't transport oxygen to the body's cells, so the body produces little to no energy and eventually dies.

CHECK YOUR KNOWLEDGE

1. Protozoa are mostly _____, meaning they gain their nutrients by ingesting other substances.

2. How are protozoa grouped?

3. How do amoebas move?

4. Besides movement, what is a function of pseudopods in amoebas?

5. What is the purpose of flagella?

6. What are heterotrophic flagellates also known as?

7. How do cilia help protozoa move?

8. Which of the two nuclei is carried over by a ciliate during reproduction?

9. How do sporozoa "move"?

10. What is the function of the apical complex in sporozoa?

ANSWERS

CHECK YOUR ANSWERS

1. heterotrophs/heterotrophic

2. Protozoa are grouped according to their methods of locomotion.

3. Amoebas extend their cytoplasm outward and grip surfaces with pseudopods.

4. Pseudopods help amoebas eat as well as move.

5. Flagella help protozoa move.

6. Zooflagellates

7. Cilia sway back and forth against a surface to push protozoa forward.

8. The micronucleus

9. They "move" by hitching a ride on other organisms.

10. The apical complex helps a sporozoa enter a host cell by tricking the host cell into thinking that it belongs there.

Chapter 21

ALGAE

Plant-like protists, or algae, live only in aquatic areas. There are many different kinds of algae. They are classified based on the quality, temperature, and salt content of the water they grow in, whether they contain flagella, or even whether or not they form colonies.

Even though algae are plant-like protists, they are not only autotrophic. There are many species of algae that gain their nutrients by ingesting other microorganisms, making them heterotrophic.

ALGAE CLASSIFICATION

There are three **PHYTA**, or classifications of algae, that represent the types of plantlike protists referred to as pond scum or seaweed. Algae are classified according to their color:

- chlorophyta are green algae
- phaeophyta are brown algae
- rhodophyta are red algae

Seaweed includes some members of the three types of algae.

Chloro, phaeo, and *rhodo* come from the Greek words *khlōrós, phaiós,* and *rhodon,* meaning "green," "gray," and "rose," respectively.

Chlorophyta

Chlorophyta can be found on the surface of lakes or ponds and some types are seaweed. Chlorophyta are mostly single-celled and prefer to form colonies, or groups. Their green color comes from the reflection of high-energy green light by their **CHLOROPHYLL**. The other colors of light are absorbed by the chlorophyta.

CHLOROPHYLL
The pigment within certain types of cells where photosynthesis occurs.

When sunlight hits water, the light splits into all the colors of the rainbow—red, orange, yellow, green, blue, indigo, and violet. The reason we see ocean water as blue is that the water molecules absorb every color except blue, which is reflected into our eyes. In the same way, chlorophyta reflect green light, but absorb all other types of light.

Phaeophyta

Phaeophyta, which includes kelps and some seaweeds, are multicellular, like plants. However, they don't contain stems, roots, or even ordinary leaves. Instead, they have long BLADES, which help the

algae collect as much light as they can from the surface. They also have rootlike appendages called HOLDFASTS, which attach themselves to rocks at the bottom of the water.

Phaeophyta have chlorophyll. They also have another pigment that they use to perform photosynthesis called **FUCOXANTHIN**. Fucoxanthin reflects brown light, which gives brown kelp its appearance.

FUCOXANTHIN
A brown pigment that phaeophyta use to perform photosynthesis.

Rhodophyta

Rhodophyta exist mostly at the bottom of bodies of water. They comprise most of Earth's seaweed. Their red color comes from a unique pigment called **PHYCOERYTHRIN**, which reflects red light. Rhodophyta are often short, with branching **FILAMENTS**, but they can also be larger.

PHYCOERYTHRIN
A red pigment.

FILAMENTS
Long chains of single-celled algae.

The larger the rhodophyta species, the more the filaments group together. These grouped filaments look like leaves, but they clump together to exchange nutrients.

One type of red algae, the coralline algae, is important for coral reefs because they produce CALCIUM CARBONATE, which is the main component of reefs.

Diatoms

DIATOMS are single-celled algae that are known for their silica cell walls, and for their diversity. This algae has more than two million species, making it the most diverse kind of protist in the Protista kingdom. Like all autotrophs, diatoms release oxygen into the environment. A third of all of Earth's oxygen comes from diatoms alone.

Like a layer of glass!

Diatoms live in environments ranging from tropical reefs to sea ice, and freshwater to very salty water. Diatoms also have chlorophyll that produce a quarter of our planet's oxygen through photosynthesis. They are valuable for organisms that use oxygen and for the life cycle of fish.

The glass-like cell walls help the cell to hold a rigid shape.

Scientists use diatoms as a gauge for the quality of a body of water. If the water is not healthy enough for diatom species to live, then it probably doesn't contain enough oxygen for other organisms to live in or use.

Dinoflagellates

DINOFLAGELLATES are the second most diverse protist in the Protista kingdom. They are the cousins of the flagellate protozoa. They are single-celled and are both heterotrophic and autotrophic, but they live primarily in oceans. Heterotrophic dinoflagellates hunt and eat other protists or protozoa, while autotrophic dinoflagellates use their chlorophyll for photosynthesis. Dinoflagellates typically have two flagella, which perform a whirling motion to move the algae forward.

Dino- is a prefix from the Greek word *dinos*, meaning "whirl." A dinoflagellate is an algae that moves using whirling flagella.

OH!

DINO MEANS "WHIRL"

Some species of dinoflagellates can be **BIOLUMINESCENT**. This can be seen in some oceans, where dinoflagellates that are disturbed by waves glow blue-green light.

BIOLUMINESCENT
A living organisms that is able to produce light.

Dinoflagellates that receive a large amount of nutrients are known to **BLOOM**, which is a

BLOOM
The rapid reproduction of microorganisms, usually due to the presence of many nutrients.

period of rapid reproduction. This rapid reproduction feeds many organisms, such as clams, crabs, shrimp, and oysters.

Some species of dinoflagellates produce toxins as they bloom. This "red tide," which infects and kills thousands of fish during a dinoflagellate bloom, is caused by toxins that are red in color. People who eat fish infected by this toxin can be poisoned as well.

CHECK YOUR KNOWLEDGE

1. What are algae?

2. Where do most protists live?

3. What causes the green color in chlorophyta?

4. How are phaeophyta different from plants?

5. What is the function of fucoxanthin?

6. What function does algae perform for coral reefs?

7. Which species of protists is the most abundant within the kingdom?

8. Why are diatoms valuable to fish and other organisms?

9. How do dinoflagellates move?

10. What is bioluminescence?

ANSWERS

CHECK YOUR ANSWERS

1. Algae are plant-like protists.

2. Most protists live in aquatic areas.

3. The reflection of green light by its chlorophyll

4. Phaeophyta have blades and holdfasts instead of leaves, stems, and roots.

5. To allow phaeophyta to perform photosynthesis

6. Rhodophyta provide calcium carbonate for coral reefs.

7. Diatoms

8. Diatoms provide oxygen for fish and other organisms.

9. Dinoflagellates spin their flagella to move themselves forward.

10. The production of light from an organism

Chapter 22

MOLDS

Molds are fungus-like protists that have no mouths or other openings, but they are able to eat. They have cell walls made of a rigid organic compound called cellulose, like plants' cell walls. However, molds' cellulose is flexible and motile—able to move. Molds are mostly single-celled, but they can also be **ACELLULAR** when many individual mold cells join together. In their acellular stage, molds are like bags of cytoplasm with thousands of individual nuclei.

> **ACELLULAR**
> Something that doesn't contain cells.

For a long time, scientists considered molds to be fungi. Today, some protists are classified as fungus-like, or "molds."

> **SPORE**
> A single-celled reproductive unit that can be created sexually or asexually.

Like fungi, molds produce **SPORES** to reproduce and they also eat organic material.

SLIME MOLDS

Slime molds behave differently in the presence and absence of food. If a single-celled slime mold is on an organism that it can eat, it slowly feeds on it, taking in nutrients through its body. However, if there is no food, single-celled slime molds will gather together and form a **SWARM**, which then searches for food together.

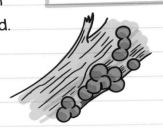

a slime mold swarm

> **SWARM**
> A collection of slime molds that form to search for food together.

If the slime molds are acellular, when they come together, they form one body with many nuclei that are enclosed by a single membrane.

Scientists are still trying to understand how slime molds find food better together than apart. Some think that slime molds become more intelligent when they swarm due to improved decision-making.

TWO HEADS—OR TWO MILLION—ARE BETTER THAN ONE.

Slime molds are mostly harmless, because they primarily eat dead things as well as bacteria and other protists. This makes them very popular to study, especially for the process of cell division—mitosis. Acellular slime molds do not undergo mitosis in the usual way. Because at one stage in their life cycle they don't have cells—only their nuclei go through cell division.

WATER MOLDS

Water molds are very different from slime molds. Instead of clumping together, they are mostly independent, single-celled organisms. Water molds tend to grow filaments, like red algae, and they will consume anything, even living matter. This means that water molds can be parasitic. Water molds, which are mostly found in moist soils and water, attack anything from plants to fish to animals.

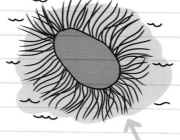

The stringy things coming from mold are filaments.

CHECK YOUR KNOWLEDGE

1. What are the cell walls of molds made of?

2. What does it mean when molds are described as motile?

3. What is an acellular slime mold?

4. How are molds similar to fungi?

5. What is a difference between molds and fungi?

6. Slime molds behave differently when in the presence of _____.

7. Why do slime molds form a swarm?

8. What happens when acellular slime molds go through mitosis?

9. In what way is water mold similar to red algae?

10. What are some organisms that water molds feed on?

CHECK YOUR ANSWERS

1. Cellulose

2. Motile means that molds are able to move.

3. An acellular mold is one that contains no cells.

4. They both are able to produce spores, and they both feed on dead organic material.

5. Fungi have rigid cell walls and molds have flexible cell walls.

6. nutrients

7. Slime molds swarm to find food.

8. Their nuclei divide.

9. They both have threadlike appendages.

10. Plants, fish, insects, and frogs

Unit 6

Fungi

Chapter 23

THE FUNGI KINGDOM

FUNGI live all around us. They can be found in soil, air, and water as well as on plants and animals. The Fungi kingdom is eukaryotic. More than 90 percent of all fungi are multicellular, with the rest being simple, single-celled fungi. Fungi are defined by their cell walls, which are made of **CHITIN**.

> **FUNGI**
> **(pl. of fungus)**
> Organisms of the Fungi kingdom that contain cell walls made of chitin.

> **CHITIN**
> **(pronounced KYT-in)**
> A tough protein that makes up the cell walls of fungi.

> Chitin can also be found in the shells of insects. It provides structure to their bodies because they have no bones.

Yeast, which is often used in baking bread, and mold, which sometimes grows on old bread, are both types of fungi.

YUM!

EWWW!

Fungi are known as **SAPROTROPHS**, a special kind of heterotroph that eats decayed or dead things. To do this, fungi give off enzymes and acids that break down material into simple substances that they can absorb. Saprotrophs are important for the recycling of nutrients in the environment from dead organisms to living organisms that can use them.

Saprotroph comes from the Greek words *sapros*, which means "rotten," and *trophe*, which means "nourishment." A saprotroph gets its nourishment from rotting/dead organisms.

Saprotrophs are also known as decomposers. Bacteria can be saprotrophs, too.

STRUCTURE OF FUNGI

Early scientists used to think that fungi were a type of plant. However, fungi have very different structures from plants.

The main part of fungi grows underground. It is made up of strands of threadlike cells called **HYPHAE**. Each hypha has a cell wall made of chitin, which contains small holes that allow hyphae to trade nutrients with one another. Fungi use their hyphae to create large underground networks called **MYCELIA** that connect them to one another. Mycelia can grow over large distances, sometimes reaching the length of small cities.

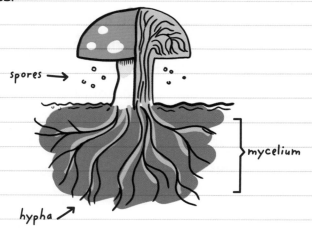

spores →

mycelium

hypha ↗

HYPHA (pl. hyphae)
The threadlike cells of fungus.

MYCELIUM (pl. mycelia)
The body of a fungus, which grows underground.

THE SPREADING OF FUNGI

The hyphae of fungi are used to expand the entire mycelium as far as possible. This helps fungi find dead organic matter for it to consume.

Hyphae are very strong due to rigid cell walls. They act like drills, tearing through soil and even rock to the places where nutrients are. Fungal hyphae are also able to bore into the cells of nearby plants.

Hyphae contain the cytoplasm and nuclei of the fungi. The relationship between some plants and some fungi is symbiotic. Hyphae can absorb nutrients that the plant cells create through photosynthesis. In return, the plants gain access to the materials that the hyphae absorb from deeper in the soil.

Plants also benefit from the presence of fungi in another way. When hyphae attach to plants, the plants gain access to the entire web of hyphae created by a fungus. This relationship allows them to communicate and even help other plants.

For example, if one plant is far away from a second plant and it does not have enough nutrients, nutrients are transported through the hyphae from the second plant to the first plant.

CHECK YOUR KNOWLEDGE

1. What does its classification as a eukaryote say about fungi?

2. What are the cell walls of fungi made of?

3. What are saprotrophs?

4. How do fungi take in nutrients?

5. What is the function of a saprotroph?

6. The threadlike cells of fungi are called _____.

7. How do hyphae exchange nutrients with one another?

8. Why do hyphae expand so far?

9. What do plant cells do for hyphae?

10. What do plant cells gain from hyphae?

ANSWERS

CHECK YOUR ANSWERS

1. The eukaryote classification means that fungi are living organisms whose cells contain nuclei and other membrane-bound organelles within a membrane.

2. The cell walls are made of chitin.

3. Saprotrophs are heterotrophs that feed on decayed or dead organic matter.

4. Fungi use acids and enzymes to break down dead matter into smaller substances that they can absorb.

5. Saprotrophs serve to recycle nutrients from dead organisms to living ones.

6. hyphae

7. Hyphae exchange nutrients through small holes in their cell walls.

8. Hyphae expand far to seek dead organic matter if they don't have enough in the immediate area.

9. Plant cells provide hyphae with nutrients that those cells create.

10. Plant cells gain the nutrients that hyphae gather from the soil and the ability to transport nutrients from plant to plant.

Chapter 24

FUNGI REPRODUCTION

Fungi are able to reproduce both asexually and sexually. Some fungi undergo asexual reproduction when their hyphae break off from the mycelium and grow on their own. Most fungi, whether they reproduce asexually or sexually, create spores, which are small reproductive cells that can create new fungi.

like seeds in plants

Because much of a fungus's mycelium exists underground, spores spread using **FRUITING BODIES**, stalks that grow aboveground, helping the fungus to reproduce.

FRUITING BODIES
Structures produced by mycelia that sprout aboveground so that the fungus can reproduce.

Many species of mushroom, a type of fungus, are called the "fruits" of the mycelium. Mushrooms grow aboveground in order to spread spores, the reproductive cells of fungi.

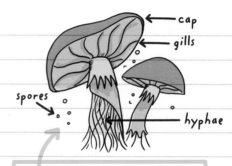

cap
gills
spores
hyphae

If a group of mushrooms are near one another, it is likely that they are a part of the same underground mycelium.

Mushrooms are made up of several hyphae that group together as one structure and grow aboveground. The ends of the hyphae, which are hidden underneath the mushroom cap, are called **SPORANGIOPHORES**. Sporangiophores make and store the fungus's spores. Sporangiophores line up in rows that scientists call "gills," because they look just like the gills of fish.

SPORANGIOPHORE
A special type of hypha that makes and stores spores.

Sporangiophore is made of the Greek words *spora*, which means "seed;" *angeion*, which means "vessel," or "container;" and *phoros*, which means "carrying." Sporangiophores are vessels that carry spores.

Sporangiophores will grow only in conditions that are good for fungi, such as moist, nutrient-rich soils. This is why so many fungi are found close to plants: The soil provides moisture, and dying plants provide nutrients.

> Mushrooms can break through concrete.

SPREADING SPORES

spread

Fungi have three main methods to **disperse** their spores from sporangiophores: wind, water, and animals.

Wind

Fungi grow their fruiting bodies close to the ground, and because the strongest currents exist only at higher altitudes, it can be very difficult for spores to be dispersed by wind currents. As a result, many species of fungi develop millions of spores. The large number of spores increases the chances that some get caught and carried by the wind. If the wind isn't strong enough or if it doesn't last long, the spores won't travel very far away from their origin. So many of these species grow close to where they started. This can be a bad thing if the area has a lot of fungi in it already, because they would have to compete for nutrients.

WOW. YOU GUYS DIDN'T GET VERY FAR!

Water

Some species of fungi that rely on water have to wait for rain to fall before sending off their spores. When rain hits the

SIGH. NO RAIN TODAY.

fruiting bodies, the impact causes spores to be released into the air. Other species grow their fruiting bodies near rivers, which can carry spores away without much effort.

> The spore's chitin cell wall prevents it from absorbing too much water, which would weigh it down.

Animals

Some fungi need the help of animals to spread. These species usually have something that attracts animals to them, like a bright color or a particular scent. The most well known example of this is the STINKHORN FUNGI, which smells like rotting meat. Although this scent is disgusting and unappealing to most animals, insects find it interesting.

Stinkhorn fungi

I JUST CAN'T SEEM TO HELP MYSELF.

These insects climb onto the fungi and, in the process, take spores onto their bodies. Those insects eventually leave the fungi and transport the spores to a new place.

Species of fungi that use this method to transport their spores often make fewer spores than species that use wind or water, because animal transportation is more reliable. Also, unlike spores spread by water or wind, spores transported by animals can often end up in locations that are far away from their starting position.

CHECK YOUR KNOWLEDGE

1. The process of fungal hyphae breaking off from the mycelium to create new fungi is a form of
   A. sexual reproduction   **B.** asexual reproduction

2. How do most fungi reproduce?

3. What is the function of fruiting bodies?

4. What are mushrooms made of?

5. What is the function of sporangiophores?

6. Why are fungi often found near plants?

7. How are spores dispersed?

8. Is wind a reliable way for spores to move large distances? Why or why not?

9. What are the two ways that water can disperse spores?

10. Why do some species of fungi that rely on animals to disperse their spores produce a smaller amount of them?

ANSWERS

CHECK YOUR ANSWERS

1. **B.** asexual reproduction

2. Most fungi reproduce using spores.

3. To help the mycelium reproduce aboveground

4. Mushrooms are made of several hyphae grouped together.

5. Sporangiophores produce and store spores.

6. Plants offer fungi nutrients while the soils that plants grow in offer moisture and nutrients from other decomposing organic matter.

7. Spores are dispersed through wind, water, and animals.

8. Wind is not a reliable way for spores to travel far, because fungi do not grow tall enough to be caught in a strong current of wind.

9. Spores can be released from fruiting bodies after being exposed to rain or carried by a river.

10. Animals provide a reliable way for spores to travel far distances.

Chapter 25

ECOLOGY OF FUNGI

Fungi have a special role in their environment. In addition to being crucial for passing nutrients from dead to living organisms, fungi also connect entire forests through their expansive mycelia. To grow this

> **ECOLOGY**
> The study of the connection between organisms in any environment.

vastly, fungi need help from the surrounding animals and plants. Biologists study the relationship that fungi have with their environment in a branch of biology called **ECOLOGY**.

MUTUALISM

Plants and fungi have a relationship that benefits each of them. This is an example of mutualism. In this type of relationship, plants and fungi benefit from one another. Plants gain nutrients from the mycelium, and the fungi gain nutrients from plant cells.

As a result, plants that have a close connection with fungi tend to grow strong, which causes the fungi that are connected to them to grow strong as well.

WE'RE BETTER TOGETHER.

Because mycelia take in nutrients and distribute them to plant cells, biologists believe that fungi played an important role in the evolution of plants' roots, which behave in the same way.

MUTUALISM
The interaction between two or more species where each benefits.

Fungi also have a mutualistic relationship with many insects. For example, leaf-cutting ants are not able to digest the leaves that they cut, but they can digest fungi. So, leaf-cutting ants create gardens of fungi and help them to grow by feeding them with bits of plants that they cut. In return for the food, the fungi become a food source for the ants, and while the ants feed, they pick up spores to create new gardens.

PARASITISM

Fungi gain a large amount of the nutrients they need by using their hyphae to penetrate other organisms' cells and absorbing any nutrients that they need. Some species of fungi use this technique in more aggressive ways, causing an interruption in the normal functions of others' cells. Instead of having a mutualistic relationship, they have parasitic relationships. Diseases caused by parasitic fungi are called **MYCOSES**.

Fungi and Plants

Fungi can damage and destroy plants in various ways. Spores can be carried from one plant to another, infecting large numbers of plants in a very short time. Hyphae can also enter a plant's cells and take all the nutrients, leaving the plant's cells unable to function properly.

This rust fungus has taken over a leaf and created new fruiting bodies to spread spores to other leaves.

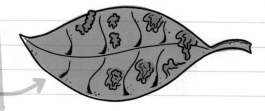

One of the most well known parasitic species of fungus are RUSTS. Rusts are fungi that latch on to plant parts such as leaves, stems, and fruits. They take over the plant's machinery with their hyphae before creating fruiting bodies to reproduce elsewhere.

Rust fungi produce rust-colored fruiting bodies, which create the orangish-brown color on infected plants.

Fungi and Animals

Fungi can also be parasitic to animals. Fungi damage animal cells in the same way they damage plant cells, by destroying the cell's ability to function. Because of the variety of cells that animals have, many different diseases can result. For example, a mammal and an insect would be affected differently.

For small invertebrates such as insects, fungi can be very aggressive. Infection can prevent insects from eating or even moving. Eventually, the fungus kills them and uses their body's cells for nutrients before creating fruiting bodies to reproduce.

For big vertebrates such as humans and dogs, fungi usually spread without doing much harm to an organism. A common example of a harmless mycosis is dermatitis, an infection that causes the skin to become irritated and itchy.

> Fungal skin infections in humans are almost always treatable with medicine and proper hygiene.

CHECK YOUR KNOWLEDGE

1. What is ecology?

2. What happens in a mutualistic relationship between plants and fungi?

3. What happens to fungi when a plant that it's benefiting from thrives?

4. How do leaf-cutting ants help fungi?

5. How do fungi help leaf-cutting ants?

6. When does a fungus become parasitic?

7. What is a disease caused by a fungus called?

8. What areas of plants do rusts inhabit?

9. What are some effects a parasitic fungus might have on an insect?

ANSWERS 227

CHECK YOUR ANSWERS

1. Ecology is the study of the connection between organisms in any environment.

2. Fungi take in nutrients from plant cells, while plant cells take in nutrients through the mycelium.

3. The fungi also thrive.

4. They provide fungi with sources of nutrients.

5. The healthy fungi provide a food source for the ants.

6. A fungus becomes parasitic when it interrupts the normal function of cells.

7. Mycosis

8. Leaves, stems, and fruits

9. The insect stops eating and moving before eventually dying.

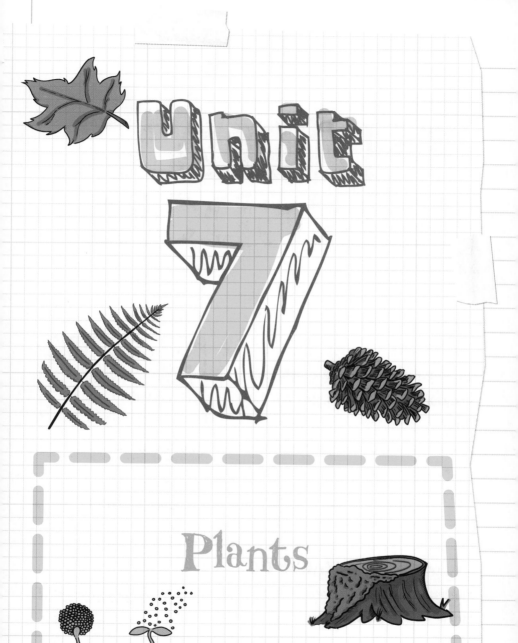

Unit 7

Plants

Chapter 26

THE PLANT KINGDOM

WHAT IS A PLANT?

The **PLANT** kingdom is one of the most recognizable of the six kingdoms. The organisms of this kingdom, plants, can grow in soil or water or even on other plants. These characteristics often trick people into believing that all things that grow in these places and look the same are plants. However, only plants are **EUKARYOTIC**, multicellular, AND have cell walls made of **CELLULOSE**.

> **PLANT**
> A eukaryotic, multicellular organism with a cellulose cell wall.

> **EUKARYOTE**
> A type of cell that has membrane-bound organelles, including a nucleus.

Cellulose can't be digested by human stomachs.

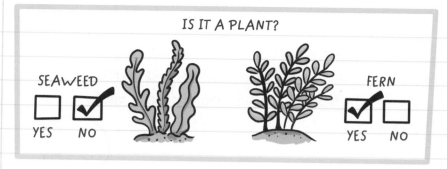

IS IT A PLANT?

SEAWEED
☐ YES   ☑ NO

FERN
☑ YES   ☐ NO

Seaweed are protists, eukaryotic, multicellular, and have cellulose cell walls. They are not considered plants because they do not have roots, stems, or leaves. Seaweed is considered an early ancestor of land plants.

PLANT CLASSIFICATIONS

Plants are characterized by how they reproduce and whether they have a **VASCULAR SYSTEM**, seeds, and flowers.

VASCULAR SYSTEM
A network made up of vessels that carry blood, nutrients, and/or water in any organism.

mostly very simple plants, like mosses

VASCULAR PLANTS have tubelike structures that carry and distribute nutrients. Most vascular plants have seeds, but some, like ferns, do not.

NONVASCULAR PLANTS don't have structures to help them carry and distribute water or nutrients. Each cell absorbs water and nutrients on its own.

231

Vascular Tissue

A vascular system is a collection of tissues that bring water and minerals up from the roots and distribute sugar from the leaves. The vascular tissue is made up of three parts:

XYLEM: tubelike cells stacked together to form vessels that distribute water from the roots to various parts of the plant. They also provide structural support.

PHLOEM: tubelike cells stacked to form tubes that distribute food

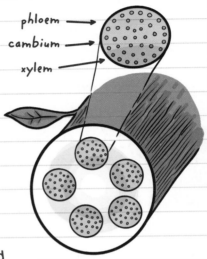

VASCULAR TISSUE

VASCULAR CAMBIUM: cells that produce new xylem and phloem cells and increase the thickness of stems and roots

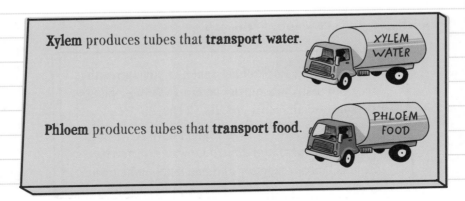

Xylem produces tubes that **transport water.**

XYLEM WATER

Phloem produces tubes that **transport food.**

PHLOEM FOOD

Most vascular plants have these structures:

LEAVES: the organs of the plant where plants capture light for photosynthesis. Some leaves are flat, others are shaped like needles, and others have different shapes.

Plant leaves are made up of:

protective layer

EPIDERMIS: the outer layer that has a waxy cuticle that prevents water loss. The leaf exchanges gases such as oxygen and carbon dioxide with the environment through openings called STOMATA.

like your lips

GUARD CELLS: structures that open and close the stomata.

PALISADE LAYER: the layer beneath the epidermis, which is composed of column-shaped cells (which themselves contain a high concentration of chloroplasts) that are packed very tightly.

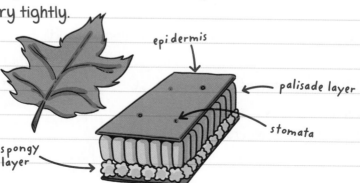

epidermis

palisade layer

stomata

spongy layer

SPONGY LAYER: cells are very loosely packed, leaving air pockets to facilitate exchange of gases, oxygen or carbon dioxide, like a sponge; most of the vascular tissue (which distributes food and water) is located in the spongy layer

STEMS: support the entire plant and deliver nutrients from the soil to the leaves and bring glucose from leaves to roots

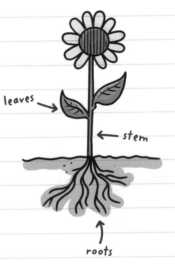

leaves

← stem

roots

ROOTS: collect nutrients and water from the soil to bring to the rest of the plant; also support the plant and prevent it from being blown or washed away

PHOTOSYNTHESIS

All plants use light, water, and carbon dioxide to make energy and oxygen. This change occurs within photosynthesis.

Photosynthesis is a collection of biochemical reactions that create glucose from molecules of carbon dioxide and water.

All life on Earth requires these producers to live.

The energy-making process of photosynthesis takes place within special structures within a plant cell called **CHLOROPLASTS**. These chloroplasts contain **PIGMENTS** that vary by plant and absorb light. In plants with green leaves, that pigment is called **CHLOROPHYLL**.

CHLOROPLAST
Structures within a plant cell, where photosynthesis occurs.

PIGMENT
The natural color of the cells and tissue.

Chlorophyll is found within green leaves. Not all plants are green, so not all plants contain chlorophyll. Fruits also gain their colors from a red pigment called LYCOPENE. CAROTENE colors oranges and pears. ANTHOCYANIN produces the blue or purple color found in eggplants.

Plant categories:

NAME	VASCULARITY	REPRODUCE WITH
Bryophytes (Mosses)	Nonvascular	Spores

All bryophytes live near or in water. This is because they have no vascular system to transport water throughout their bodies.

| Pteridophytes (Ferns) | Vascular | Spores |

Pteridophytes hold their spores on the bottom of their leaves.

| Gymnosperms (Cones) | Vascular | Seeds |

Each seed in a cone is called a "scale." Gymnosperms also have leaves that are shaped like needles.

| Angiosperms (Flowers/Fruits) | Vascular | Flowers and seeds |

Many flowers have a section that holds seeds, called a pistil. If the plant creates fruits, the seeds are usually held within the fruits.

Bryophytes

Bryophytes, which include MOSSES, LIVERWORTS, and HORNWORTS, are the earliest types of plants. Bryophytes have no stems or traditional roots. They grow in moist soil and in wide COLONIES. Colonies of mosses are called "carpets" because they look like green carpets on the floors of jungles and forests.

> *Bryophyte* comes from the Greek words *bruon* and *phuton*, which mean "moss" and "plant."

Pteridophytes

Pteridophytes include ferns and horsetails and are the earliest category of plants that have stems and roots. They reproduce using spores. Because pteridophytes don't produce flowers or seeds, they are sometimes referred to as "cryptogams," meaning that their reproduction is hidden.

> *Pteridophyte* comes from the Greek words *pteris* and *phuton*, meaning "fern" and "plant."

Gymnosperms

Gymnosperms are a category of plants that have either exposed seeds or seeds that are open to the environment (not enclosed in fruit). Gymnosperms have the smallest number of species when compared to the other three types of plants.

Their seeds, which are held in cones, contain not only a plant **EMBRYO**, but also store food, which the seeds use as food to start growing.

> ## EMBRYO
> The part of a seed that contains the earliest forms of a plant's roots, stem, and leaves.

> *Gymnosperm* comes from the Greek words *gymnos* and *sperma*, meaning "naked" and "seed."

Angiosperms

Angiosperms are flowering plants. Angiosperms hold their seeds within **OVARIES**. The ovary develops into the fruit once the flower is pollinated.

> ### OVARY
> Protective seed-carrying vessel.

> More than 80 percent of all plants are angiosperms.

> *Angiosperm* comes from the Greek words *angeion* and *sperma*, which mean "vessel" and "seed." Seeds are held in a vessel such as a flower or a fruit.

CHECK YOUR KNOWLEDGE

1. Where can plants grow?

2. What traits do plants share?

3. What is the structure in which photosynthesis occurs?

4. What is a plant's vascular system made of?

5. Pteridophytes are the earliest category of plants that have true _____.

6. How do pteridophytes reproduce?

7. What is the category of seeding plants called?

8. What do the seeds of gymnosperms contain?

9. What structures hold seeds in angiosperms?

ANSWERS

1. In soil or water or on other plants

2. All plants are eukaryotic, multicellular, and have cellulose cell walls.

3. Chloroplast

4. Xylem, which provides structural support and transports water; phloem, tubes that distribute food; and vascular cambium, which produces xylem and phloem

5. stems and roots

6. Pteridophytes reproduce using spores.

7. Gymnosperms

8. The seeds contain embryos and nutrients for the embryo.

9. Seeds are held in the plant's fruits.

Chapter 27

PLANT STRUCTURE AND FUNCTION

STRUCTURE AND FUNCTION

Each of the four major categories of plants have structures that are different from one another. Their structures determine how each of them function.

Bryophytes

Bryophytes have no roots to move nutrients over large distances, so they are forced to live in places that have nutrients available for them, such as moist or rich soils. Even if bryophates had roots, without stems they would be unable to move water from the ground to the rest of the plant. The leaves of bryophytes are very thin; in some species, harsh sunlight can cause them to dry up or burn. These sun-sensitive species grow in shady areas, away from harm.

Bryophytes have learned to adapt. To anchor themselves, they use **RHIZOIDS**.

RHIZOID
A tiny, stringy, rootlike growth that helps anchor bryophytes to surfaces.

Bryophytes don't grow in areas where there might be competition for nutrients. Instead, they might grow in areas that other plants can't survive even if that area is rocky. Bryophytes know how to take moisture directly from the air with their thin leaves, helping them survive in their environments. Many bryophytes are able to survive during periods of extreme dryness or cold by becoming dormant. They can become active again with just a little water.

Bryophytes are very strong plants. Every cell performs all the functions needed to keep it alive.

Moss, liverwort, and hornwort are examples of bryophytes.

Pteridophytes

Pteridophytes have structures that make them better at finding nutrients than bryophytes. Their roots allow them to draw nutrients and water from farther away. Pteridophytes' tough stems allow these plants to climb, which, together with their wide leaves, helps the plants capture more sunlight and create more food through photosynthesis.

Pteridophytes have RHIZOMES, underground stems that can produce new roots and store food for the plant.

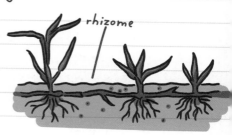
rhizome

Gymnosperms

Gymnosperms were the first vascular plants to evolve to have SEEDS. Seeds are reproductive units adapted to land. Seeds contain everything a plant needs to survive. The plant embryo inside the seed is sustained by the food inside the seed and protected by a tough seed coat that breaks only when in the presence of water and nutrients.

Because seeds are strong, they are usually able to withstand the digestive systems of animals that eat them. This means that when those animals pass their waste, some seeds end up being passed intact with it. Seeds that are dispersed this way go wherever the animal that eats them goes.

Some trees, like ginkgo and conifers, fall into the gymnosperm category. Trees are plants with a trunk and supporting branches. The trunk of a tree is a large stem that is composed of wood, a strong material that consists of phloem and years' worth of xylem (the rings seen in a cross section). The strength of wood also allows a tree to grow taller than other plants.

Angiosperms

branches
leaves
trunk
stem

Because trees are so tall, they are often the first to get sunlight, helping them create enough food to support their size through photosynthesis.

There are more angiosperms on Earth than any other category of plant. Angiosperms are seed plants that have seeds enclosed in fruit. Angiosperms have developed ovaries, which protect their seeds and further ensure the species' survival. Some ovaries develop into fruits, which attract animals that eat them, and then these animals deposit the seeds in a different location.

More than 90 percent of tree species and all grasses are angiosperms.

A angiosperms can attract animals through color. Insects, particularly those with well-developed eyes, are attracted to colorful flowers because they offer a food source called **NECTAR**. Nectar is a sugary fluid that flowers produce to attract insects that help them with the first stages of reproduction.

1. How do the physical structures of bryophytes help them to survive?

2. What do bryophytes do when their ability to gain nutrients is threatened?

3. How do bryophytes with thin leaves get moisture in dry soil?

4. What is unique about the cells of bryophytes versus the cells of more evolved plants?

5. What did pteridophytes evolve to make them better at gaining nutrients than bryophytes?

6. What structure helps pteridophytes produce new roots?

7. How do seeds help a plant species survive?

8. How does the tough coat of a seed help it spread?

9. Why are there more angiosperms than any other type of plant?

ANSWERS   245

CHECK YOUR ANSWERS

1. Bryophytes don't have roots through which they can ingest nutrients. Instead, they have thin leaves that are used to take in moisture from the air.

2. Bryophytes can survive dormant during harsh periods and become active again when water and nutrients are available.

3. They pull moisture from the air.

4. The cells of bryophytes perform all functions that the plant needs to survive.

5. True roots and stems

6. Rhizomes

7. They protect the plant embryo and provide the food it needs.

8. The tough seed coat is able to survive the digestive systems of most animals that eat it. The animal carries the seed and passes it along with its waste at a different location.

9. Their seeds are protected by angiosperms' ovaries.

Chapter 28

PLANT REPRODUCTION

One of the characteristics that separates plants are their methods of reproduction.

Bryophytes and **pteridophytes** use **spores**, reproductive cells that spread through the wind and water.

Gymnosperms and **angiosperms** use **seeds**, reproductive units that contain plant embryos and the food that they need to survive.

Seeds evolved from spores and succeeded in helping plant species survive, which is why seed plants make up the majority of plants today. Species that use spores have unique methods of dispersing their spores that have helped them stay around, even millions of years after the evolution of newer plants.

SPORES

Spores usually are single-celled and contain all necessary **CHROMOSOMES** that make up a species' **GENOME**. They can be created either through sexual reproduction or asexual reproduction.

CHROMOSOME
A structure held within cells that contains part of the genetic information that makes up an organism.

GENOME
The complete set of genes that make up an organism.

offspring come from a combination of genetic information from two parents

offspring come from a single organism

Spores are made and stored in the SPORANGIUM. When the spores are mature, the sporangia (pl.) open, releasing the spores into the wind.

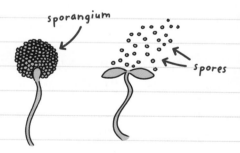
sporangium

spores

Bryophytes, which need moist soils to grow, use water to spread spores. Some species of plants use insects to carry spores away for them.

Seeds

While spores can be created by just one parent, seeds need two parents. Species that reproduce using seeds are sexual reproducers.

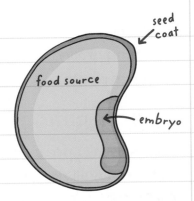

seed coat

food source

embryo

Seeds are made up of the seed embryo, a tough coat that protects it, and its food source. A seed is created in the ovary. When ovaries are **POLLINATED**, they develop into fruits, which encase the seeds.

POLLINATE
To transfer pollen to an ovule.

Some plants are able to pollinate themselves! Self-fertilization means the egg is fertilized by the sperm from the same plant. The plant creates countless genetic varieties of egg/sperm (via meiosis), so the resulting offspring is not a clone of the parent.

The reproduction of seeds begins with **POLLEN** grains that contain sperm. Pollen is produced in a **POLLEN CONE** if the seed plant is a gymnosperm, or a **STAMEN** if the plant is an angiosperm.

POLLEN
A substance that contains half of the chromosomes that a species needs to live.

STAMEN
The part of the angiosperm that produces pollen.

When pollen is produced, it is released from the plant and dispersed ← spread to another plant's **OVULE**. The ovule contains the other half of the necessary chromosomes. When the egg,

> **OVULE**
>
> The structure within the ovary of a plant that houses the egg. It develops into the seed coat when pollinated.

which resides in the ovule, is pollinated, it develops into a seed coat. In gymnosperms, ovules are inside seed cones; in angiosperms, they are inside a PISTIL in the flower.

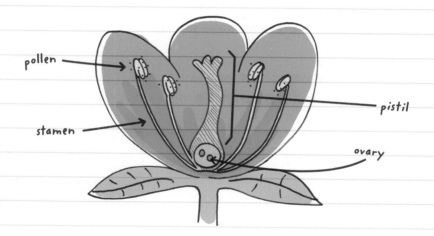

Plants have various methods of SEED DISPERSAL:

- **WIND:** Seeds are light and have feathery bristles that can be carried by the wind (like a dandelion).

- **WATER:** Seeds can float down rivers and streams.

- **ANIMALS:** Seeds can hook on to the fur, feathers, or skin of animals, or they may be eaten and then emerge in the animals' droppings.

- **BURSTING:** The fruits of the seeds can dry and split open, throwing the seeds in various directions.

A PLANT'S LIFE CYCLE

There are two stages in a plant's life cycle. Plants alternate between producing gametes and producing spores.

> **STAGE 1:** Gametophyte phase—sexual reproduction—the plant produces **GAMETES**, or sex cells.

> **STAGE 2:** Sporophyte phase—asexual reproduction—the seed or spore is created after fertilization.

> **GAMETE**
> Sex cells, or sperm and egg cells.

The two-stage plant life cycle is called **METAGENESIS**.

Sexual Reproduction

After a plant's spore is carried by wind or water to moist soils, it buds into a GAMETOPHYTE.

Plants that make egg cells
are "female" gametophytes.

just like with animals

Plants that make sperm cells
are "male" gametophytes.

GAMETOPHYTE (pronounced guh-**mee**-tow-fait)
A plant body that can produce egg or sperm cells.

When the sperm cell of a
male meets with the egg cell
of a female, it can become
FERTILIZED.

FERTILIZE
The combining of a sperm
cell and an egg cell.

Gametophyte comes from the Greek words *gamos*,
meaning "marriage," and *phyte*, meaning "plant."
Gametophytes create different types of cells that, when
brought together, make a new organism.

Asexual Reproduction

The asexual stage begins with the
the creation of a **SPOROPHYTE**.

SPOROPHYTE
A plant that produces
spores or seeds.

253

As the sporophyte grows, it creates spores within its sporangia or seeds within its ovaries. When the sporophyte becomes an adult plant, spores or seeds are dispersed to new environments. When the spores or seeds find a suitable environment to grow in, the cycle restarts from the creation of a new gametophyte.

DOMINANT LIFE STAGE

A plant's "dominant" life stage, or the stage that it spends the most time in, is determined by the type of species it is. Mosses spend more time in the gametophyte stage. Ferns, angiosperms, and gymnosperms spend more time in the sporophyte stage.

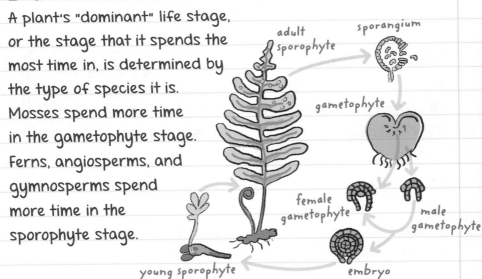

Depending on the climate where the species exist, gymnosperms and angiosperms can produce pollen at different times. But the pollen is usually produced only for a few months, once a year.

CHECK YOUR KNOWLEDGE

1. What types of plants reproduce using seeds?

2. Compare the methods of reproduction for species that create spores and those that create seeds.

3. In what structure are spores produced?

4. In what structure are seeds produced?

5. What two parts from separate seed plants interact to result in pollination?

6. What is the two-stage life cycle of plants called?

7. What is the function of a gametophyte?

8. How do gametophytes lead to the next stage in the plant's life cycle?

9. What is the function of sporophytes?

10. What is the dominant life stage of an angiosperm?

ANSWERS

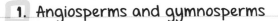

CHECK YOUR ANSWERS

1. Angiosperms and gymnosperms

2. Species that create spores use both asexual and sexual reproduction, while those that create seeds use only sexual reproduction.

3. Spores are produced in the sporangia.

4. Seeds are produced in the ovaries.

5. Pollen (contains sperm); ovule (contains egg)

6. Metagenesis

7. A gametophyte creates sex cells, such as the sperm or egg cells.

8. The sperm cells made by male gametophytes fertilize the egg cells made by female gametophytes and lead to the creation of a sporophyte.

9. Sporophytes create spores or seeds.

10. The sporophyte stage

Chapter 29

PLANT ADAPTATION

Plants, like all life-forms, need to adapt to survive.
These adaptations can come in the form of:

- changes in behavior
- changes in shape
- production of chemicals

ANNUALS, BIENNIALS, AND PERENNIALS

Different plant species can have life cycles that begin at different times and last for varying amounts of time.

Type: annual
Life-Cycle Span: one year

Annuals have one season of growth before dying.

Type: biennial
Life-Cycle Span: two years

Plants spend their first year growing their
roots and stems before going dormant ← alive, but
in colder months.   not actively
                                           growing

During their second year, in warmer months, biennials grow
leaves, flowers, and fruits with seeds before they die.

Type: perennial
Life-Cycle Span: more than two years

Perennial plants grow from their seeds and grow flowers,
leaves, and fruits in warmer months.

During colder months, angiosperms typically lose their
flowers, leaves, and fruits and go dormant. Gymnosperms
can survive colder months without losing their leaves.

Perennials can take a long time to grow to adulthood.

Many plants' life cycles begin in response to their
environment. For example, seeds will grow only in the

presence of water. If there is no water around, the seed will remain dormant.

> Some species germinate only after extreme conditions. For example, there are seeds that germinate only after forest fires. This happens because certain chemicals within smoke trigger the seed's germination.

BIOMES

The environment doesn't only determine when and how plants grow, but it also determines which species grow.

Plants have adapted various structures to help them survive in particular environments. For example, mosses can absorb moisture through their thin leaves and their rhizoids. This means that they can survive anywhere there is water, whether it is cold or hot.

In places like deserts, where rainfall is rare, the thin mosses, which can't hold water, would die quickly. Succulent plants, such as cacti, which can store large amounts of water in their cells, can survive the deserts' dry seasons. If these plants were placed in a rain forest, their

ENOUGH ALREADY!

roots, which are used to handling only small amounts of water, would rot, killing the plant.

Plants that live in the same environment all have similar traits that allow them to survive in that environment. The environment is called a **BIOME**.

There are eight main biomes:

TEMPERATE FOREST

- Temperate forests have four distinct seasons

- Trees include deciduous trees, which shed their leaves in colder months, and evergreen trees, which never shed their leaves

- Types of plants: mosses, ferns, short plants, trees, flowers

TROPICAL RAIN FOREST

- Forests where rain falls throughout the year

- Species of plants are still being discovered in rain forests

- Types of plants: trees, mosses, ferns, flowers

GRASSLAND ← *think prairie, pasture, plains*

- Plains that are dominated by grasses

- There is very little rain, which can cause fires; little rain and the presence of fires prevent trees from growing

- Types of plants: grasses, short plants

SAVANNA

- Plains that receive ample rain to support grasses and trees
- Types of plants: grasses, mosses, short plants, trees, flowers

TAIGA

- Frigid forest lands

- The soils contain permafrost (frozen soils) and bedrock, an impenetrable layer of rock; both keep water at the top layers of the soil

- Pine needles lose less water than normal leaves, which helps them survive in the harsh environment

- Trees are flexible and cone-shaped, which helps them stay strong under the weight of snow and ice

- Types of plants: gymnosperm trees, mosses

TUNDRA

- Cold plains that contain permafrost

- In cold months, the plains freeze over

- Types of plants: grasses, mosses

DESERT

- Two main seasons: a hot, dry season and a harsh, cold season

- There is very little rainfall, preventing most life from taking hold

- Types of plants: cacti

AQUATIC ← it's underwater!

- The largest biome on Earth

- Clear waters allow light to penetrate it; plants grow on surfaces of the seafloor

- Types of plants: sea grasses, mangrove trees, mosses

CHECK YOUR KNOWLEDGE

1. What drives the adaptation of plants?

2. For how long does an annual plant live?

3. During which year does a biennial plant go dormant?

4. What months do most perennial plants grow leaves, flowers, and/or fruits?

5. What is needed for a seed to grow?

6. What is a biome?

7. Compare the number of seasons between a temperate forest and a desert.

8. What's the difference between savannas and grasslands?

9. Why do gymnosperms do so well in the taiga biome?

10. Which is the largest biome?

ANSWERS

CHECK YOUR ANSWERS

1. The adaptation of plants is driven by the environment.

2. Annual plants live for one year.

3. Biennial plants go dormant in their first year.

4. The warmer months

5. Water

6. A biome is any environment in which a specific community of plants live.

7. There are four seasons in temperate forests, but two in deserts.

8. Savannas get more rainfall than grasslands, which allows for trees to grow.

9. Gymnosperm trees are cone-shaped and flexible, which helps snow and ice slide off without breaking them.

10. Aquatic biome

Unit 8

Animals

Chapter 30

THE ANIMAL KINGDOM

ANIMAL CHARACTERISTICS

Animals are all:

MULTICELLULAR: have more than one cell;

HETEROTROPHIC: get their nutrients from another source;

and animal cells are supported by COLLAGEN, a tough protein that forms the structure of animal cells.

Animal cells also don't have rigid cell walls like plants and bacteria do. Because of this, animal cells are flexible and fluid.

Most animals have symmetry, which means they look identical across a line that divides them. BILATERAL SYMMETRY means that if you drew a line down their bodies, each side would look the same.

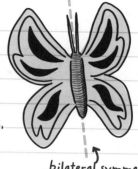

bilateral symmetry

same
same
same

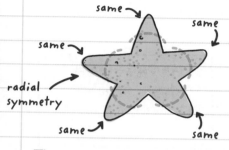

radial symmetry

same
same

Other animals have RADIAL SYMMETRY, which means that they have identical parts arranged in a circle.

There are a few ASYMMETRICAL animals—like the sea sponge, which is the simplest of multicellular animals.

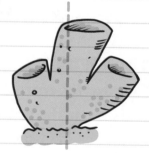

Most animals reproduce sexually, meaning they require two parents to reproduce. There are a few that can reproduce both sexually and asexually, like the Komodo dragon, which, depending on conditions, can lay unfertilized eggs that develop to maturity without a mate.

komodo dragon

PROCESSES

All animals participate in certain processes (functions) that allow them to live and survive within their environments. These functions are:

- ## NUTRITION

  Animals gain their nutrients from eating other organisms.

- ## RESPIRATION

  Respiration is the breakdown of nutrients to get energy. It is a part of **METABOLISM**.

  > **METABOLISM**
  > The set of all chemical reactions that maintain an organism's life.

- ## TRANSPORT

  In order for energy to be made inside the body, nutrients need to be transported from where they are broken down to the cells. The process of transporting nutrients is called **CIRCULATION**.

  > Humans have a circulation system made of vessels that transport blood. The blood transports nutrients to cells.

- ## EXCRETION

  In the energy-making process, waste products are created. The process of excretion removes these waste products from the body and keeps it healthy.

ADAPTATION

Adaptation is the process of change that helps an organism suit itself to its environment. Organisms that properly adapt to changes in their environment survive longer than organisms that do not adapt.

An environment can be internal or external.

In INTERNAL ENVIRONMENTS—inside the body— adaptation is guided by **HOMEOSTASIS**, which regulates everything from blood pressure to how nutrients are used.

HOMEOSTASIS
The tendency of an organism to be internally stable.

In EXTERNAL ENVIRONMENTS—outside the body— adaptation uses, among other features, **LOCOMOTION**, the ability to move from one place to another.

If the external environment changes too fast, a species may die out. There is also a small chance that the species may **EVOLVE**. Evolution is the process of adaptation that causes changes in the characteristics of a species over several generations.

REPRODUCTION

The purpose of reproduction is to maintain a species. Animals normally reproduce sexually, which means that two parents are required to create a new organism.

Each parent has its own GAMETE, or sex cell. Each cell has half the amount of genetic material that an organism needs to live. When both gametes come together, fertilization occurs, and a new organism is created.

Sexual Reproduction

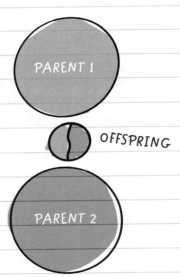

PARENT 1

OFFSPRING

PARENT 2

CHECK YOUR KNOWLEDGE

1. What protein supports the cells of animals?

2. How do animals get their nutrients?

3. What is the function of respiration?

4. What process brings nutrients from their place of metabolism to the cells?

5. What is the purpose of excretion?

6. What drives an organism to adapt to its environment?

7. What regulates internal environments?

8. What is the easiest way for an organism to adapt to changes in an external environment?

9. What is one way that a species can adapt to an external environment's changes?

10. Why do animals reproduce?

ANSWERS

1. Collagen

2. Animals get their nutrients by eating other organisms.

3. Respiration helps an animal break down nutrients to get energy.

4. The process of circulation brings nutrients to the cells.

5. Excretion helps an organism stay healthy by removing waste products.

6. Survival

7. Homeostasis

8. The easiest way for an organism to adapt to changes in an external environment is to move away from that environment to a better suited one.

9. Evolution

10. Animals reproduce to maintain their species.

Chapter 31

INVERTEBRATES

Animals that do not have a backbone are called
INVERTEBRATES. Invertebrates make up more than
95 percent of the animal kingdom. Examples of invertebrates
include insects, shellfish, worms, snails, and sponges.

Invertebrates are broken up into several categories. Most of
the animals in the categories live in
MARINE, or seawater, environments.

> that yellow, holey,
> squishy-when-wet
> object we wash with

SEA SPONGES (Poriferans): Sea sponges live under
the water and have pores (holes) and channels
in their bodies that allow water and nutrients
to pass through. Sponges clean the water
around them by filtering plankton out of
the water for food. Sea sponges were
once thought to be plants because they
are SESSILE, or unmoving. But unlike
plants, all sponges are heterotrophs.

Porifera comes from the Latin words *porus* and *fera*, which mean "pore" and "bearing," respectively.

Sponges are pore-bearing animals.

Reproduction in sea sponges is both sexual and asexual.

- **Sexual Reproduction:** Most sponges are HERMAPHRODITES, which means they produce both sperm and eggs. Sponges combine male and female genetic material to produce offspring that have recombined genetic information.

- **Asexual Reproduction:** Sponges produce BUDS, which are parts of a parent sponge that fall off and grow into new sponges that are identical to the parent.

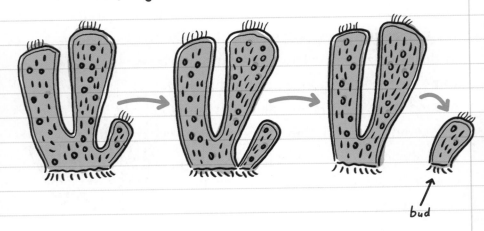

bud

pronounced Ni-DAR-ee-ans

CNIDARIANS: Cnidarians are made up of more than 10,000 species of animals, including jellyfish, sea anemones, hydras, and corals. They are named after specialized cells that they all contain, called **CNIDOCYTES**. Cnidocytes are found in the tentacles that the animals use to capture prey and to defend against predators. The cnidocyte injects a toxin, or poison, into anything nearby.

Because cnidarians offer a valuable method of protection, some types of fish hide behind them and even live among anemones or corals. These fish either avoid the cnidocytes entirely or are immune to their toxin. In return for the natural protection provided by the cnidarians, the fish keep the coral clean by eating the algae that grows on the coral.

CNIDOCYTES
Cells that inject toxins into prey.

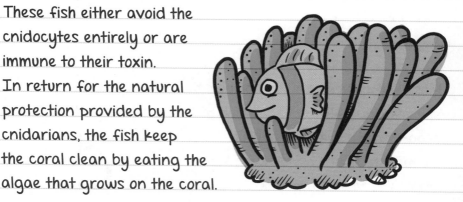

Toxins are why jellyfish stings continue to hurt after a while and can even cause a numbing feeling. Smaller organisms can be paralyzed or even killed by it.

Reproduction in cnidarians is both sexual and asexual.

- Some sexually reproductive species are **MONOECIOUS**, which means that they are able to produce both egg and sperm cells. They cannot fertilize their own sex cells; so, two parents are still needed.

Cnidarian comes from the Greek word *knidē*, meaning "nettle." Nettles are plants that have stinging hair.

FLATWORMS (Platyhelminths): These are flat organisms that move by slithering and gliding through the water. Their bodies are held together with a spongy connective tissue called MESENCHYME.

Most flatworms can live on their own, but a few of the species are PARASITIC, which means they need other organisms to live, and can be harmful to their host or even kill them. The tapeworm is one type of parasitic flatworm. It lives in the host's intestines, eating its food.

tapeworm

Reproduction is sexual and asexual.

- Some sexually reproducing flatworms can be monoecious.

- Asexual reproduction occurs through BUDDING, where they create buds that fall off the parent and create new worms, and FRAGMENTATION, in which they tear themselves into pieces that each grow into new worms. Like cnidarians, many flatworms have both sperm and egg cells and are able to fertilize.

fragmentation

ROUNDWORMS, PINWORMS, HOOKWORMS (Nematodes):
Nematodes are like two long tubes layered within each other. They can live in nearly every kind of environment. Nematodes can live on their own or as parasites. They can be **CARNIVOROUS** (meat-eating) or **HERBIVOROUS** (plant-eating). Carnivorous nematodes have sharp cuticles in their mouths that allow them to attach to other organisms.

like teeth!

Reproduction is sexual.

- Nematodes can also be monoecious.

ANNELIDS: Annelids are earthworms, leeches, and marine worms. Annelids are known as SEGMENTED WORMS because their bodies are made up of small connected rings, or segments. They often have bristles around their bodies that they use to move. The ringlike segments on their bodies can stretch and expand, which, when combined with their bristles, gives them a large amount of flexibility. Annelids often dig into the ground and eat organic materials within the soil. Their waste, when decomposed, enriches the soil and helps plants grow, making them valuable for any environment.

EARTHWORMS are usually found in soil and eat living or dead organic matter.

Gardeners love earthworms because they improve the condition of the soil in their gardens.

MARINE WORMS live on the ocean floor and scavenge tiny food particles. LEECHES are parasitic, feeding off the nutrient-rich blood of other animals, but they can also capture and eat other invertebrates.

Annelid reproduction is both sexual and asexual. Some annelids like earthworms are monoecious, but cannot self-fertilize.

MOLLUSKS: Mollusks are soft-bodied organisms that usually have a shell. A layer of tissue called a mantle surrounds their bodies. Their shells can be made of chitin, a tough carbohydrate, or calcium carbonate. In mollusks with shells, the mantle protects the mollusks' internal organs and secretes the chemicals that form the shell. Examples of mollusks include snails, slugs, oysters, squid, and octopuses. CEPHALOPODS and APLACOPHORA are two classes of mollusks that don't have shells. Octopuses are examples of cephalopods.

Mollusks reproduce sexually and some species are monoecious. They cannot self-fertilize.

ECHINODERMS: Echinoderms are scavengers with spiny skins that eat anything, making them **OMNIVOROUS**. Echinoderms have radial symmetry. They don't have heads or brains. They can regenerate damaged organs and even entire limbs.

OMNIVORE (adj. omnivorous)
An animal that can eat plants or meat.

Examples of echinoderms are sea urchins, sea cucumbers, and starfish.

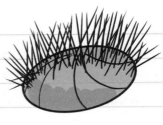

Echinoderm reproduction is both sexual and asexual.

- Both male and female echinoderms release sperm and egg cells into the water, where fertilization occurs externally.

- Some species can divide into two different organisms. These two organisms then grow into two adult organisms. For example, a starfish species can reproduce an entirely new starfish from one of its arms.

> Each arm carries an equal share of vital organs.

Echinoderms like sea cucumbers move by using their small tentacle-like tube feet to pull themselves forward or flex their bodies to inch forward along the ground.

Asexual reproduction in echinoderms usually involves the division of the body into two or more parts—FRAGMENTATION—and the REGENERATION of missing body parts.

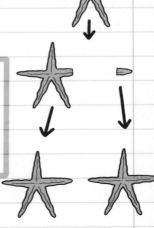

CHECK YOUR KNOWLEDGE

1. How do sea sponges eat?

2. Cnidarians are _____, which means that the same individuals can produce both sperm and egg cells.

3. What are the cells that contain the toxin that cnidarians secrete called?

4. What happens to flatworms that reproduce through fragmentation?

5. What do annelids eat?

6. Name two mollusk classes that do not have shells.

7. What two materials might mollusk shells be made of?

8. How do sea cucumbers move?

9. Where do starfish hold their vital organs?

10. Are echinoderms carnivorous, herbivorous, or omnivorous?

ANSWERS

CHECK YOUR ANSWERS

1. They filter nutrients from the water that flows through their pores.

2. Monoecious

3. Cnidocytes

4. They tear themselves into pieces that each grow into a new flatworm.

5. Organic matter within the soil

6. Cephalopods and Aplacophora

7. Chitin or calcium carbonate

8. Sea cucumbers can use their tentacle-like tube feet to pull themselves forward or flex their bodies to inch forward along the ground.

9. Starfish house an equal share of vital organs in each arm.

10. Omnivorous

Chapter 32

ARTHROPODS

Arthropods have segmented bodies, which allow them to turn and bend. Their limbs have joints, enabling them to take long strides and climb. This helps them to quickly move over land and water.

Arthropods have an **EXOSKELETON**, which protects their vital organs and supports their bodies. It acts like armor for the arthropod. As arthropods grow, they shed and rebuild their exoskeletons. This process, which occurs frequently over the life of an arthropod, is called **MOLTING**.

EXOSKELETON
A hard outer body covering.

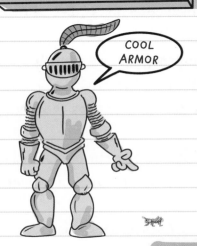

COOL ARMOR

Arthropods are the most abundant phylum in the animal kingdom, composing 85 percent of all animals. They live in salt water, fresh water, and on land. They hunt other smaller organisms or scavenge dead organisms for food.

Most TERRESTRIAL, or land-based, arthropods lay eggs after external fertilization and reproduce sexually, either through direct breeding or using **SPERMATOPHORES**, capsules that contain sperm cells. With terrestrial arthropods, male arthropods pass sperm cells internally to a female arthropod's egg cells, and the females then lay their fertilized eggs. AQUATIC, or water-based, arthropods use mostly external fertilization. They pass their sperm cells into the water, where they enter the bodies of nearby female arthropods.

Arthropods are usually categorized by how many segments their bodies have, the number of legs they have, and any additional organs that individual species may share.

Classes of arthropods include:
- **Crustaceans**, such as crabs, shrimp, and lobsters

- **Chelicerates**, such as scorpions, spiders, and ticks

- **Myriapods**, such as centipedes and millipedes

- **Insects**, such as flies and bees

CRUSTACEANS

Crustaceans are arthropods that contain three segments: a head, a **THORAX**, and an **ABDOMEN**. In some species, the head and thorax are fused into one segment called the CEPHALOTHORAX.

> **THORAX**
> The part of an animal's body between the neck and the abdomen, which usually contains the heart and lungs.

> **ABDOMEN**
> The part of an animal's body that contains the stomach and intestines.

abdomen · thorax · head

Cephalon comes from the Greek word *kephalē*, meaning "head."

There are more than 65,000 species of crustaceans, many of which are capable of living on both land and water. DECAPODS are crustaceans that live in water, like crayfish, crabs, lobsters, prawns, and shrimp.

from the Greek words *deca* and *pod*, meaning "ten" and "foot"

CHELICERATES

Chelicerates are arthropods that have two body segments—a cephalothorax and an abdomen—and a jawlike structure called the CHELICERA, which is where this arthropod's name comes from. Many have **PEDIPALPS**, which are appendages that are close to the chelicerae and help chelicerates taste and smell, or work as weapons, such as pincers.

structures that are attached to something larger

chelicerae   cephalotorax

pedipalps→

↖abdom

There are approximately 77,000 species of chelicerates, most of which live on land. All scorpions and most spiders are predators. Ticks and mites have adapted to feed on host organisms and some chelicerates have adapted to scavenging—eating decaying matter.

MYRIAPODS

Myriapods are among the most ancient of the living arthropods. They have segmented bodies and a pair of antennae. Each segment of their bodies has a pair of legs attached to it. Depending on the species, their bodies can be short or very long, supporting anywhere from 10 to 750 legs. Centipedes and millipedes are examples of myriapods.

Myriapod comes from the Greek words *murios* and *poda*, meaning "ten thousand" and "feet."

There are about 16,000 species of
myriapods. Most of them live on land.

INSECTS

Insects are the most numerous of the arthropods.
The number of species is estimated at between six
and ten million, with more than
a million described so far. Their
bodies are clearly divided into
three segments: a head with a pair
of antennae; a thorax that contains
six legs and, sometimes, one or two
pairs of wings; and an abdomen.

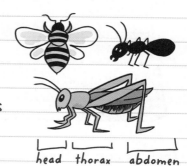

head   thorax   abdomen

Insects are the only type of animal to have species that
undergo complete **METAMORPHOSIS**, a process in which
an organism passes through three or four distinct life phases.

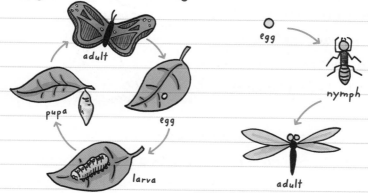

adult

pupa

egg

larva

egg

nymph

adult

After changing into their adult stage, insects look completely
different than they did at their larval stage. Each stage has

its own needs and focus. For example, in the larva stage the insect focuses completely on eating. In the adult stage insects focus completely on reproduction.

LARVA
A young, immature insect.

PUPA
An insect in the inactive, immature state between larva and adult.

The transformation of a caterpillar into a butterfly or moth is the most well-known example of metamorphosis.

Insects can be found in every environment in the world, and on land or in water, and they can perform many environmental roles. Insects such as ants form complex, cooperative societies that allow them to transform entire environments and defend their territory against much larger organisms, including humans.

STAND YOUR GROUND!

Insects such as bees help flowers spread to new environments by pollinating flowers. Grasshoppers can break down plants, helping them decompose, ensuring that the plants that grow after are stronger.

CHECK YOUR KNOWLEDGE

1. What provides protection and structure to the bodies of arthropods?

2. What percentage of the animal kingdom consists of arthropods?

3. Name three ways that arthropods are categorized.

4. What are decapods?

5. What are the jawlike appendages of chelicerates called?

6. What characteristics do insects share?

7. Explain the process of metamorphosis.

ANSWERS

CHECK YOUR ANSWERS

1. Exoskeletons

2. About 85 percent of all animals are arthropods.

3. Arthropods are categorized by how many segments their bodies have, how many legs they have, and which organs that species may share.

4. Decapods are crustaceans that have ten legs and live in water.

5. Chelicerae

6. Insects have bodies that are composed of three segments: a head, which has a pair of antennae; a thorax, containing six legs and, sometimes, one or two pairs of wings; and an abdomen.

7. Metamorphosis is a process in which an insect goes through distinct phases: an egg stage, a larva stage, a pupa stage, and an adult stage (or an egg, nymph, and adult).

Chapter 33

CHORDATES

Chordates make up only about 5 percent of all animal species.

> The word part *chord* is used in the names of many organisms in this phylum, either as a body part or in the name of a species. Humans, for example, contain a spinal "cord."

Chordates are animals that at some stage in their development have a:

■ **NOTOCHORD**, a supporting rod (like a backbone) that runs the length of the body. The notochord is a structure that helps bone and cartilage grow. In vertebrates, like humans, the notochord develops into the vertebral column.

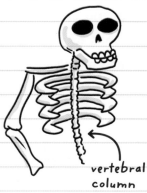

vertebral column

- **NERVE CORD**, a nerve in the "back," or dorsal, of the body that is also a structure that contains **NEURONS**. This structure is part of the animal's nervous system and contributes to its survival by creating a network of nerves that helps the organism to better sense its environment.

> **NERVE CORD**
> A hollow supporting structure that runs along the dorsal side of an animal.

> **NEURON**
> A cell that transmits electrical messages to and from the brain.

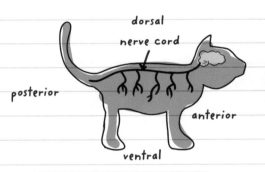

- **PHARYNGEAL SLITS**, openings along the sides of some chordates' heads. In fish, these slits support the gills, while in humans, these slits are briefly present during embryonic development, then develop into the bones of the jaw and the inner ear. The name is based on their position close to the **PHARYNX**, part of the throat.

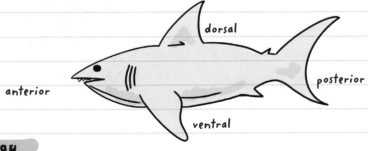

Chordates are sometimes divided into two categories: nonvertebrate and vertebrate. ←

any animal that has a vertebral column

- **POST-ANAL TAIL**, a muscular tail that extends backward behind the anus.

NONVERTEBRATE CHORDATES

Nonvertebrate chordates are made up of two groups: TUNICATES and CEPHALOCHORDATES. Organisms in both of these groups have a notochord; however their notochords do not develop into a vertebral column as in humans.

Tunicates

Tunicates make up a group of 2,000 different species that attach themselves to a rigid object, such as a rock or coral. They filter feed, using one of their two openings to suck in water and the other to push out water, separating any food from the water within their bodies.

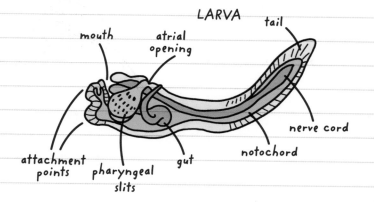

LARVA

mouth   atrial opening   tail

attachment points   pharyngeal slits   gut   notochord   nerve cord

Tunicate **larvae**, or young, look a lot like tadpoles. They contain a notochord, nerve cord, tail, and pharyngeal slits. They lose their tails as they develop into adults and develop the openings that they use to filter feed.

Cephalochordates

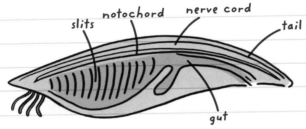

slits notochord nerve cord tail gut

Cephalochordates, also known as **LANCELETS**, have about thirty different species in their group. Instead of attaching themselves to surfaces, they burrow into the sand at the bottom of the seas and poke their heads out of the sand to filter feed. Water that goes into their mouths is filtered out through their pharyngeal slits, while any food enters their gut. Lancelets reproduce sexually, shedding eggs and sperm cells directly into the water, where they meet.

like a fishing net

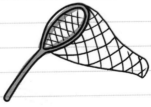

Lancelets are so named because of their straight, lancelike appearance.

VERTEBRATE CHORDATES

In vertebrates, the notochord is a principal element of the early embryo, in which it plays an organizational role in nervous system development. In later vertebrate development, it becomes part of the vertebral column. In vertebrates, the spinal cord, along with the brain, make up the central **NERVOUS SYSTEM**. It carries electrical messages to and from the brain to the rest of the body.

> **NERVOUS SYSTEM**
> A body system that brings electrical messages to and from the brain.

SPINAL CORD

nerve root: stimulates movement and feeling

spinal cord disc: protects the spine

All vertebrate chordates are sexual reproducers. Aquatic, or water-based, species fertilize egg cells externally, with males of a species passing their sperm cells into the water and females releasing their eggs into the water where they join with the sperm cells. Terrestrial, or land-based, species fertilize egg cells internally, with direct contact between males and females.

There are seven classes of vertebrates.

CLASSES OF VERTEBRATES

CLASS	ANIMALS	DESCRIPTION
AGNATHA **Common name:** Jawless Fish	Lampreys and Hagfish	Fish without jawbones.
CHONDRICHTHYES **Common name:** Cartilaginous Fish	Sharks, Rays, Skates	Fish with skeletons that are made of CARTILAGE instead of bone.
OSTEICHTHYES **Common name:** Bony Fish	Catfish, Salmon, Tuna, Clown Fish	Fish with skeletons that are made of bone instead of cartilage.
AMPHIBIA **Common name:** Amphibians	Frogs, Toads, Salamanders	COLD-BLOODED animals that spend part of their time on land and part of their time in the water. Cold-blooded animals need sunlight to regulate their body temperature. (WARM-BLOODED animals can regulate their own temperature.) Organisms breathe through their skin and lungs. Most amphibians, like insects, undergo metamorphosis.
REPTILIA **Common name:** Reptiles	Lizards, Turtles, Crocodiles, Snakes, most of the dinosaurs	Scaled, cold-blooded animals. Most reptiles produce eggs, although some give birth to live young.

CLASS	ANIMALS	DESCRIPTION
AVES **Common name:** Birds 	Parrots, Eagles, Owls, Penguins	Animals that have beaks, or bills, made of a bony material, wings, and bodies covered with feathers. They reproduce by laying eggs. Birds have a four-chambered heart.
MAMMALIA **Common name:** Mammals Octupuses have three hearts; earthworms have five heart-like structures! → 	Dogs, Cats, Humans	Animals that have hair or fur on the body, produce milk to feed young, have glands that give off sweat and scent, and have different types of teeth. Organisms have a four-chambered heart. Most organisms walk on four legs, but some can walk on two. Some aquatic mammals, such as whales, seals, and otters, have limbs that evolved into fins. Mammals mostly give live birth, but a few lay eggs.

CHECK YOUR KNOWLEDGE

1. What are chordates?

2. What is a notochord?

3. What is the function of the nerve cord?

4. What is the difference between a chordate and a vertebrate?

5. What are the two main groups of nonvertebrate chordates?

6. What happens when tunicates develop from larvae to adult?

7. How do lancelets feed?

8. What system is the spinal cord a part of?

9. What class of vertebrate were the dinosaurs?

10. What two classes of vertebrates can reproduce by internally fertilizing eggs?

CHECK YOUR ANSWERS

1. Chordates are animals that at some point in time have a notochord, a nerve chord, pharyngeal slits, and a post-anal tail.

2. The notochord is a flexible, skeletal support that runs along the back (dorsal side) of an animal.

3. The nerve cord helps the organism to better sense the environment and sends electrical messages to the brain.

4. Vertebrates have a vertebral column.

5. Tunicates and cephalochordates

6. Tunicates lose their tail and develop openings used to filter food as they grow to adulthood.

7. Lancelets burrow into the sand and stick their heads out to take in food. Water is filtered out of their pharyngeal slits.

8. The nervous system

9. Reptilia/Reptiles

10. Reptilia/Reptiles and Aves/Birds

Chapter 34

VERTEBRATES: ANAMNIOTES

Anamniotes are made up of fish and amphibian species because **EMBRYOS** are not enclosed by an **AMNION**, a thin membrane in amniotes that protects the embryo from the outside world. The lack

like in the seed of a plant!

> **EMBRYO**
> An organism in its early stages of development.

of an amnion means that the soft, jellylike eggs laid by fish and amphibians would dry out without water.

Fish and amphibians are sexual reproducers, creating their offspring through the fertilization of egg cells with sperm cells.

WHY DO WE ALWAYS HAVE TO GO TO YOUR PLACE TO HANG OUT?

Fish live only in aquatic environments and at every depth, from the water's surface to the bottom of oceans. However, most amphibians spend only part of their lives in water and the rest of their lives on land.

FISH

All fish live successfully in water. They breathe underwater using GILLS, which are a structure that carries out gas exchange with water. Fish have fins on their sides to help them steer in water. They also have fins on the tops and bottoms of their bodies for stability. The bodies of some fish contain a special air bladder, which is filled with a gas that helps the fish stay afloat. Fish that do not contain an air bladder must constantly swim or take time to rest and recover at the bottom of the water.

Some fish without air bladders survive by blending themselves into the sand to avoid predators and to sneak up on prey.

Fish can be predators or prey, eating or being eaten by other organisms or even fellow fish. As fish die or are eaten, their bodies nourish all other organisms in the sea, including plants and smaller organisms.

YIKES!

Three main classes of fish include:

CLASS	ANIMALS	DESCRIPTION
AGNATHA **Common name:** Jawless Fish	Lampreys and Hagfish	Their mouths are round due to the lack of a jawbone. Fish like the lamprey have a mouth full of sharp teeth that they use to hook into other fish. They either feed on the flesh or the blood of their host. Hagfish are scavengers, feeding on things that are dead or dying.
CHONDRICHTHYES **Common name:** Cartilaginous Fish	Sharks, Rays, Skates	Their skeletons are made of ~~CARTILAGE~~, which is a firm but flexible kind of connective tissue. Your ears and nose are made out of cartilage, which is why you can twist and bend them with your hands. Some species of cartilaginous fish can give birth to live offspring, like humans, instead of laying eggs. Some cartilaginous fish have a sucker-like mouth with claws or teeth inside. They can attach to another fish and suck its blood!
OSTEICHTHYES **Common name:** Bony Fish	Most fish (Catfish, Salmon, Tuna, etc.)	Bony fish have skeletons made of bone. Most bony fish have scales that are made of thin, bony plates. They are also covered in a layer of mucus that helps them glide through the water.

AMPHIBIANS

Amphibians are animals that spend their larval, or young, stages in the water and their adult stages on land. Biologists believe that amphibians were the first kinds of animals to develop bodies suited to living on land.

Most amphibians use external fertilization. For amphibians to transition between water and land, they have to undergo metamorphosis. The process can include developing:

- limbs that allow them to move on land;
- eyes that allow them to see farther out of water; and
- lungs that they use to breathe and process air.

Amphibians breathe in air through their skin (along with their lungs), which must remain moist and flexible. This prevents them from traveling too far away from water. Because amphibians must keep their skin wet, scientists can use amphibians to determine the health of the environment. If conditions are too dry, amphibians will not live there, which can let scientists know that an area does not receive enough rain. Amphibians cannot fully function in conditions that are too cold, so they hibernate in colder months.

The main groups of amphibians are:

ORDER	ANIMALS	DESCRIPTION
ICHTHYOSTEGALIA	Ichthyostega	An extinct species that is theorized by scientists to be the first amphibians on land. Clumsy and slow, with four legs and poorly developed feet. They had a muscular tail that helped them move along land to make up for their weak leg muscles.
ANURA	Frogs and Toads	Their larvae (tadpoles) lose their tails during metamorphosis from larva to adult. Their feet are webbed, allowing them to push their limbs against the water to swim faster.
URODELA	Salamanders and Newts	Salamanders keep the same appearance from their larval stages into their adult stages. They use their legs and arms, as well as their tail, to help them swim. Their limbs are so short that their bellies drag along the ground.

YOU'D BE CLUMSY AND SLOW, TOO, IF YOU WERE BUILT LIKE THIS.

ORDER	ANIMALS	DESCRIPTION
APODA	Caecilians ↑ Latin for "blind ones"	Apoda are limbless and snakelike. They are burrowers that "see" using their skin to feel for vibrations, which guide their movement.
		They have strong skulls that help them burrow through mud and sand.
		They have sharp teeth but swallow their food whole, like snakes.
		Like frogs, they grow lungs during metamorphosis and breathe through their skin.

1. What is an anamniote?

2. How do fish and amphibians reproduce?

3. What is the function of an air bladder?

4. Why are the mouths of Agnatha round?

5. What do lampreys eat?

6. Chondrichthyes have skeletons made of _____.

7. What can amphibians gain after undergoing metamorphosis?

8. What substance must amphibians always have nearby?

9. How do the sightless caecilians "see"?

ANSWERS

CHECK YOUR ANSWERS

1. Anamniotes are organisms that don't have embryos encased in an amnion.

2. Fish and amphibians reproduce sexually, creating offspring through the fertilization of egg cells.

3. The air bladder helps a fish float in water.

4. The round mouths of Agnatha are due to the fact that they don't have a jawbone.

5. Lampreys feed on the blood and flesh of their hosts.

6. Cartilage

7. Better eyes, limbs that help them move on land, and lungs to help them breathe

8. Water

9. Caecilians use their skin, feeling for vibrations in the ground.

Chapter 35

VERTEBRATES: AMNIOTES

EMBRYO PROTECTION

Amniotes are made up of reptiles, birds, and mammals and are among the most recently evolved species on Earth. Their name comes from the thin membrane, called the amnion, that protects their embryos from their outside environment. A fluid forms within the amnion that protects the embryo from being damaged by shock from external forces. This adaptation allows offspring to be born on land, which is more changeable and is more dangerous than underwater environments.

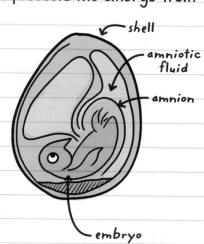

shell

amniotic fluid

amnion

embryo

AMNIOTE—with amnion
ANAMNIOTE—without amnion

The amnion is further protected by eggshells, like those of reptiles and birds, or by a womb, like those of mammals like humans.

Body Temperature

The most important difference between amniotes is their body temperature, which can determine how their bodies function. Many species can regulate their own body temperature within a certain range; however, some need heat from outside sources.

An amniote that needs heat from outside sources, such as the sun, is called ECTOTHERMIC. Most reptiles are ectotherms, or cold-blooded.

An amniote that can create its own heat is called ENDOTHERMIC. All birds and mammals are endotherms, or warm-blooded.

The cells of some endotherms go through an energy-making process that generates heat as waste, which is why they can create their own heat.

REPTILES

Modern reptiles are the descendants of the dinosaurs. Like reptiles, dinosaurs came in many shapes and sizes, laid eggs, and could be **HERBIVOROUS**, **CARNIVOROUS**, or **OMNIVOROUS**.

HERBIVOROUS
Species that eat only plants.

CARNIVOROUS
Species that eat only meat.

OMNIVOROUS
Species that eat both plants and meat.

The eggs of amphibians and fish are soft sacs. In order to keep these eggs healthy, they need to be laid in water. However, the eggs of reptiles and birds have shells. This helps protect the egg from conditions on land.

Reptiles also have scales, made of a tough protein called **KERATIN**. These scales help reptiles retain their bodies' moisture and heat, while also being flexible enough to allow their bodies to move.

Keratin is the same protein that human hair and nails are made of.

As reptiles grow, they molt, shedding their scales and growing new ones. When they shed their scales, reptiles can be vulnerable. So they hide while they shed, emerging only after they grow more scales.

I FEEL SO NAKED.

Reptiles are predators of pests, eating many insects and rodents like rats and squirrels. Reptiles have sharp teeth and good vision, which help them as they hunt.

MODERN REPTILE GROUPS

ORDER	ANIMALS	DESCRIPTION
SPHENODONTS	Tuataras	May be the oldest living reptile, having bones like those of fish and amphibians. Unlike other lizards, they have no external ears and poorly developed eardrums.
SQUAMATA	Snakes and Lizards	This is the largest order of reptiles.
TESTUDINES	Turtles and Tortoises	Turtles are one of the few kinds of reptiles that can live in water and spend most of their time in water. Tortoises, unlike turtles, do not live in water, spending all their time on land. Tortoises and some species of whales are the longest-living animals in the world. Both tortoises' and turtles' shells are completely connected to their bodies, containing nerve endings that allow them to feel whatever touches their shell.

ORDER	ANIMALS	DESCRIPTION
CROCODILIA	Crocodiles and Alligators	Crocodiles prefer salt water, and alligators prefer fresh water.
		Crocodiles have pointed snouts, while alligator snouts are rounder.
		When crocodiles' mouths are closed, their teeth are mostly visible. Alligators' teeth are mostly hidden.
		Alligators naturally fear humans and will avoid them, attacking only if provoked. Crocodiles are instinctively aggressive, attacking anything nearby.

BIRDS

Birds are endothermic vertebrates. They are also descendants of dinosaurs. Several winged dinosaurs were covered in feathers. There were also many dinosaurs that had beaks made of keratin. As these dinosaurs lost many of the characteristics that made them closer to reptiles, they gained many other characteristics—such as improved hearing and sight, more effective wings, and smaller bodies—eventually becoming birds.

All birds have beaks, wings, and feathers; however, not all birds are able to fly. Flightless birds, like penguins and ostriches, have bodies that are more suited to other tasks, such as swimming or running.

IF ONLY.

SOME OF THE MODERN BIRD GROUPS

ORDER	ANIMALS	DESCRIPTION
PELECANIFORMES	Pelicans and Herons	Have webbed feet, which they use to swim. Their light bodies enable them to float on the water. They use their large beaks to scoop fish from the water.
PSITTACIFORMES	Parrots and Cockatoos	Among the most intelligent birds, parrots can imitate human voices. Parrots have a curved bill. Their legs are incredibly strong, allowing them to tightly grip thin branches while staying upright.
GALLIFORMES	Chickens, Turkeys, Quail, Pheasant, Partridge	Heavy-bodied, ground-feeding birds. They are reluctant flyers, which means that they can fly, but are not comfortable doing so. They flap their wings when they are afraid, prepared to fly away if necessary.

ORDER	ANIMALS	DESCRIPTION
FALCONIFORMES	Eagles, Falcons, Hawks, Vultures, Condors, Harriers	These are the top predators of all birds. They are strong, with curved, sharp talons on their feet, allowing them to pick up, secure, and fly away with prey.
STRIGIFORMES	Owls *active mostly at night*	Owls are a nocturnal species. Owls' eyes and ears can locate prey at far distances and in low-light areas. The large number of bones in an owl's neck allows it to rotate its head almost in a full circle.

MAMMALS

Mammals have hair or fur covering their bodies, produce milk to feed their young, have jawbones that help them both tear and chew food, and have different types of teeth.

Mammalian bodies share many other characteristics, including a four-chambered heart, which separates blood that has no oxygen from blood that does; well-developed limbs or fins; and the ability to create their own heat.

Mammals have an advanced **DIAPHRAGM**, which is a thin muscle that expands and contracts the lungs and separates them from the stomach and intestines; **MAMMARY GLANDS**, which are ducts that female mammals use to feed milk to their young; and a well-developed brain.

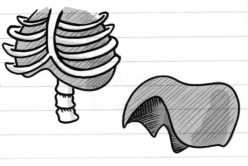

Crocodiles and alligators are two of the only nonmammals that have a diaphragm.

Modern mammals include:

- **MONOTREMES**, which is an order of primitive mammals that lays eggs instead of giving birth to live young. Examples include the echidna (spiny anteater) and platypus. Monotremes' legs are on the sides of their bodies, rather than underneath them like most mammals.

- **MARSUPIALS**, which give birth to underdeveloped embryos that continue to mature inside the pouch of their mother. Examples include the koala, opossum, wombat and kangaroo. Most marsupials— about 70 percent—live in Australia. Most of the remaining 30 percent live in South America.

- **EUTHERIANS**, also known as PLACENTALS, which develop their young inside a **PLACENTA**—an organ that connects the mother with their developing embryo. Humans are eutherians.

> Ninety-five percent of all mammals are eutherians.

Eutherians develop their embryo within their bodies and a saclike organ called the placenta. The placenta has an **UMBILICAL CORD**, which carries food, water, and oxygen to the embryo and returns waste to the mother. Your belly button is where your umbilical cord connected you to your mother.

I THINK I HAVE AN INNIE.

SOME TYPES OF EUTHERIANS

ORDER	ANIMALS	DESCRIPTION
RODENTIA	Mice, Rats, Squirrels	Mammals that have sharp teeth that help them gnaw through tough food. Many are herbivorous, but some can be carnivorous.
PRIMATES	Humans, Apes, Monkeys	The mammals with the most developed brains of the entire animal kingdom. Many species are tree climbers, using hands, feet, and tails to climb.
ARTIODACTYLA	Cows, Deer, Camels, Pigs	Herbivorous animals that comprise most of the world's large land mammals. They all have an even number of toes. Are MIGRATORY, moving from one place to another in search of food.
PERISSODACTYLA	Horses, Donkeys, Zebras, Rhinos	Mammals with an odd number of toes. Are migratory, moving from one place to another in search of food. There are only seventeen species remaining, and this number continues to drop.
CARNIVORA	Dogs, Cats, Bears, Seals	Predatory mammals with teeth specialized for tearing meat. They are very intelligent, having the ability to solve problems and remembering the solutions to those problems if they occur again.

ORDER	ANIMALS	DESCRIPTION
SCANDENTIA	Tree Shrews	Omnivorous, small mammals. Tree shrews are closely related to primates. Not all species of tree shrew live in trees.
LAGOMORPHA	Rabbits, Hares	Herbivorous, small mammals, closely related to rodents. Breed many times throughout the year and produce large numbers of offspring.
EULIPOTYPHLA	Hedgehogs, Shrews, Moles	Small, nocturnal, burrowing mammals that feed primarily on insects. Have long snouts, which they use not only to look for food but also to detect danger.
CINGULATA	Armadillos	Mammals that have a rough shell and long claws for digging. When threatened, they roll into their shell for protection.

ORDER	ANIMALS	DESCRIPTION
PILOSA	Anteaters, Sloths	Mammals with claws used to tear into tough insect mounds or climb trees.
		Anteaters and sloths sustain their environment by choosing to feed at one place for only a short time before relocating.
		Sloths move slowly to conserve energy and to avoid predators like owls and hawks.
PHOLIDOTA	Pangolins	Pangolins are the only mammals completely covered in scales, which they use to protect themselves from predators.
		When threatened pangolins curl into a tight ball, like armadillos.
		Pangolins feed on insects like ants and termites.
		They live in trees and on the ground.
CHIROPTERA	Bats	Bats are the only mammals that can actually fly.
		They are nocturnal, like owls, but they have terrible vision. Instead, they locate objects using reflected sounds to "see."
		This is called echolocation.
		Bats are herbivorous and carnivorous.
		They live in trees and on the ground.

CHECK YOUR KNOWLEDGE

1. What is an amniote?

2. An amniote that can generate its own heat is called an _____.

3. What are the scales of reptiles made of?

4. What is the largest order of reptiles?

5. What two types of amniotes are the descendants of dinosaurs?

6. What are the beaks, or bills, of birds made of?

7. What are the large beaks of Pelecaniformes used for?

8. Name two things that mammals have that no other type of animal has.

9. What do biologists call the mammals that protect their developing young in a pouch?

10. Which order has the most developed brains?

ANSWERS   323

CHECK YOUR ANSWERS

1. An amniote is a species whose embryos are encased in an amnion.

2. Endotherm

3. Keratin

4. Squamata

5. Reptiles and birds

6. Keratin

7. Plucking fish out of the water

8. A well-developed brain, mammary glands to deliver milk to its young, and an advanced diaphragm to expand and contract lungs

9. Marsupials

10. Primates

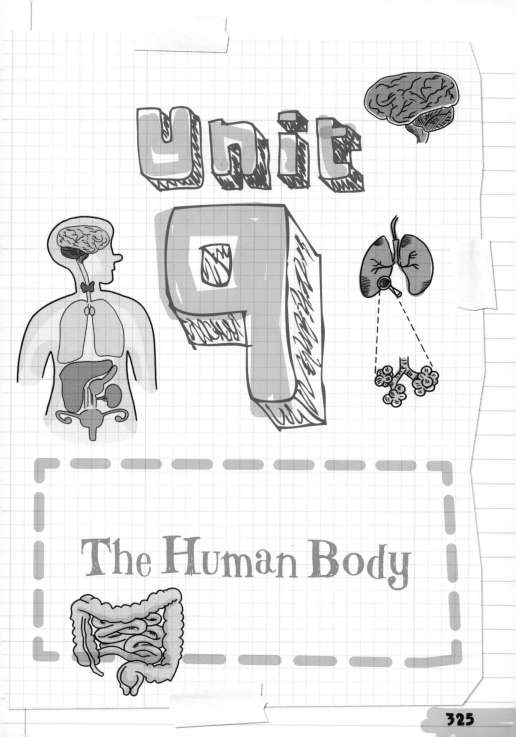

Unit 9

The Human Body

Chapter 36

BODY SYSTEMS AND HOMEOSTASIS

ORGAN SYSTEMS

The human body has five levels of organization: The most basic unit of the human body is a single cell. When groups of cells work together on a similar job, they are called **TISSUES**. There are various types of tissues—for example, skin tissue, muscle tissue, and nerve tissue.

When tissues work together on a single job, they are called **ORGANS**. The kidneys, the heart, the liver, and the intestines are examples of organs.

Organs work with one another to form **ORGAN SYSTEMS**, which exist to keep an organism healthy.

| CELLS | TISSUE | ORGAN | ORGAN SYSTEM | HUMAN BODY |

There are eleven organ systems:

THE INTEGUMENTARY SYSTEM

- This is the external system that protects the body from damage and absorbs nutrients. This organ system includes the skin, hair/scales/feathers, and nails.

THE NERVOUS AND ENDOCRINE SYSTEMS

- The NERVOUS SYSTEM detects sensory information and is responsible for generating responses to a given stimulus, in the form of reflexes or planned motor behaviors. It is the control center of everything you do and think.

- The ENDOCRINE SYSTEM is a collection of **GLANDS** that regulate many of the body's functions, such as growth, sleep, as well as the function of organs.

GLANDS
Organs in the body that secrete chemicals.

THE MUSCULAR AND SKELETAL SYSTEMS provide
the structure for the body and allow it to move.

THE RESPIRATORY AND CARDIOVASCULAR SYSTEMS deliver oxygen and nutrients to the body.
The lungs and heart are the centerpieces of these systems.

THE DIGESTIVE AND EXCRETORY SYSTEMS

- process and metabolize food for the body.

- remove waste while maintaining proper levels of nutrients in the body.

THE IMMUNE SYSTEM

- includes the lymphatic system, which not only removes waste, but also returns any extra fluids to the blood.

- is responsible for providing defense against infectious agents that do harm to the body.

THE REPRODUCTIVE SYSTEM

- for male humans, reproduction involves the production of sperm cells in the testes.

- for female humans, reproduction involves the production of egg cells in the ovaries.

HOMEOSTASIS

The human body's organ systems all work together to keep an organism healthy. **HOMEOSTASIS** refers to any behavior that allows an organism to maintain its internal balance despite what is going on in the outside environment. This balanced state is known as **EQUILIBRIUM**.

Homeostasis comes from the Greek words *homoios*, meaning "equal," and *stasis*, meaning "state." Homeostasis is the tendency of the body to remain in an "equal state," or equilibrium.

Organ systems work together to keep the body in equilibrium through the use of SIGNAL TRANSDUCTION, the transmission of molecular signals into cells from the outside. These signals make sure that each cell works together for the proper function of each organ and organ system. If the body's equilibrium is thrown off, signals are sent out to correct any problems. If the body can't maintain homeostasis, the organ systems can fail, which can lead to the death of the organism.

Homeostasis works through a reaction to **STIMULI**. The body might react to a stimulus by trying to decrease the effects of that stimulus. This action is called NEGATIVE FEEDBACK. Negative feedback is the result of the body understanding that the effects caused by a stimulus must be stopped in order to maintain homeostasis.

STIMULUS
(pl. STIMULI)
Anything in an environment that causes a reaction.

For example, when the body's core temperature drops too low, you might shiver. Shivering is part of a negative feedback loop. It is the result of muscle spasms that result in generating heat. Your hands and feet might also feel cold as blood flow is restricted to the extremities (fingers and toes) to keep blood and heat directed toward important organs like the heart and lungs.

IT'S F-F-FREEZING!

When a body receives a stimulus that causes a reaction it wants to continue, this is called POSITIVE FEEDBACK.

For example, during childbirth a chemical called oxytocin is released into the body. Oxytocin speeds up the muscle contractions that push a baby out of its mother's womb. The body increases the contractions. This increase causes more oxytocin to be released. The positive feedback is broken only when the baby is born, and contractions stop.

DISEASE

Diseases are conditions within cells, organs, or organ systems that affect the normal function of the human body. This includes not only serious illnesses, caused by viruses or bacteria, but also minor injuries such as cuts. Diseases are characterized by their SYMPTOMS, or signs.

CHECK YOUR KNOWLEDGE

1. What are organs?

2. What body system is responsible for reflexes?

3. How does the endocrine system communicate with the body?

4. What role does the respiratory system play?

5. Besides removing wastes, what else does the lymphatic system do?

6. How do the reproductive systems in male and female humans differ?

7. What is homeostasis?

8. How is the body kept in equilibrium?

9. What is the effect of a negative feedback response?

10. What is the purpose of a positive feedback response?

ANSWERS

331

CHECK YOUR ANSWERS

1. Organs are structures within the body that perform specific tasks.

2. The nervous system

3. The endocrine system communicates through glands, which secrete chemicals.

4. The respiratory system delivers oxygen and nutrients to the body.

5. The lymphatic system also returns extra fluids to the blood.

6. The male reproduction system produces sperm in the testes. The female reproductive system produces eggs in the ovaries.

7. Homeostasis is the tendency of the body to remain in a balanced state.

8. The body regulates its organ systems to keep the body in equilibrium.

9. Negative feedback responses reverse the effects caused by a stimulus.

10. Positive feedback responses help a reaction continue.

Chapter 37

THE INTEGUMENTARY SYSTEM

The integumentary system refers to all the parts that cover the body, including hair, fur, nails, and skin.

Integumentary comes from the Latin word *integumentum*, which means "a covering." The integumentary system is the system of organs that covers the body.

Words dealing with the skin often begin with the prefix *derma-*, which is based on the Greek word *derma*, which means "skin." For example, *dermatitis* is a disease that causes irritation in the skin.

The integumentary system is the covering on the body that protects the inside of the body from damage, including from **PATHOGENS**. Another important function is that it regulates the amount of water released from the body.

> **PATHOGENS**
> Infectious organisms such as bacteria or viruses.

THE SKIN

Skin, hair, and nails make up the outermost layer of all humans. All three are made of **KERATIN**, which forms the structure that prevents stress and damage.

> **KERATIN**
> A tough, structural protein that makes up the hair, nails, and outer layer of the skin.

The skin is the outermost layer on your body; it is also the largest organ.

THE SKIN

Protects the body from injury

Forms a barrier to prevent bacteria and other organisms from entering the body

Prevents water loss

Releases waste

Regulates temperature

Has nerve endings to relay information about temperature, pressure (touch), and pain to the brain

The skin is made up of three layers. The outermost layer is called the **EPIDERMIS**. The epidermis doesn't contain any blood vessels. This means that a cut in the epidermis will not bleed.

> *Epidermis* comes from the Greek words *epi* and *derma*, which mean "on top of" and "skin."
> The epidermal layer is the top layer of the skin.

This is the part that bleeds when cut.

Below the epidermis is the **DERMIS**. The dermis contains nerves and blood vessels. It has two layers: The **PAPILLARY LAYER**, the upper layer of the dermis, is connected to the epidermis and is responsible for providing nourishment to the epidermis. The lower layer, the **RETICULAR LAYER**, is more densely populated by nerves and blood vessels. It also contains connective tissue made of ELASTIN, a stretchy protein, and COLLAGEN, a tough protein. The combination of the two proteins makes skin both flexible and firm.

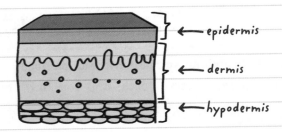

← epidermis

← dermis

← hypodermis

The last layer of the skin is the **HYPODERMIS**, a flexible layer where both connective tissue and fat are stored. The fatty tissue in the hypodermis helps keep the heat generated within the body inside. The hypodermis also serves as a connection between the higher layers of the skin and the muscles underneath.

Hypodermis comes from the Greek word *hypo*, meaning "under." The hypodermis is under the dermis.

Accessory Organs of the Skin

Hair, nails, sebaceous glands, and sweat glands are some of the ACCESSORY ORGANS of the skin, which means that they help the function of the skin, but are not a part of the skin and its layers.

Hair is a mass of tightly packed keratin that grows from a FOLLICLE, a small cavity (hole) in the dermis. As the hair grows from the bottom of the follicle, it pushes upward, eventually coming out of the skin.

hair

follicle

Hair protects the body in two ways:

- It helps the skin maintain the body's heat.

- It keeps the sun's radiation, which is harmful to the body, from directly hitting the skin.

Nails grow from the epidermis. Keratin gathers at the NAIL MATRIX and forms plates. These eventually push outward, forming nails on your fingers and toes. Nails exist to protect the fingers and toes from damage.

NAIL MATRIX
The place from which nails grow.

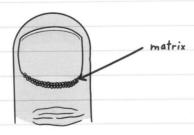

matrix

1. What is the integumentary system?

2. What does the integumentary system do?

3. What disease can result in irritated skin?

4. What is the function of keratin?

5. What is the function of the epidermis?

6. What is the role of the dermis?

7. What is the reticular layer?

8. What is the function of the fatty tissue in the hypodermis?

9. How does hair help the skin?

10. Where do nails grow from?

1. All parts that cover the body

2. Among other functions, the integumentary system protects the body from pathogens and damage.

3. Dermatitis

4. Keratin forms the structure of skin, hair, and nails and prevents damage to the integumentary system.

5. The epidermis protects the other layers of tissue from infection.

6. The dermis provides nourishment as well as movement and flexibility to the skin.

7. The lower layer of the dermis, which is densely packed with blood vessels and nerves

8. To keep the heat that the body generates inside

9. Hair helps the skin maintain body heat and blocks the sun's radiation from directly hitting the skin.

10. The epidermis

Chapter 38

THE MUSCULAR AND SKELETAL SYSTEMS

MUSCULAR SYSTEM

The muscular system is located under the skin. It is responsible for the flexibility of the body's motion and helps the body maintain its posture. The muscular system is also responsible for the actions taken by the circulatory, respiratory, digestive, and excretory systems, because all of them involve organs that are made of muscles.

Words related to the muscular system often begin with the prefix *myo-*, which is based on the Greek word *mys*, which means "muscle." For example, myocardia are muscles of the heart. People whose muscles don't function properly have a disease called "myopathy."

Muscles are like springs that move by contracting and relaxing.

contracted

relaxed

Muscle cells use energy to contract and relax. The contraction and relaxation of some muscles can also pull bones, which allows the human body to move.

Types of Muscular Tissue

Certain muscles can be moved *voluntarily*, meaning that they can be moved when the organism chooses to move them. Muscles that must be moved voluntarily are called VOLUNTARY MUSCLES.

There is only one type of voluntary muscle, SKELETAL MUSCLES. These are muscles that are attached to the body's skeleton, like the muscles that move your arms or legs.

SKELETAL MUSCLES:

- help the body move by moving the bones.

- work in pairs. When one pair contracts, the other relaxes and vice versa.

> **SKELETAL MUSCLES**
> Muscles that are attached to the body's skeleton.

Biceps and triceps are types of skeletal muscles.

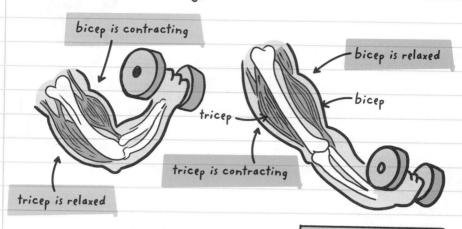

bicep is contracting

bicep is relaxed

bicep

tricep

tricep is contracting

tricep is relaxed

The connective tissues that attach muscle to bone are called TENDONS.

Skeletal muscles make up over a third of the human body's muscle.

Muscles that are not moved voluntarily, or INVOLUNTARY MUSCLES, make up the remaining muscles of the body. The two types of involuntary muscles are SMOOTH MUSCLES and CARDIAC MUSCLES.

SMOOTH MUSCLES:

■ Make up the stomach, lungs, small and large intestines, bladder, uterus, and blood vessels.

■ Smooth muscle cells move as a group, either fully contracting or fully relaxing.

CARDIAC MUSCLES:

- Found only in the heart.

- Cardiac muscle cells contract in a highly coordinated manner with the neighboring cells, working to efficiently keep the heart pumping and blood circulating throughout the body.

Some of the body's muscles need to contract and relax more often than others do. For example, the heart must keep beating in order to pump blood to the different parts of the body. So it must contract and relax very quickly. For organs like the heart, muscle cells are organized in a way that bundles them together, forming grooves, or **STRIATIONS**, in their structure, which increases the speed of contracting and relaxing. Both skeletal and cardiac muscles are striated muscle types.

Smooth muscle gets its name because it has no striations.

SKELETAL SYSTEM

The skeletal system provides the body with everything that it needs to move and support that movement.

- It supports the body and gives it shape.
- It protects the internal organs.
- It stores calcium and other minerals.

The skeletal system is able to perform these functions with **BONE**, collagen and calcium that make up the skeleton. The skeletal system is represented by the SKELETON, the collection of all bones in the human body.

> Words related to bone have the prefix *osteo-*, based on the Greek word *osteon*, which means "bone."

Bone is made of four main parts:

| around | | bone |

THE PERIOSTEUM

- The tough outer shell of the bone, which protects everything within.

THE COMPACT BONE

- The area of the bone where calcium is stored, making it very hard and dense.

- It is made of layers that surround hollow caverns, which allow blood vessels to enter the bone.

THE SPONGY BONE

- Light bone that is filled with many spaces that provide flexibility to the bone.

- Spongy bone is surrounded by and can harden into compact bone.

- The spaces are filled with blood vessels and bone marrow.

BONE MARROW

- Major site of new blood cell production. Marrow can either be red or yellow.

- Red marrow is responsible for the production and destruction of red blood cells platelets and white blood cells.

- Yellow marrow contains fat cells, which are yellowish in color.

All marrow is red in humans until the age of seven, because the need for new blood cells is very high in younger children.

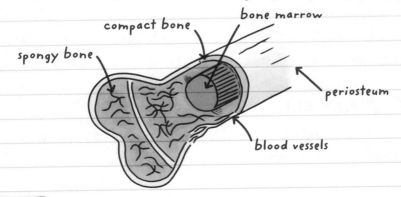

As humans age, most of their marrow becomes yellow marrow, except in a few bones, such as the ribs and skull.

> **OSTEOBLAST**
> A cell that constructs new compact bone.

New bone tissue is created by special cells called **OSTEOBLASTS**, which use elements such as calcium

> **OSTEOCLAST**
> A cell that breaks down damaged compact bone.

to construct the new bone. If the bones break, **OSTEOCLASTS** break down the damaged compact bone, creating new surfaces for bone to grow and harden into. Bones are very dynamic in nature: New bone tissue is constantly formed, and old, injured, or unnecessary bone is dissolved for repair or for calcium release.

> Some people have a disease called osteoporosis (pronounced ah-stee-oh-po-RO-sis), where bone is broken down faster than it is constructed. This causes bones to break more often.

New bones are softer than bones that are many years old. This is why doctors tell people to not put stress on newly repaired bones, because they are not yet strong.

MOVEMENT OF THE SKELETAL SYSTEM

Humans have 206 bones, separated by **JOINTS**. Joints allow us to move our bodies.

> **JOINTS**
> Flexible connections made between bones.

There are different types of joints:

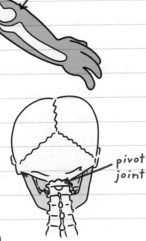

pivot joint

- **PIVOT JOINTS**—joints that allow bones to move around a single point.

    Pivot joints allow the skeleton to rotate.

    Examples: the joints at the top of the spinal cord, which allow the head to turn; the wrists; and the elbows.

pivot joint

- **GLIDING JOINTS**—joints that allow bones to slide past one another.

    Gliding joints are usually located between bones that meet at flat or nearly flat surfaces.

gliding joint

Examples: the joints between vertebrae of the spinal cord and between the bones of the wrist (also known as the carpal bones).

- **HINGE JOINTS**—joints that allow bones to flex and extend along an axis.

> like hinges on a door

Hinge joints allow body parts such as the arms and legs to stretch, giving the body height and reach.

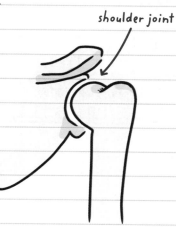

hinge joint

Examples: the joints between the knee, elbow, ankle, finger, and toe bones.

- **BALL-AND-SOCKET JOINTS**—the ball is in a socket so that it can rotate in a circle.

shoulder joint

Examples: the joints between the shoulder and torso and between the hip and leg.

CARTILAGE, a spongy material, makes up part of human joints. The cartilage helps to cushion bones when pressure, caused by weight or stress, is placed on them.

For the joint to bend, connective tissues called **LIGAMENTS** are needed to hold the joint in place and the bones together.

The skeletal muscles of the muscular system are responsible for moving bones around joints. The skeletal muscles must be connected to the bones. Another type of connective tissue, **TENDONS**, connects muscles to bone.

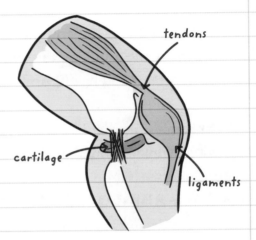

At birth, many of a baby's bones are made entirely of cartilage, which is more flexible than bone. This is why babies have more flexibility than adults.

CHECK YOUR KNOWLEDGE

1. What is the muscular system responsible for?

2. What does skeletal muscle do?

3. Which muscle type composes the majority of organs in the human body?

4. How do the movements of cardiac muscles differ from the movements of smooth muscles?

5. What benefit does striated muscle offer?

6. What color of bone marrow creates blood cells?

7. What breaks down old bone tissue?

8. What skeletal disease is characterized by bones that are broken down more than they are created?

9. What do joints allow humans to do?

10. What tissue connects bone to muscles?

ANSWERS

CHECK YOUR ANSWERS

1. The muscular system is responsible for the body's flexibility and posture, as well as the actions of the respiratory, circulatory, digestive, and excretory systems.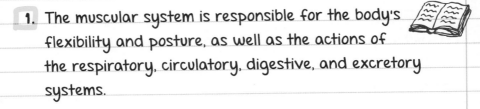

2. Skeletal muscle moves the body's bones.

3. Smooth muscle

4. Cardiac muscle is striated and smooth muscle is nonstriated.

5. Striated muscle can compress and relax quickly.

6. Red bone marrow

7. Osteoclasts

8. Osteoporosis

9. Joints allow humans to move.

10. Tendons

Chapter 39

THE NERVOUS AND ENDOCRINE SYSTEMS

THE NERVOUS SYSTEM

The nervous system is like a highway that runs through all other organ systems. This highway allows communication between the **BRAIN** and the rest of the body. Senses, such as sight, touch, and smell, need to be understood by the brain, which is the body's processing organ. The nervous system uses **NEURONS** to transmit information to the brain and within the brain. Neurons are special cells that translate information from senses into ACTION POTENTIALS, or electrical signals around the body along pathways called NERVES.

Neuron is a Greek word that means "nerve." Words relating to nerves or the nervous system begin with the prefix *neuro-*.

A neuron is made of a cell body, an axon, and dendrites.

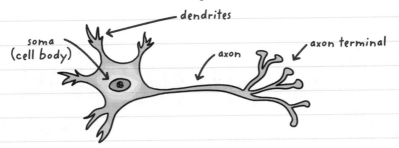

Neurons have a main body and tentacle-like extensions called **AXONS**, which communicate the electrical signals from the body of one neuron to the body of another.

Electrical signals are created by charged potassium and sodium moving into and out of neurons. These ions move through transport proteins in the cell membrane called SODIUM-POTASSIUM PUMPS. As sodium and potassium move through the pumps, they generate a disequilibrium of the concentrations of these ions inside and outside of cells. This generates a RESTING ELECTRIC POTENTIAL. When a stimulus reaches a resting neuron, there is a sudden shift from resting to an active state. Specialized channels in the membrane open and sodium and potassium move through them, changing their concentrations inside the cell and the electric potential. This impulse is called an action potential. Neurons can transmit these signals, which can travel through neurons at speeds up to 270 miles per hour—faster than almost any car ever made!

The Movement of an Electrical Signal

A STIMULUS triggers your sense of touch, sight, smell, taste, or hearing. That stimulus, or message, begins to move along the nervous system highway.

1. The body of the neuron receives an electrical signal from the sense that was triggered.
2. The electrical signal moves along an axon through action potentials.
3. The electrical signal reaches the end of an axon and enters an area called the **SYNAPSE**, which is a connection between neurons.
4. At the synapse, the electrical signal releases **NEUROTRANSMITTERS**—chemical substances that relate to the strength of the electrical signal.
5. Neurotransmitters then flow across the synapse onto the next neuron's **DENDRITES**. The dendrites translate the chemical substance back into an electrical signal.
6. The electrical signal moves into the body of the next neuron, where the process repeats until it reaches the brain, where it is analyzed.

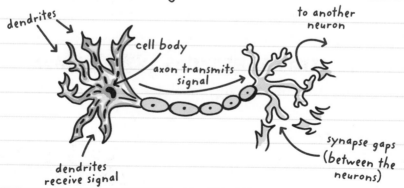

dendrites

to another neuron

cell body

axon transmits signal

dendrites receive signal

synapse gaps (between the neurons)

This process repeats across many neurons and creates **NEURAL PATHWAYS**, or chains of neurons, from a sensory organ, such as the eyes or nose, to the brain.

If the brain experiences something new, it can create an entirely new neural pathway so that it will remember the new experience. When that experience is repeated, electrical signals travel more quickly to and within the brain through more direct pathways, like traveling on a known highway instead of a longer, unfamiliar, local route. This is why tasks that are done repeatedly, such as reading or writing, are almost automatic, taking little thought to perform.

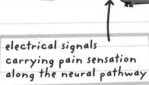

OUCH

electrical signals
carrying pain sensation
along the neural pathway

THE CENTRAL NERVOUS SYSTEM

The brain is not the only organ that can process a reaction. The spinal cord, which is connected to the brain, also contains neurons. Together, the brain and the spinal cord make up the **CENTRAL NERVOUS SYSTEM (CNS)**, which coordinates the activity of all parts of the body.

The Brain

The brain is made of many small parts that perform various functions. Each part of the brain relies on the others to understand the messages that neurons send to it.

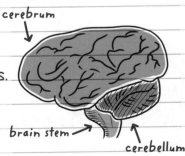

cerebrum

brain stem

cerebellum

THE BRAIN

PART	FUNCTION
THALAMUS	■ Receives and sends signals from sensory organs to other parts of the brain. ■ Allows us to feel pain and feel sleepy or alert. ■ Coordinates movement and balance.
CEREBRUM	■ The largest and most developed area of the brain. ■ Controls fine acts of movement, like those done with fingers. ■ Helps with speech, emotions, learning, memory, movement, sensation. ■ Many of the thalamus's messages are sent here. ■ Controls what the body does in response to what we see, hear, touch, taste, and smell.
BRAINSTEM	■ Because it is connected to the spinal cord, it's important for the transfer of messages between the brain and the rest of the body. ■ Is in control of the functions of the body that occur without conscious thought, such as breathing, digestion, and heart rate.

PART	FUNCTION
CEREBELLUM	▪ Receives information from sensory organs. ▪ Keeps muscle activity smooth and coordinated, helping the human body to remain constantly balanced.
HYPOTHALAMUS	▪ Manages homeostasis by releasing and limiting hormones that control how the body reacts. ▪ Affects heart rate, blood pressure, body temperature, appetite, and body weight.

The Spinal Cord

The spinal cord receives information from neural pathways all over the body and transfers that information to the brain. It is also responsible for transferring the information from the brain to the rest of the body through the same neural pathways.

The spinal cord is protected by **VERTEBRAE** (singular: vertebra), which are rows of bone that go from the brain stem down to the lower back.

Vertebrae are divided according to which regions of the body the nerves under them control. For example, underneath the first seven vertebrae are eight nerves that control the head, neck, and arms.

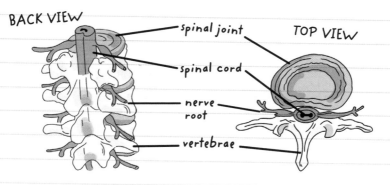

BACK VIEW

spinal joint

TOP VIEW

spinal cord

nerve root

vertebrae

THE SPINAL CORD	
VERTEBRAE	**TASK**
CERVICAL VERTEBRAE (top 7 vertebrae)	■ Protect 8 CERVICAL nerves (the first 2 are both behind the first vertebrae). ■ Control the head, neck, arms, and hands.
THORACIC VERTEBRAE (middle 12 vertebrae)	■ Protect 12 THORACIC nerves. ■ Control the chest, arms, heart, lungs, liver, and abdominal muscles. *relating to the chest*
LUMBAR VERTEBRAE (5 vertebrae)	■ Protect 5 LUMBAR nerves. ■ Control the leg muscles, reproductive organs, and bowels. *relating to the lower part of the back*

VERTEBRAE	TASK
SACRAL VERTEBRAE (5 vertebrae)	■ Protects 5 SACRAL nerves. ■ Controls the bladder, buttocks, knees, reproductive organs, legs, thighs. *relating to the bottom of the spine*
COCCYGEAL (bottom of the vertebral column)	■ Protects 1 COCCYGEAL nerve. ■ Supplies nerves to the skin over the coccyx.

THE PERIPHERAL NERVOUS SYSTEM

means "around the edge"

All neural pathways outside of the brain and spinal cord make up the **PERIPHERAL NERVOUS SYSTEM (PNS)**. The PNS is responsible for delivering information *from* or *to* the brain and spinal cord *to* the rest of the body.

The peripheral nervous system is made up of the SOMATIC NERVOUS SYSTEM and the AUTONOMIC NERVOUS SYSTEM.

THE SOMATIC NERVOUS SYSTEM
■ Made of nerves that allow for voluntary muscle control (skeletal muscle).

- Takes in information from AFFERENT NEURONS, or neurons that travel from sensory organs to the central nervous system. After the information is processed, a return signal is sent to the relevant muscles along EFFERENT NEURONS, instructing them on how to move.

Somatic comes from the Greek word *somatikos*, which means "of the body." The somatic nervous system is the system that allows for voluntary control of the body.

THE AUTONOMIC NERVOUS SYSTEM
- Made of nerves that control the involuntary muscles of the body (cardiac and smooth muscle).

- Controls actions needed to continuously occur for an organism to survive, such as the beating of the heart or the digestion of food.

- The hypothalamus delivers the commands to the heart and digestive system through the autonomic nervous system.

- Controls the REFLEXES, or the involuntary, rapid movements in muscles, in response to stimuli.

THE NERVOUS SYSTEM

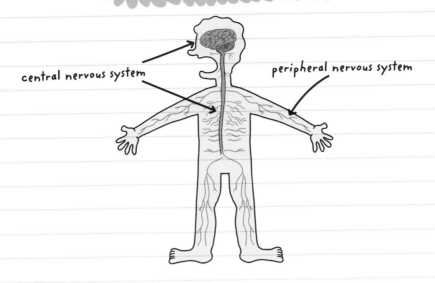

central nervous system

peripheral nervous system

THE ENDOCRINE SYSTEM

The endocrine system controls the body's metabolism, growth, water content, body temperature, blood pressure, and reproduction.

The endocrine system does not rely on electrical signals. Instead, it relies on HORMONES, chemical substances that regulate the body by controlling behavior and actions. These hormones are released from **GLANDS**.

The HYPOTHALAMUS, the part of the central nervous system that controls hormones, is the link between the nervous system and the endocrine system.

> **GLAND**
> An organ that secretes hormones.

362

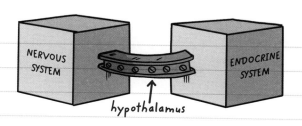

hypothalamus

GLAND	HORMONES SECRETED
THYROID GLAND Part of your throat; where the vocal cords are located.	Thyroid hormone **FUNCTION:** regulates metabolism and how the body uses the energy it creates
PITUITARY GLAND Attached to the brain. About the size of a pea.	Several hormones, including the growth hormone **FUNCTION:** stimulates the growth of the human body; controls other glands such as the ovaries or testes
PANCREAS	Insulin **FUNCTION:** produces the hormone that controls blood glucose
TESTES (MALES)	Testosterone **FUNCTION:** controls puberty and a male's ability to produce sperm, as well as facilitating other functions

GLAND	HORMONES SECRETED
OVARIES (FEMALE)	Estrogen and progesterone FUNCTION: estrogen controls puberty; progesterone and estrogen help manage a female's ability to bear children, as well as facilitating other functions
PINEAL GLAND	Melatonin (sleep hormone) FUNCTION: regulates feelings of sleepiness at night and wakefulness in the morning

ENDOCRINE SYSTEM

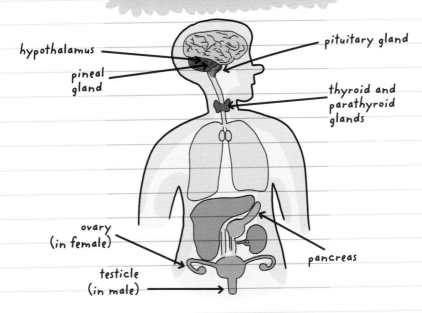

hypothalamus

pineal gland

pituitary gland

thyroid and parathyroid glands

ovary (in female)

testicle (in male)

pancreas

CHECK YOUR KNOWLEDGE

1. What is the nervous system?

2. What special cells make up the nervous system?

3. What is the function of axons?

4. What happens when an electrical signal reaches a synapse?

5. What parts make up the central nervous system?

6. Which part of the brain does the thalamus send most of its messages to?

7. What part of the peripheral nervous system allows for voluntary muscle control?

8. What part of the central nervous system does the autonomic nervous system rely on?

9. What links the nervous system and the endocrine system?

10. What are hormones?

ANSWERS

CHECK YOUR ANSWERS

1. The nervous system allows communication between the brain and the rest of the body.

2. Neurons

3. Axons carry action potentials from the body of one neuron to the body of another.

4. The electrical signal is converted to a chemical signal (neurotransmitter), which can then cross the synapse.

5. The brain and the spinal cord

6. The cerebrum

7. The somatic nervous system

8. The spinal cord

9. The hypothalamus

10. Hormones are chemical substances secreted from glands that regulate behavior and actions.

Chapter 40

THE RESPIRATORY AND CIRCULATORY SYSTEMS

THE RESPIRATORY SYSTEM

Cellular respiration is a series of reactions that break down glucose, a simple sugar, releasing chemical ATP for the body to use. The body needs oxygen to oxidize glucose. Cellular respiration uses oxygen and releases carbon dioxide and water as waste. Blood is the delivery system used to carry oxygen to all the cells from the lungs and returns to the lungs with carbon dioxide waste.

The central organs of the respiratory system are the **LUNGS**, which contain smooth muscles that expand and contract.

When the lungs expand, they create a difference in pressure between the inside of the human body and the outside environment, which causes air to rush into them. When the lungs contract, the pressure inside the body increases, causing air to flow out.

Words related to the respiratory system have the prefix *pneumo-* in them, which is based on the Greek word *pneumōn*, which means "lung." For example, pneumonia is a disease caused by an infection of the lungs.

Breathing

BREATHING is the mechanical process of taking in air. You breathe automatically—you don't have to think about it. If you need more oxygen, you breathe faster (which is why you get out of breath when you exercise—your body needs more oxygen to burn more glucose for energy).

There are two **CAVITIES**, or openings, where air can enter into the body: the nose and the mouth. When you breathe in, oxygen flows in through the **PHARYNX**, the cavity behind the nose and the mouth that leads into the throat.

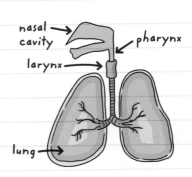

The cavity between the nose and the top of the mouth is called the NASOPHARYNX, and the cavity between the top of the mouth and the beginning of the throat is called the OROPHARYNX.

Air with oxygen enters the **LARYNX**, an open, muscular passage that connects the entry points of the pharynx to the lungs. The larynx also holds and protects the vocal cords. The area that connects the pharynx and the larynx is called the LARYNGOPHARYNX.

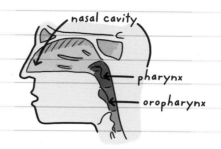

If there was only one cavity, any food that was eaten would end up in the lungs and damage them. To prevent this, the larynx splits into two cavities:

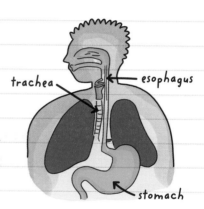

■ the **ESOPHAGUS**, which is a cavity that leads into the stomach for food digestion, and

also known as the windpipe

■ the **TRACHEA**, which leads into the lungs. The EPIGLOTTIS, a flap (the little punching bag in the back of your throat), prevents food from going into the trachea. When you breathe, the epiglottis remains open.

Swallowing closes the trachea, which is why you can't swallow and breathe at the same time.

As air enters the lungs, it must first go through the **BRONCHI** (pronounced bron-key; singular: bronchus).

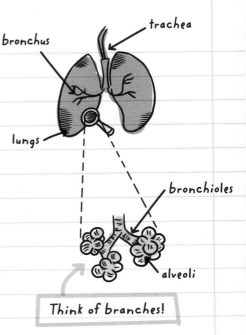

The bronchi divide the trachea into two branches, with each branch leading to either the left or right lung.

Think of branches!

Air moves through smaller branches, called BRONCHIOLES, before ending up in the **ALVEOLI**. The alveoli, also known as air sacs, exchange oxygen between the lungs and the blood, which takes the oxygen to the body's cells.

Protection of the Lungs

The respiratory system, and each of its organs, is protected by two things:

- **CILIA**, thin hairs that line the body's cavities

- **MUCUS**, a thick and sticky liquid

Both cilia and mucus keep any harmful substances, including dust, bacteria, and viruses, out of the lungs. In order to move the dirty mucus out of the lungs, cilia move it up, past the trachea.

Mucus can be blown out through the nose, spit out, or swallowed (yuck!). Stomach acid then kills any microorganisms.

Cilia move back and forth in wavelike motions and are always moving mucus.

Smoking kills the cilia in your trachea and respiratory system, which is why smokers have a mucousy-sounding cough. They have to physically cough all the mucus out of their lungs.

THE CIRCULATORY SYSTEM

The circulatory system moves nutrients throughout the body. The central organ, the engine, is the **HEART**, which is a pumping organ made of cardiac muscle. The heart pumps **BLOOD** to different parts of the body. Blood is a fluid that contains cells that can fight infection, carry oxygen and waste, and seal off damage to skin and muscle.

The heart is made of four chambers: a left and right ATRIUM and a left and right VENTRICLE. Blood always flows from the atrium to the ventricle.

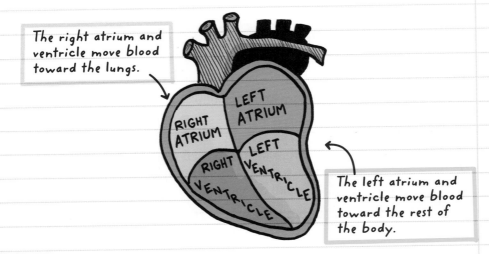

The right atrium and ventricle move blood toward the lungs.

RIGHT ATRIUM

LEFT ATRIUM

RIGHT VENTRICLE

LEFT VENTRICLE

The left atrium and ventricle move blood toward the rest of the body.

Words related to the circulatory system have the prefix *hemo-* or *hemato-*, which is based on the Greek word *haima*, which means "blood." For example, *hemophilia* is a disease in which a person experiences excessive bleeding due to poor blood clotting.

Parts of the Blood

Blood is produced in bones and is made up of two parts:

- **PLASMA**, which is made of water and some dissolved proteins and makes up about 55 percent of blood.

- **SALT**, **PROTEINS**, and **CELLS**, which make up the remaining 45 percent of blood.

Cells include red blood cells, white blood cells, and **PLATELETS**.

Because 45 percent of the blood is made up of salt and cells, blood is a lot thicker than a solution like salt water, which contains about only 4 percent salt and other substances, and a much higher percentage of water than blood.

RED BLOOD CELLS are the most common cell type in blood. They bring oxygen to the body's cells and also remove waste from them.

PLATELETS are the body's repairers. If any part of the body is damaged, platelet cells rush to the scene to form clots, or clumps, to prevent further blood flow to cuts.

A "scab" over a cut in your skin is evidence of platelets working.

When any part of the circulatory system is damaged, platelets move to the area and release chemicals to call more platelets to the area of damage. This is an example of positive feedback.

WHITE BLOOD CELLS help to protect the body from harmful bacteria or viruses that get trapped in the circulatory system.

There is about 1 platelet for every 20 red blood cells and about 1 white blood cell for every 700 red blood cells.

Oxygen Circulation

The circulatory system relies on the skeletal system to create blood cells. Blood cells of all types are formed in the bone marrow, where they travel outward into the circulatory system through **CAPILLARIES**, the tiniest blood vessels in the body.

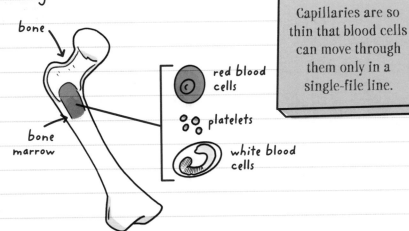

bone

bone marrow

red blood cells

platelets

white blood cells

Capillaries are so thin that blood cells can move through them only in a single-file line.

The red blood cells that are **DEOXYGENATED** contain no oxygen. For the blood cells to receive oxygen, they must first travel through **VEINS** toward the heart's right atrium.

> **VEIN**
> A blood vessel that moves deoxygenated blood.

Once the blood reaches the heart, the right ventricle pumps the deoxygenated blood toward the lungs, where it enters a new set of capillaries. In these capillaries, the lungs' alveoli exchange oxygen and carbon dioxide during the process of breathing. Oxygen then enters the blood and is taken up by the red blood cells.

> The spontaneous movement of gases without the use of energy between the gas in the alveoli and the blood in the capillaries in the lungs is called **diffusion**.

Red blood cells take in oxygen by using **HEMOGLOBIN**, a molecule within red blood cells that contains iron. The iron within hemoglobin attracts oxygen like a magnet, allowing it to stick to the red blood cells through its journey in the body. This blood is **OXYGENATED BLOOD**, due to its carrying oxygen.

The circulation continues as the oxygenated blood reenters the heart through the left atrium and ventricle. The left ventricle forcefully pumps the blood out through an **ARTERY** called the **AORTA**, which branches out to various parts of the body.

> **ARTERY**
> A vessel that pumps oxygenated blood.

As the red blood cells move through the arteries, they enter capillaries that lead to the various cells of the body. When the red blood cells enter oxygen-poor environments, the oxygen carried by the hemoglobin separates from the blood cell and is taken into the cells. Deoxygenated blood then leaves the capillaries, restarting the circulation cycle.

Blood's Journey Through the Body

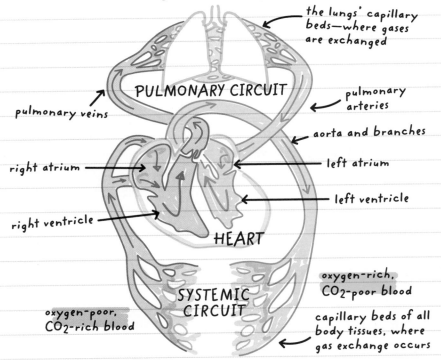

the lungs' capillary beds—where gases are exchanged

PULMONARY CIRCUIT

pulmonary veins

pulmonary arteries

aorta and branches

right atrium

left atrium

left ventricle

right ventricle

HEART

SYSTEMIC CIRCUIT

oxygen-rich, CO₂-poor blood

oxygen-poor, CO₂-rich blood

capillary beds of all body tissues, where gas exchange occurs

Oxygenated blood from the lungs ➡ left atrium ➡ left ventricle ➡ aorta to other arteries ➡ capillaries ➡ right atrium ➡ right ventricle ➡ lungs for oxygenation. Then the cycle begins again.

CHECK YOUR KNOWLEDGE

1. What organ processes oxygen?

2. What is the pharynx?

3. Why does the larynx split into two different cavities?

4. What do the alveoli do?

5. How does the body deal with dirty mucus?

6. What are the functions of blood?

7. What substance makes up the majority of blood, and what percentage of blood does this substance make up?

8. In what vessel does oxygen enter the circulatory system from the lungs?

9. What kind of blood flows through veins?

10. How is oxygen carried within blood?

ANSWERS

1. The lungs

2. The pharynx is the cavity behind the nose and mouth that leads into the throat.

3. The larynx splits into two cavities to allow food to enter the stomach instead of the lungs and to prevent food from entering the lungs and damaging them.

4. The alveoli exchange oxygen and carbon dioxide with the blood.

5. Cilia move dirty mucus up and past the trachea so that it can be swallowed and any captured microorganisms can be destroyed in the stomach.

6. Blood contains cells that can fight infection, carry oxygen and waste, and seal damage to skin and muscle.

7. Plasma, which makes up 55 percent of blood

8. Capillaries

9. Deoxygenated blood

10. Oxygen is attracted to the iron in hemoglobin. The oxygen attaches to the red blood cells as it journeys through the body.

Chapter 41

THE DIGESTIVE AND EXCRETORY SYSTEMS

THE DIGESTIVE SYSTEM

The DIGESTIVE SYSTEM takes in food, breaks it down, and absorbs nutrients into the body. There are two types of digestion:

MECHANICAL DIGESTION: when the body physically increases the surface area of food by breaking it down (such as when you chew your food) or when the stomach churns and compresses the food, improving chemical digestion (enzymatic) efficiency.

CHEMICAL DIGESTION: when the body breaks down food using **ENZYMES**, special proteins that produce chemical reactions.

DIGESTIVE SYSTEM

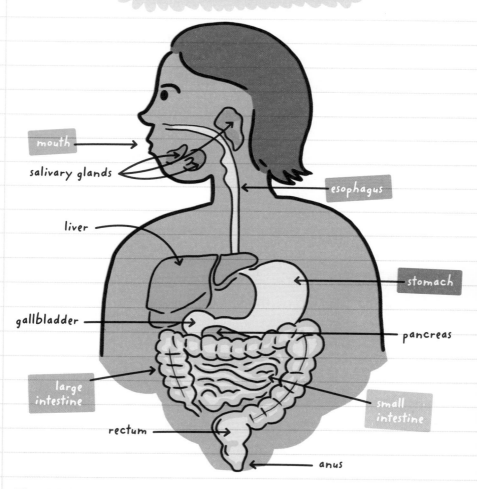

mouth

salivary glands

esophagus

liver

stomach

gallbladder

pancreas

large
intestine

small
intestine

rectum

anus

The DIGESTIVE TRACT includes the:

mouth   esophagus   **stomach**
small intestine   large intestine

THE DIGESTIVE PROCESS

Step 1: When food is placed in the mouth, teeth aid in mechanical digestion by breaking it down into smaller pieces. At the same time, **SALIVA** lubricates it with a mixture of water, mucus, and enzymes to begin chemically digesting food. Saliva also contains white blood cells that fight bacteria and other pathogens. Because of this, saliva helps defend the body from taking in harmful organisms.

Words related to the digestive system have the prefix *gastro-*, which is based on the Greek word *gastēr*, which means "stomach." For example, gastritis is a disease caused by the swelling of the stomach lining.

Step 2: As food is swallowed, the trachea, which carries air into the lungs, closes, while the esophagus opens. The esophagus is a muscle that is lubricated with mucus, and it involuntarily contracts and relaxes, pushing food down into the stomach. This type of muscle contraction is called **PERISTALSIS**.

Peristalsis is what allows you to swallow things, even when hanging upside down.

Don't do this!

This process happens thoroughly the digestive tract, to move food along.

Step 3: As food moves from the esophagus into the stomach, it passes through the **ESOPHAGEAL SPHINCTER**, a ring of muscle that separates the esophagus and stomach. When food leaves the esophagus, the sphincter closes, preventing stomach acid and partially digested food from moving back into the esophagus.

Step 4: The **STOMACH** is a giant muscle that both chemically digests food using a mixture of acids and enzymes that break down food into smaller components and mechanically digests food by shaking, compressing, and churning. Digested food mixed with stomach acid is called **CHYME**.

> Thick mucus prevents the stomach from eating through itself with its own acids.

Step 5: After food is properly digested, the **PYLORIC SPHINCTER** opens. The pyloric sphincter separates the stomach and the **SMALL INTESTINE**. As chyme moves through the small intestine, it begins to absorb nutrients, taking them into the circulatory system to go where they're needed.

> **PYLORIC SPHINCTER**
> (pronounced pie-LORE-ic sfink-ter)
> A ring of muscle that separates the stomach and small intestine.

ACCESSORY ORGANS, such as the liver, pancreas, and gallbladder, help the small intestine absorb nutrients. The pancreas and gallbladder secrete enzymes and bile to further chemically digest chyme to make absorbing the nutrients easier. The liver processes the nutrients that the small intestine absorbs and filters the blood coming from the digestive tract. The liver also detoxifies chemicals that enter the body.

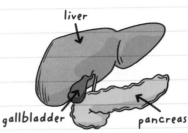

At this point in digestion, the only substance passing through the digestive tract is food residue that cannot be digested. As this indigestible food moves into the **LARGE INTESTINE**, any water that it still contains is absorbed.

LARGE INTESTINE
An organ that is responsible for absorption of water from indigestible food matter.

As the remaining water is absorbed, the large intestine forms **STOOL**, solid waste that must be removed from the body.

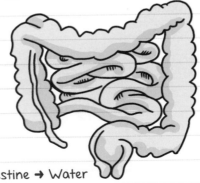

Small Intestine → Nutrients; Large Intestine → Water

Solid waste is removed by passing through another sphincter—the **ANUS**, a sphincter that separates the large intestine and the outside of the body, completing the process of digestion.

THE DIGESTIVE TRACT

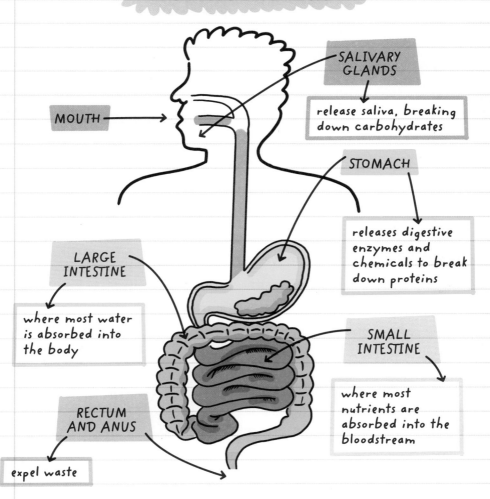

SALIVARY GLANDS

release saliva, breaking down carbohydrates

MOUTH

STOMACH

releases digestive enzymes and chemicals to break down proteins

LARGE INTESTINE

where most water is absorbed into the body

SMALL INTESTINE

where most nutrients are absorbed into the bloodstream

RECTUM AND ANUS

expel waste

THE EXCRETORY SYSTEM

The EXCRETORY SYSTEM removes waste from the body in order to help it maintain homeostasis. It includes skin, lungs, nails, hair, and kidneys. As food moves through the small intestines, all nutrients are absorbed into the blood. Substances left over after cellular respiration and digestion are transported by blood to the **KIDNEYS**. The body excretes METABOLIC WASTE, such as excess water, carbon dioxide, and nitrogen compounds.

> **KIDNEYS**
> A pair of organs that filter waste out of the blood.

The Urinary System

The URINARY SYSTEM filters blood and gets rid of metabolic wastes and excess water, salt, and minerals. The blood containing waste moves into the kidneys through the **RENAL ARTERY**. This artery leads to the **NEPHRONS**, which remove waste. In the nephrons, the waste is filtered and any water or nutrients that may still be useful to the body are reabsorbed. The unabsorbed waste is passed into the **URETER**, a tube that carries URINE (liquid waste) into the bladder, where it is stored until it leaves the body through the URETHRA. The cleaned blood leaves the kidneys through a renal vein and goes back into the body.

renal = relating to kidneys

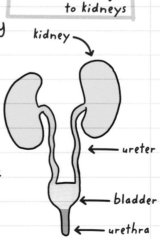

kidney

ureter

bladder

urethra

CHECK YOUR KNOWLEDGE

1. What is the first step of digestion?

2. What involuntary process moves food through the esophagus and into the stomach?

3. What prevents stomach acid from moving into the esophagus?

4. How does the stomach break down food?

5. Which digestive organ is responsible for the absorption of nutrients?

6. What function does the liver perform?

7. What is the purpose of the large intestine?

8. Where does the blood take waste?

9. Where does the freshly cleaned blood go?

10. What function do the kidneys perform?

ANSWERS

CHECK YOUR ANSWERS

1. Breaking down and lubricating food in the mouth

2. Peristalsis

3. The esophageal sphincter

4. The stomach compresses and uses a mixture of acids and enzymes to break down food.

5. The small intestine

6. The liver filters the blood coming from the digestive tract. It also detoxifies chemicals that enter the body.

7. The large intestine absorbs any remaining water from indigestible food.

8. The blood takes waste to the kidneys.

9. The freshly cleaned blood passes though a renal vein back into the body.

10. The kidneys filter waste out of the blood.

Chapter 42

THE IMMUNE SYSTEM

The IMMUNE SYSTEM protects and fights against infection and disease. The immune system is an organism's personal army, battling against harmful invaders.

LET'S GO!

Diseases can be caused by pathogens, infectious organisms such as bacteria, viruses, and other parasites. All diseases function by preventing the body from performing normally.

Pathogens can be caught from anything that a human interacts with, including food and even other humans.

Because the pathogens are so infectious, it is very easy for any organism, not just humans, to be infected by them.

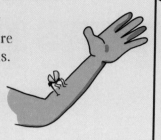

Many organisms cannot be harmed by certain pathogens. Those organisms are called CARRIERS for those pathogens. For example, a mosquito cannot be harmed by many viruses; however, it can carry those viruses into a human when it feeds on their blood.

Because pathogens are so dangerous, the body must be able to find and remove them before they do harm. This is the role of the **IMMUNE SYSTEM**, which detects the presence of pathogens and reacts to them. The two actions together are called the **IMMUNE RESPONSE**.

> detection + reaction = immune response

The immune system's goal upon infection by a pathogen is to:

1. kill the pathogen.

2. prevent the pathogen from having any influence over the body's homeostasis.

IMMUNE RESPONSE
The detection by and reaction of the immune system to pathogens.

In order to achieve its goal, the immune system uses two lines of defense. The first line includes PASSIVE METHODS, which try to prevent as many pathogens from getting into the body as possible. The second line of defense uses **LEUKOCYTES**, or white blood cells, to digest and destroy bacteria and other pathogens that made their way into the body. Leukocytes become active only if pathogens make it past the first line of defense.

> **LEUKOCYTES**
> White blood cells, which fight pathogens in the body.

There are five main types of leukocytes:

LYMPHOCYTES: detect pathogens

NEUTROPHILS: the first cells to arrive at the site of infection after a pathogen is detected

MONOCYTES: help destroy pathogens and clean up dead or old cells

EOSINOPHILS: destroy certain bacteria and parasites

BASOPHILS: protect against **ALLERGENS**, substances that cause an allergic reaction, by releasing **HISTAMINES** (chemicals), which alert various defenses, causing blood vessels to dilate (open wider).

NONSPECIFIC IMMUNITY

The body has several defense mechanisms that prevent the growth and entrance of pathogens. There are physical and chemical barriers, as well as responses like coughing, tearing up, and producing mucus. These make up the first line of defense.

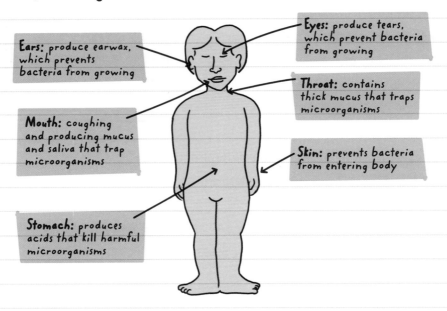

Ears: produce earwax, which prevents bacteria from growing

Eyes: produce tears, which prevent bacteria from growing

Throat: contains thick mucus that traps microorganisms

Mouth: coughing and producing mucus and saliva that trap microorganisms

Skin: prevents bacteria from entering body

Stomach: produces acids that kill harmful microorganisms

If a pathogen enters the body, past the first line of defense, the body engages nonspecific defenses, which are physical and chemical barriers to ensure that pathogens do not get further into the body. They are called "nonspecific" because, no matter what foreign organism enters the body, the reactions are the same. Examples of these responses include inflammations and fevers. If these nonspecific responses fail, the body engages its second line of defense.

SPECIFIC IMMUNITY

The Lymphatic System

If a pathogen gets past the first line of defense, then the second line defends the body. The second line is the **ADAPTIVE IMMUNE RESPONSE**, which is the immune response involving the actions of white blood cells.

For the body to activate the adaptive immune response, a pathogen must first be detected. The lymphatic system plays a key role in finding pathogens that have infected the body. This system operates by using a special fluid called **LYMPH**. Lymph, contained within special lymph vessels, passes through the body's cells, collecting and discarding waste.

> **LYMPH**
> A fluid that collects waste from the body's cells.

Lymph comes from the Latin word *lympha*, which means "water." The lymphatic system "washes" cells with lymph to clean them.
Lymph vessels travel along veins and arteries, which allows the blood to constantly be filtered and cleaned.

Lymph takes the cell's waste to LYMPH NODES, which filter the waste, determining if there are any pathogens that have infected the body. If there are, the lymph nodes create

LYMPHOCYTES, which are sent into the blood to look for an infection.

The adaptive immune system allows for a stronger immune response, as well as **IMMUNOLOGICAL MEMORY**, where pathogens can be "remembered" by a signature antigen. Antigens are parts of pathogens that can trigger an immune response. Depending on the kind of foreign invasion, two different types of adaptive immune responses can occur: the HUMORAL IMMUNE RESPONSE and the CELL-MEDIATED IMMUNE RESPONSE.

The Humoral Immune Response

The humoral immune response is a type of adaptive immunity defense that involves the secretion of free-floating antibodies by B cells into the blood and lymph nodes. One type of lymphocytes, which originate in bone marrow, are released by lymph nodes and are known as B CELLS. As B cells move through the blood, they look for **ANTIGENS**, parts of pathogens that can trigger an immune response. If a B cell bumps into an antigen, it surrounds the antigen in a process called **PHAGOCYTOSIS**.

After the antigen is surrounded, the B cell places fragments of the antigen on its surface. Another lymphocyte, the T CELL, binds to the B cell and activates it.

Because T cells "help" B cells by activating them, this type of T cell is also called the "helper" T cell.

When a B cell is active, it begins to undergo rapid cell division into one of two types of cells:

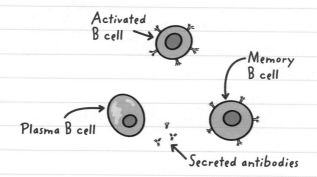

Activated B cell

Memory B cell

Plasma B cell

Secreted antibodies

- **MEMORY B CELLS** clone, or duplicate, the pathogen the original B cell bonded to. If the organism becomes reinfected by a pathogen, memory B cells help the body respond more quickly. These memory B cells are responsible for the body's immunity to illnesses that it has already recovered from.

- **PLASMA B CELLS** create **ANTIBODIES** and send them out into the blood.

Antibodies are proteins that bind to the specific antigen that the original B cell surrounded at the beginning of the immune response. When the antibodies and antigens bind, the antigens activate, behaving like a signal for **MACROPHAGES**, monocytes that, like B cells, eat pathogens, preventing them from infecting the body.

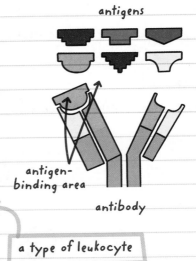

antigens

antigen-binding area

antibody

a type of leukocyte

Memory B cells divide and create plasma B cells if they come across a familiar antigen, without the need of a T cell.

Antibodies can also come from a parent. If a mother has antibodies against specific antigens, many of those can be passed on to her children during pregnancy or through her breast milk. This is called **PASSIVE IMMUNITY**.

The creation of new proteins and cells that target specific antigens is an example of the body's ADAPTIVE IMMUNITY, which makes sure that the body's immune system continues to grow over the course of an organism's life.

Cell-Mediated Immunity

Cell-mediated immunity is an adaptive immune response that does not involve antibodies. It is the activation of antigen-specific T cells and other nonspecific cells of the immune system. Cell immunity protects the body by activating:

* **helper T cells** that help B cells produce antibodies and also promote the spread of other T cells.
* **cytotoxic T cells** that destroy infected body cells before virus or internal pathogens have the chance to multiply.
* **"killer cells"** that destroy pathogens and release toxic chemicals to kill pathogens.
* **phagocytes** and **macrophages** that perform the same functions as in the humoral immune response.

This response also generates an immune response when a pathogen is reintroduced to the body through the activation of memory T cells.

MODERN MEDICINE AND THE IMMUNE SYSTEM

In modern times, biologists and doctors develop new ways to prevent pandemics. These new ways involve using ANTIBIOTICS, ANTIVIRALS, and VACCINES.

widespread disease

> There are many bacteria that are good for you, for example, ones that help the human body perform important functions, like digestion. Antibiotics kill those types of bacteria, too.

Antibiotics are medicines that are effective at killing or slowing the growth of bacteria, while **antivirals** are medicines that are effective at stopping a virus from multiplying. Both medicines work by attacking processes or molecules that bacteria and viruses have that normal human cells don't. For example, many types of antibiotics work by stopping bacteria from making cell walls, but they don't affect human cells because animal cells do not have cell walls.

A VACCINE is a substance that stimulates the body's immune system to work against infection. It contains the antigen of the pathogen that it is created to protect against. Vaccines use dead or weakened bacteria or viruses to stimulate the production of antibodies. The vaccine imitates an infection and triggers the immune system to produce T cells and antibodies. The immune system identifies the surface proteins of the pathogen. Once the infection goes away the body is left with memory T cells and memory B cells that have learned how to fight the disease and have a "record" of the pathogen's surface proteins. The vaccine prepares the body's immune system to recognize and fight future attacks of that same surface protein.

> The flu shot is a vaccine, made of several current strains of flu virus for that year.

If a pathogen enters your body after you've been vaccinated, your memory B cells make antibodies right away and are able to fight and kill the pathogen.

CHECK YOUR KNOWLEDGE

1. What are pathogens?

2. What actions make up the immune response?

3. What type of cell does the immune system work through?

4. What type of cell is responsible for detecting pathogens?

5. Name parts of the immune system's first line of defense.

6. What are antigens?

7. What is the function of antibodies?

8. Why are some T cells called helper cells?

9. What is the purpose of an antiviral?

10. How do vaccines work?

ANSWERS

399

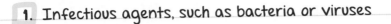

CHECK YOUR ANSWERS

1. Infectious agents, such as bacteria or viruses

2. The detection of and the reaction to pathogens

3. The immune system works through leukocytes, or white blood cells.

4. Lymphocytes

5. Skin, mouth, eyes, ears, stomach

6. Antigens are parts of pathogens that can trigger an immune response.

7. Antibodies bind to antigens and provide a signal for macrophages.

8. T cells "help" B cells by activating them.

9. Antivirals fight viruses.

10. Vaccines use dead or damaged viruses to stimulate the body's production of antigens, allowing the body to gain immunity against pathogens.

Chapter 43

THE REPRODUCTIVE SYSTEM

An important consideration of any organism is how they pass their genetic information to the next generation. The creation of new organisms allows a species to continue.

The **REPRODUCTIVE SYSTEM** is responsible for producing a new organism. Male and female humans each have different reproductive systems that allow for the combining of genetic information and for production of a new organism.

FEMALE REPRODUCTIVE SYSTEM

The main organs of the female reproductive system are the **OVARIES**, the **UTERUS**, and the **VAGINA**.

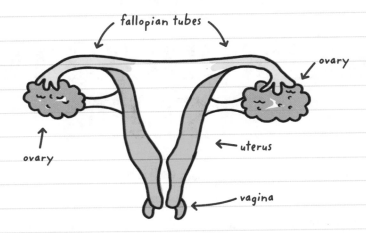

fallopian tubes

ovary

ovary

uterus

vagina

The ovaries are two structures in which the **EGG CELLS** reside and mature. Eggs are cells that contain half the necessary genetic material needed to create human offspring. As an egg matures, it travels from the ovary down the **FALLOPIAN TUBE** to the uterus, where it joins with the male sperm cells, beginning the process of **FERTILIZATION**.

EGG CELLS
Female sex cells, which contain half the genetic information needed to create offspring.

FALLOPIAN TUBE
A duct that transports the egg cell from the ovary to the uterus.

FERTILIZATION
The fusion of male and female sex cells.

A process called *in vitro fertilization* allows for the fertilization of an egg cell with a sperm cell outside of the female reproductive tract.

The release of a mature egg from the ovaries is called OVULATION.

Every twenty-one to thirty-five days, the uteran walls and uterus fill with blood to provide a protective environment for any fertilized egg cells. If an egg cell is not fertilized, the uterus discards its lining and blood in the process known as MENSTRUATION.

Female humans are born with all their eggs—1 to 2 million of them. They do not create any more eggs over their lives.

The ovaries also produces hormones like ESTROGEN, which is responsible for the development of the reproductive system and characteristics like pubic hair and breasts.

Menstrual blood leaves the **VAGINA**, a canal that leads into or out of the uterus. Sperm cells also use the vagina to travel to the uterus to fertilize an egg cell.

MALE REPRODUCTIVE SYSTEM

The main organs of the male reproductive system are the **TESTES** and the **PENIS**.

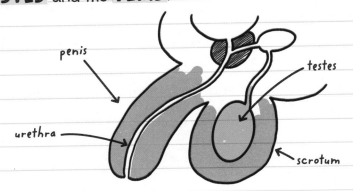

The testes are two organs that are contained in the **SCROTUM** and generate **SPERM**, cells that contain half of the genetic material needed to create human offspring. Sperm is made of a head and a tail. The head contains the genetic information (DNA) and the tail provides mobility. Sperm are generated in SEMINIFEROUS TUBULES, which exist all throughout the testes. As the sperm mature, they leave the tubules and travel to the EPIDIDYMIS, where they are stored.

a duct that transports and stores sperm cells

SCROTUM
A saclike organ that contains the testes.

SPERM
Male sex cells that contain half the genetic information needed to create offspring.

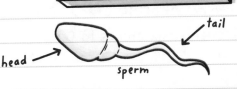

In order for the sperm to leave the body, they must travel out of the epididymis and into the **VAS DEFERENS**, a tube that transfers sperm to the penis. As sperm move through the vas deferens, they are fed nutrients through **SEMINAL FLUID**. Seminal fluid provides sperm cells with the energy they need to leave the penis through the process of ejaculation. Generally, for reproduction to occur, semen must be ejaculated into the female reproductive tract.

The combination of seminal fluid and sperm is called SEMEN.

The testes also produce hormones, such as **TESTOSTERONE**, the sex hormone responsible for hair growth, muscle mass, and fat distribution.

Vas deferens is a Latin phrase that means "carrying-away vessel." The vas deferens carries sperm away from the testes.

FERTILIZATION AND PREGNANCY

When the sperm and egg cells meet, their genetic material combines, creating one complete human cell known as a **ZYGOTE**, and beginning the nine-month period of pregnancy. Approximately thirty hours after fertilization, the zygote begins the process of cell division, which the organism will continue to do until its death.

ZYGOTE
A fertilized egg cell.

After about three weeks of cell division, the zygote becomes an **EMBRYO**. At that time, cells begin to transform into different types. For example, some cells develop into the cells of the heart, while others develop into the cells of the eyes and ears.

> **EMBRYO**
> An early stage of development in which cells begin to transform into different types.

After nine weeks of development, the embryo is considered a **FETUS**. The fetus continues to grow for seven more months, until it becomes a fully developed human.

> **FETUS**
> A developing human that contains all critical organs and body structures.

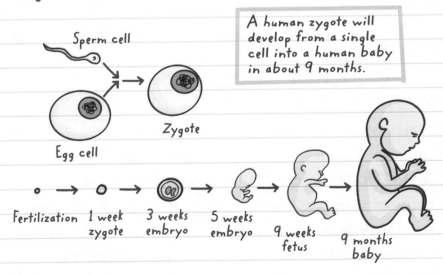

A human zygote will develop from a single cell into a human baby in about 9 months.

Sperm cell

Egg cell

Zygote

Fertilization → 1 week zygote → 3 weeks embryo → 5 weeks embryo → 9 weeks fetus → 9 months baby

Human Development

After a baby is born, it grows and develops in stages:

- **NEONATAL PERIOD**: the first four weeks after birth. The baby adjusts to being outside the body.

- **INFANCY**: from birth to about age 2. Initially the baby's homeostatic functions are not well developed. As the baby matures, its body learns to regulate itself better. The baby also undergoes rapid brain development. The baby also becomes more mobile—crawling, walking, running.

- **CHILDHOOD**: from age 2 to about age 12. The nervous system matures. Muscle skills and coordination improve. Language and reasoning also improve.

- **PUBERTY AND ADOLESCENCE**: Puberty is the beginning of sexual maturity and the development of sexual characteristics. Humans experience rapid growth, stimulated by the hormones testosterone (males) and estrogen (females). Adolescence begins at sexual maturity—the occurrence of the first menstrual cycle

in females and the presence of sperm in semen in males. Usually both males and females experience greater strength and increased physical endurance.

- **ADULTHOOD:** bones stop growing and, as adulthood progresses, become weaker. Digestion and metabolism slow down. It becomes more important to increase physical and mental activity to slow down the effects of aging.

Sex (the determination of an organism as male or female) does not necessarily determine a person's gender. Sex and gender are related for some people, but not for others. A person may be:

- **cisgender**—their gender corresponds with the sex they were assigned at birth (a man assigned as male or a woman assigned as female at birth)

- **transgender**—their gender differs from the sex they were assigned at birth (a man assigned as female or a woman assigned as male at birth)

- **nonbinary**—their gender doesn't fall under the category of man or woman

- **gender fluid**—their gender varies on the spectrum of man and woman at any given moment (gender fluid people may also use the terms genderqueer, bigender, multigender, or polygender)

- **agender**—they don't identify with any gender

Intersex, a label for a biological variation that develops as a fetus matures, describes a person who is born with reproductive anatomy that doesn't fit the traditional idea of female or male. It's used to describe:

- a person born with a combination of genes so that some cells have XX (female sex) chromosomes and some have XY (male sex) chromosomes

- a person born with genitals or sex characteristics that seem to be both male and female or a variation of one or the other (some, but not all, people who fit this description may be transgender)

CHECK YOUR KNOWLEDGE

1. What is the function of reproduction?

2. What are the main organs of the male reproductive system?

3. The scrotum contains the _____.

4. What is the function of the epididymis?

5. What structure transfers sperm from the epididymis to the penis?

6. What are the main organs of the female reproductive system?

7. Where does the egg cell meet the sperm cell?

8. What process occurs if an egg is not fertilized?

9. What occurs as the zygote becomes an embryo?

10. What is the difference between a zygote and an embryo?

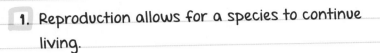

CHECK YOUR ANSWERS

1. Reproduction allows for a species to continue living.

2. The testes and the penis

3. testes

4. The epididymis stores sperm cells.

5. The vas deferens

6. The ovaries, uterus, and vagina

7. The uterus

8. The menstruation process, in which the lining and blood of the uterus is discarded

9. Cells begin to transform into different types.

10. The zygote is the fertilized cell and the embryo is the developing human organism that the zygote grows into.

Unit 10

Genetics

Chapter 44

INTRODUCTION TO GENETICS

TRAITS AND ALLELES

Genetics is the study of **HEREDITY**, or the passing of traits from parents to their offspring. The units that contain the hereditary information of organisms are called **GENES**.

Genetic traits include all the characteristics an organism has. In humans, this would include hair type, eye color, skin color, behavior, and so on.

Mendel's Experiment

GREGOR MENDEL (1822–1884) is widely considered the father of modern genetics because of his genetic experiments. In 1856, he studied genetics by using the pea plant to figure out how genes are transferred from parent to offspring.

Gregor Mendel's pea plant experiments involved observing many **GENERATIONS** of pea plants. During his study, Mendel discovered that there are two

GENERATION
A set of members of a group that are born around the same time.

types of traits: a **DOMINANT TRAIT**, the main trait that appears in the HETEROZYGOUS GENOTYPE—inheriting different forms of a particular gene from each parent, and a **RECESSIVE TRAIT**, the hidden trait that is not expressed in the heterozygous genotype; it's only seen when HOMOZYGOUS—inheriting identical forms of a particular gene from each parent.

> Genes are "expressed," or shown, when a trait appears.

DOMINANT TRAIT
The main trait that appears in an organism's offspring.

RECESSIVE TRAIT
The hidden trait that is not expressed by an organism's offspring.

When the sex cells of parents combine, the offspring randomly gets one gene of a specific type from each parent. In his experiment, Mendel bred pea plants (parents) that had different characteristics (alleles) and observed their offspring.

ALLELE
The varying forms of a gene. Organisms have two alleles, one from each of their parents.

He wanted to see which characteristics from the parents would appear in the offspring.

GENERATION	PARENT PLANTS BRED	OFFSPRING (F1)	MENDEL'S THOUGHTS
1	One tall and one short pea plant Parental generation	All tall pea plants F1	Tallness is the dominant trait for plant height. Mendel wondered if the offspring of tall plants were the same genetically as the parent tall plant.
2	Two tall plants from Generation 1's (F1) offspring	75 percent of offspring were tall, 25 percent were short F2	The recessive trait from F1 must be preserved, even if it does not appear. the "short trait"

Generations are called parental, F1, F2, and so on. F comes from "filial" (first filial generation, second filial generation, etc.). F1 generation is produced by the breeding of two parental organisms, while F2 generation is produced by the interbreeding of two F1 generation offspring.

The offspring of the second generation provided the basis of the idea of **ALLELES**, which are the different forms of a gene. Organisms receive one allele from each of their parents, giving them two different genes for the same characteristic. (Like the height allele in the pea plant experiment.) Alleles can either be dominant or recessive. The gene that is always expressed in the organism is the dominant trait.

the one that shows up

If two parents, one with blue eyes and one with brown eyes, had a child, each parent would give the child one allele for eye color. The child's eye color would be determined by which allele had the dominant trait. In this case, because brown eyes are the dominant trait and blue eyes are the recessive trait, the child would have brown eyes.

B
Dominant allele
for brown eyes

b
Recessive allele
for blue eyes

BB   Bb
eyes will be brown

bb
eyes will be blue

Mendel's second-generation offspring also proved that recessive genes are preserved even if they don't appear. If the opposite was true and the dominant genes erased the recessive genes, then the offspring in the second generation should all have been tall, because the parents were all tall.

This meant that the tall parent plants of generation 1 and the tall parent plants of generation 2 did not have the same **GENOTYPE**, even though they had the same **PHENOTYPE**. In other words, their genes were different, even though they were both tall. You can't observe an organism's genotype, but you can observe its phenotype.

> **PHENOTYPE**
> Physical characteristics expressed by genes.

> **GENOTYPE**
> The genetic composition of an organism.

The reason for the different genotypes was because the tall parent plants bred in generation 1 were **HOMOZYGOUS**. This means that their two alleles were the same.

like BB and bb

However, the offspring tall plants were **HETEROZYGOUS**, due to their different alleles.

like Bb

THE PUNNETT SQUARE

Because all characteristics are created by two alleles, it is possible to predict the genotypes of offspring with a PUNNETT SQUARE. This tool is used to figure out the probability that an offspring will express a certain trait.

REGINALD PUNNETT (1875–1967) was a British geneticist who developed the Punnett Square, the tool used to predict the genotype of offspring.

Monohybrid Punnett Square

MONOHYBRID PUNNETT SQUARES examine only one trait, such as the tallness trait observed by Mendel. These diagrams consist of four boxes, each of which represents a 25 percent likelihood of getting offspring with a certain genotype. All the boxes add up to 100 percent.

> It doesn't matter which parent is on the side or top.

Parent 1		Parent 2	
		Allele 1	Allele 2
	Allele 1	25%	25%
	Allele 2	25%	25%

To analyze Punnett squares, take one letter from one parent's allele and one letter from the other parent's allele and put them together in the box where those two letters meet. So it should look like this:

		Parent 2	
		A1	A2
Parent 1	A1	A1-A1	A1-A2
	A2	A2-A1	A2-A2

The monohybrid Punnett square can be used to explain the genotypes of all the offspring in Mendel's experiment. The two alleles for height can be represented as *T* for tall and *t* for short.

In the first part of the experiment, Mendel bred a homozygous tall and a homozygous short plant. The homozygous tall plant can be represented as TT, while the homozygous short plant can be represented as tt.

		Parent 2	
		t	t
Parent 1	T	Tt	Tt
	T	Tt	Tt

So, all offspring will be tall: Tt. The dominant allele, T, is the characteristic that will be expressed by the offspring.

Monohybrid Cross

The cross (breeding) done by Mendel in the next stage of his experiment was between two heterozygous tall offspring (Tt and Tt). This is also known as a **MONOHYBRID CROSS**.

MONOHYBRID CROSS
Tracking a single gene
[Aa × aa]

		Parent 2	
		T	t
Parent 1	T	TT	Tt
	t	Tt	tt

This result explains why 75 percent of Mendel's second-generation offspring were tall, while the other 25 percent were short. Three of the four boxes contain the tall dominant trait (TT, Tt, Tt), while the remaining box contains the recessive short trait (tt).

These Punnett squares represent only the probability of each outcome. These parent plants that produced four offspring might not have exactly three tall and one short offspring. They might have two and two or four and zero. But as numbers of offspring increase they tend to reflect the probability. So, plants that had 400 offspring would likely have around 300 tall and 100 short.

Dihybrid Punnett Square

DIHYBRID PUNNETT SQUARES examine two traits. It refers to tracking two genes (AaBb × aabb). These Punnett squares have 16 boxes, with each box representing a 6.25 percent likelihood of the offspring having that genotype.

		Parent 2			
		Allele 1	Allele 2	Allele 3	Allele 4
Parent 1	Allele 1	6.25%	6.25%	6.25%	6.25%
	Allele 2	6.25%	6.25%	6.25%	6.25%
	Allele 3	6.25%	6.25%	6.25%	6.25%
	Allele 4	6.25%	6.25%	6.25%	6.25%

If Mendel had wanted to test for both pea color and tallness in his experiment, the homozygous parents have a TTYY and ttyy genotype, where Y represents the dominant yellow allele and y represents the recessive green allele for pea color. So, TTYY, TTYy, TtYY, TtYy, would be the alleles for tall, yellow pea plants.

For dihybrid Punnett squares, we use combinations of alleles for both parents. We can use the FOIL METHOD to create the combinations listed on the side and top of the square for each parent.

- For the TTYY parent, we:
    F: Take the first letter of each trait—TTYY (TY),
    O: Take the outside letters—TTYY (TY),
    I: Take the inside letters—TTYY (TY),
    L: Take the last letters of each trait—TTYY (TY).

- For the ttyy parent, we do the same:
    F: First—ttyy (ty),
    O: Outside—ttyy (ty),
    I: Inside—ttyy (ty),
    L: Last—ttyy (ty).

	Parent 2			
Parent 1		ty	ty	ty	ty
	TY	TtYy	TtYy	TtYy	TtYy
	TY	TtYy	TtYy	TtYy	TtYy
	TY	TtYy	TtYy	TtYy	TtYy
	TY	TtYy	TtYy	TtYy	TtYy

The square shows that there is a 100 percent likelihood of heterozygous alleles (TtYy) for both traits.

Dihybrid Cross

Crossing the offspring from the monohybrid parent together results in a **DIHYBRID CROSS**, or a cross between two genes.

> **DIHYBRID CROSS**
> The breeding of two genes.

To find the allele combinations for this cross, use the FOIL method again.

For both TtYy parents:
    First—TtYy (TY),
    Outside—TtYy (Ty),
    Inside—TtYy (tY),
    Last—TtYy (ty).

		Parent 2			
		TY	Ty	tY	ty
Parent 1	TY	TTYY	TTYy	TtYY	TtYy
	Ty	TTYy	TTyy	TtYy	Ttyy
	tY	TtYY	TtYy	ttYY	ttYy
	ty	TtYy	Ttyy	ttYy	ttyy

The result of the dihybrid cross shows that there is:

- a 56.25 percent chance that the offspring will be tall and yellow
  TTYY, TTYy, TtYY, TtYy, TTYy, TtYy, TtYY, TtYy, TtYy
  (6.25 x 9 = 56.25)

- an 18.75 percent chance that the offspring will be tall and green
  TTyy, Ttyy, Ttyy (6.25 x 3 = 18.75)

- an 18.75 percent chance that the offspring will be short and yellow
  ttYY, ttYy, ttYy (6.25 x 3 = 18.75)

- a 6.25 percent chance that the offspring will be short and green
  ttyy (6.25 x 1)

Punnett squares do not work in situations where one gene causes the appearance of another. For example, if the gene for black hair influenced the gene for eye color, then a Punnett square can't help to determine the probability of a different eye color.

1. Genetics is the study of what?

2. What contribution did Gregor Mendel make to the field of genetics?

3. What are genes?

4. What is the difference between dominant and recessive traits?

5. How are recessive traits preserved across generations?

6. What is the genotype of an organism?

7. What is the difference between a homozygous tall plant and a heterozygous tall plant?

8. What is the function of a Punnett square?

9. What is a monohybrid cross?

10. What is a dihybrid cross?

CHECK YOUR ANSWERS

1. Genetics is the study of heredity.

2. Gregor Mendel found out how genes were transferred from parent to offspring.

3. Units containing an organism's hereditary information

4. Dominant traits are main traits that are expressed (in heterozygous conditions), while recessive traits are traits that are hidden (in heterozygous conditions).

5. Genes have two alleles each. If one of these is a recessive allele, then it can be passed to the next generation.

6. The genotype is the genetic combination of an organism.

7. The heterozygous tall plant contains a recessive allele.

8. A Punnett square helps predict the genotype and phenotype of offspring.

9. A monohybrid cross is the tracking of a single gene.

10. A dihybrid cross is the tracking of two genes.

Chapter 45

DNA AND RNA

DNA, which stands for deoxyribonucleic acid, is the molecule that contains every gene within an organism. DNA holds the instructions for the growth and function of every organism.

James Watson, Rosalind Franklin, and Francis Crick identified the structure of DNA in 1953.

DNA has a unique shape called a DOUBLE HELIX—two helixes, or strands, held together by paired **BASES** and hydrogen bonds between the bases.

like a curvy ladder

The nucleotides within a single strand are held together by covalent bonds (stronger than hydrogen bonds holding two separate strands together).

BASE
One of four units of DNA.

The two strands of DNA are ANTIPARALLEL. This means the head of one strand is always laid against the tail of the other strand of DNA.

In DNA, there are four nitrogen bases: ADENINE (A), THYMINE (T), GUANINE (G), and CYTOSINE (C). The strands are complementary. This means that they fit together but are opposite of each other. The order of the letters is the "language" that tells a cell how to build an organism. In RNA, thymine is replaced by uracil (U).

One helix contains a row of nitrogen bases, while the other contains bases that correspond to those nitrogen bases. Together they form **BASE PAIRS**.

BASE PAIR
Bonded bases, such as adenine and thymine pairs or cytosine and guanine pairs.

DNA has two kinds of base pairs. The bases always pair up the same way:

- adenine-thymine (A-T)—two hydrogen bonds between each pair

- cytosine-guanine (C-G)—three hydrogen bonds between each pair

PURINES and PYRIMIDINES are nitrogenous bases that make up the two different kinds of nucleotide bases in DNA and RNA. The purines in DNA and RNA are adenine and guanine. The pyrimidines in DNA are cytosine and thymine; in RNA, they are cytosine and uracil. Purines pair with pyrimidines because their size and shape make them a perfect fit for hydrogen bonding.

Use this mnemonic to remember base pairing:

A Trait Could Grow.

Adenine + Thymine / Cystosine + Guanine

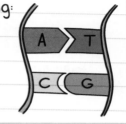

IT'S LIKE LOOKING IN THE MIRROR.

NOT QUITE!

The order of base pairs makes each person's DNA unique. Even identical twins have different DNA, although their DNA is similar.

DNA IN THE CELL

Because DNA holds so much information, it needs to be compressed into a form that can fit within an organism's cells. DNA is held in the cell in the form of **CHROMATIN** in the nucleus. Chromatin is a structure made of DNA wrapped around proteins called **HISTONES**. Chromatin wraps around histones repeatedly, creating a compact structure that can hold many feet of DNA in one chromatin fiber.

CHROMATIN
Structure made of DNA tied around histones.

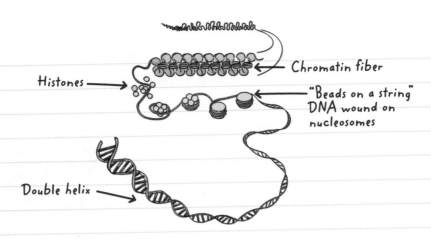

Histones →

Chromatin fiber

"Beads on a string"
DNA wound on
nucleosomes

Double helix →

DNA is six and a half feet long. Despite that, chromatin is so compact that all of an organism's DNA can fit into something as small as one cell.

THE HUMAN GENOME PROJECT was a global project to map the human **genome**, the library of all an organism's genes. The project determined that DNA holds the information of around 25,000 genes.

DNA REPLICATION

When a cell divides, each cell must have the same amount of DNA to properly function. This means that the DNA must be copied. This copying happens during **DNA REPLICATION**.

> **DNA REPLICATION**
> The process of copying DNA.

During DNA replication, the paired bases of the double helix are broken apart and each strand is copied.

The DNA Replication Process:

1. During cell replication, the DNA is "unzipped" by a protein called **HELICASE**, causing the paired bases to separate. The separated DNA creates a Y shape called a **FORK**. Another protein, **DNA POLYMERASE**, attaches to both separated strands. Replication begins on both strands at the same time.

> **HELICASE**
> The protein that "unzips" DNA by separating bond pairs.

> **DNA POLYMERASE**
> Enzymes that create DNA molecules by copying genetic information.

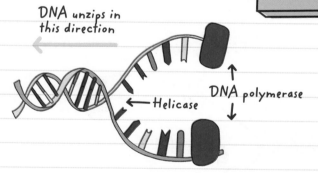

DNA unzips in this direction

← Helicase

DNA polymerase

2. The two strands are each replicated in opposite directions, continuing the antiparallel formation of DNA. The first, the LEADING STRAND, replicates in the direction that the unzipping occurs in. The second, the LAGGING STRAND, replicates away from the direction of the unzipping.

The leading and lagging strands are called "template" strands. A template is a model for copying.

3. For the leading strand, another protein—PRIMASE— creates a short single strand called a primer, which attaches itself to the leading strand. Primers act as the starting point for replication. DNA polymerase moves continuously from the end of the primer toward the direction that the DNA is unzipping in, creating new strands that connect to the leading strand and form A-T and C-G base pairs.

4. On the lagging strand, primers attach at different points of the strand, and DNA polymerase add bases after it in

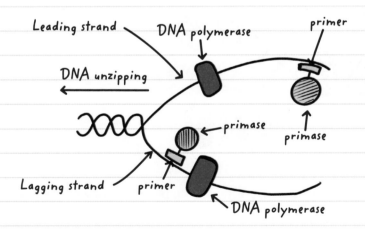

the same way it does in the leading strand. The polymerase moves in the opposite direction from the direction that the DNA molecule unzips in. This means that:

- New primers are added as the molecule unzips, unlike the leading strand, which just uses one primer.

- The DNA polymerase must stop each time it hits the beginning of another primer and move to the end of the next primer.

The DNA polymerase reads the template strand and adds the matching base to create a base pair. For example, if the template has an adenine (A) base, the polymerase would add a thymine

> It's called the lagging strand because the polymerase has to stop and reset each time a new primer is added, unlike the leading strand, which adds bases continuously.

(T) base, creating an adenine-thymine (A-T) base pair. If the template has a cytosine (C) base, the polymerase would add a guanine (G) base, creating a cytosine-guanine (C-G) base pair.

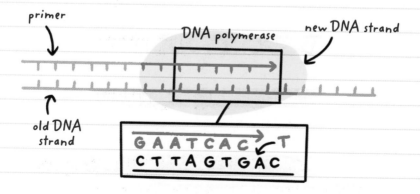

primer

DNA polymerase

new DNA strand

old DNA strand

GAATCAC→T
CTTAGTGAC

The bases that are made in between each primer on the lagging strand are called OKAZAKI FRAGMENTS, after REIJI OKAZAKI, who, in 1968, discovered the differences between how the two DNA strands replicated.

5. When the DNA has been fully replicated on both the leading and lagging strands, another protein, which has properties of **EXONUCLEASE** in addition to its polymerase activity, uses its exonuclease activity to degrade the RNA primers ahead of it as it extends the DNA strand behind it and removes the primers so that they can be used for replication of other DNA strands. DNA polymerase returns to replace the primers' bases. Two double strands of DNA are now formed.

6. At the end of replication, there are several gaps in the replicated strands due to the removal of the primers and addition of new bases. These gaps must be sealed. The sealing is done by the enzyme **DNA LIGASE**.

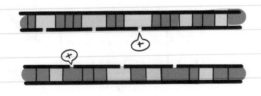

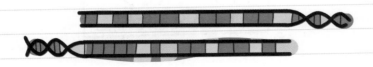

TRANSCRIPTION

The instructions in DNA must be read and used by the cell. The first step of this process is **TRANSCRIPTION**, which happens within the cell's nucleus. During transcription, the two strands of DNA are separated by helicase (just like in DNA replication) and an enzyme called **RNA POLYMERASE** attaches to one of the strands and begins to read it. This strand is called a **TEMPLATE STRAND**.

As the RNA polymerase reads the template strand, it builds a new strand that is similar to the DNA strand that was originally attached to the template. This new strand is called **mRNA**. For RNA to be effective, it needs to use the same bases as DNA, with the exception of thymine (T), which is replaced by uracil (U). The RNA's bases pair with the template strand, just like the base pairs that attach two DNA strands together.

> Base pairs in RNA strand: cytosine and guanine (C-G), and uracil and adenine (U-A).

> Think of RNA as a temporary copy of DNA that has been changed slightly and is read by the cell.

RNA

Template strand

To "transcribe" means to write. RNA polymerase "writes" new RNA strands based on DNA.

After the RNA strand is created, it detaches from the DNA, and the two DNA strands pair once again. The RNA then exits the nucleus, where the DNA resides, and is read by a **RIBOSOME** to create the proteins that the cell needs to properly function.

RIBOSOME
A structure within a cell that reads RNA and creates proteins.

Mutations

The cell checks for any problems after replication or transcription and corrects errors where they happen. Sometimes, though, mistakes happen. Random errors or changes in the genetic code are called **MUTATIONS**.

If a mutation goes undetected, it is possible that the cell containing the mutated DNA can produce harmful proteins and cause disease. Sometimes, however, these mutations are harmless and may even help an organism to survive better in their environment.

Cancer is a well-known disease caused by mutations within cells.

TYPES OF MUTATIONS

MUTATION TYPE	DESCRIPTION
POINT MUTATION • substitution • silent • missense • nonsense	■ Point mutation: change in single nucleotide pair ■ Substitution mutation: one base pair is switched to another **EXAMPLE:** 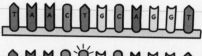 ORIGINAL SEQUENCE  MUTATED SEQUENCE *See the highlighted C (cytosine)? The second DNA strand, which would have an A (adenine) base, is expecting a T (thymine) base to pair with. The presence of the cytosine will prevent pairing from occurring.* This error can happen due to mistakes in DNA replication or RNA transcription.
FRAMESHIFT MUTATION	■ Mutations that are the result of a deletion or insertion. **EXAMPLE:** This type of mutation is more drastic and damaging than point mutations.

There can also be mutations where not just a few bases of DNA have a problem, but entire parts of the molecule do. These are called **CHROMOSOMAL MUTATIONS**. They are caused by changes in the structure of CHROMOSOMES, the tightly packed form of chromatin.

Chromatin forms chromosomes during cell division. Chromosomes are so tightly packed that they can be seen under a microscope.

There are several types of structural changes that can happen within a chromosome:

ERROR	DESCRIPTION	EXAMPLE
DUPLICATION	The chromosome has extra DNA that it does not need. *The chromosome has received more than necessary amounts of DNA.*	
DELETION	A part of the chromosome is lost. *A part of the chromosome is deleted.*	

ERROR	DESCRIPTION	EXAMPLE
INVERSION	The base pairs of the DNA are reversed.	
	The middle part of the chromosome has been flipped.	
TRANSLOCATION	A part of one chromosome is transferred to another chromosome.	

If these mutated chromosomes were to be passed down to offspring, GENETIC DISEASES, or disorders, could result. Genetic diseases are diseases that are caused by problems within genes.

SEX-LINKED GENES

Two of the forty-six human chromosomes are SEX-DETERMINING CHROMOSOMES. Biologists call these sex-determining chromosomes the **XY CHROMOSOMES**.

Humans that have two paired X chromosomes (XX) usually develop female characteristics, while humans that have an XY pair of chromosomes usually develop male characteristics.

Like all chromosomes, the XY chromosomes carry information about specific genes. However, because the XY chromosomes affect sex, the genes that they carry information for are called **SEX-LINKED GENES**. When these genes have a mutation, disorders that are unique to the sex of the organism result.

Sex-linked gene disorders include:

DISORDERS	DESCRIPTION
X CHROMOSOME	
Hemophilia	Inability for blood to clot.
Duchenne Muscular Dystrophy	Loss of muscle cells due to the absence of proteins that help keep the muscle cells intact.
Deuteranopia	Also known as red-green color blindness, the most common form of color blindness.
Y CHROMOSOME	
Y Chromosome Microdeletion	Reduced fertility or sperm count.
XYY Syndrome	Larger bodies and learning difficulties.

Because Y chromosomes are usually present only in males, these disorders can be passed down only to males.

442

CHECK YOUR KNOWLEDGE

1. What is DNA?

2. What bases make up DNA?

3. What proteins compress chromatin to make it even more compact?

4. Why does DNA need to be copied?

5. What is the role of a primer?

6. How does the cell handle gaps from the removal of primers at the end of DNA replication?

7. What is RNA?

8. What possible problems can mutations cause?

9. What is a genetic disease?

10. Why are the genes carried by the X and Y chromosomes referred to as "sex-linked genes"?

ANSWERS

CHECK YOUR ANSWERS

1. DNA, or deoxyribonucleic acid, holds the instructions for the growth and function of every organism.

2. There are four DNA bases: adenine, thymine, guanine, and cytosine.

3. Histones

4. To ensure that all cells receive the same amount of DNA

5. A primer acts as a starting point for DNA replication on both strands.

6. The cell uses DNA ligase to seal the gaps with the addition of new bases.

7. RNA is a single strand of genetic code that is read by the cell.

8. Mutations can produce harmful proteins and cause disease.

9. A disease caused by a problem in an organism's genes

10. The X and Y chromosomes affect the sex of an organism.

Chapter 46

GENETIC ENGINEERING

Each gene is used, or expressed, to create a product within an organism's cells. This **GENE EXPRESSION** can be controlled based on what the body needs and environmental signals. Gene expression controls all chemical reactions in the body.

> **GENE EXPRESSION**
> The use of a gene to create a product.

For example, when you eat food, the body's chemistry immediately begins to change in response. Your mouth generates saliva, your stomach churns, and your cells prepare to receive nutrients from the food. However, when you've gone a long time without eating, your body generates a completely different signal. You retain more water and begin to burn your stores of fat, which turn into the sugars that your body needs to create energy.

GENETIC ENGINEERING

Biologists can use biological or chemical processes to alter the genes of a cell. The process is called

GENETIC ENGINEERING. Using genetic engineering, scientists can manipulate the DNA of an organism to produce various behaviors within the organism.

Through genetic engineering, plants and animals:
- have been changed to be resistant to disease
- are able to grow faster
- are more nutritious

Engineering organisms for our purposes can improve the quality of our food, but at the same time, organisms may lose genes that help them live in their particular environment. If a species dies due to the lack of necessary genes, their absence could have a large impact on the environment that they are a part of.

Scientists have a set of rules they follow that are based on what they determine is right for people, animals, or an environment. The advances in genetic engineering resulted in the creation of many of those rules.

GENETICALLY MODIFIED ORGANISMS (GMOs), are examples of plants and animals that have been genetically engineered. Most genetically modified foods were created to make plants resistant to disease. Corn and soybeans are examples of genetically modified foods.

HMMM. COMING ALONG NICELY.

Genetic engineering involves several techniques practiced by molecular biologists, like the removal and addition of DNA strands. The DNA strands are often artificially made by molecular biologists, who add their desired number and order of base pairs.

To remove and add DNA, RESTRICTION ENZYMES, special proteins that cut at one end of a DNA sequence between two bases on the same strand, then cut on the opposite end of the complementary strand. Restriction enzymes leave behind "sticky ends," single-stranded overhangs, resulting in two ends of DNA that will have some nucleotides without any complementary bases. These DNA fragments can easily attach to other sticky ends.

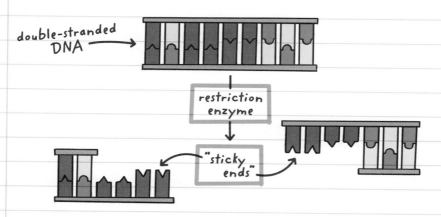

double-stranded DNA →

restriction enzyme

"sticky ends"

Transformation of DNA

Many bacteria have freely floating circular DNA molecules called **PLASMIDS** within their membranes, in addition to their ordinary chromosomes. Plasmids contain genes that help the bacteria stay alive. Plasmids, unlike chromosomal DNA, can replicate themselves, even if the bacterial cell is not dividing. Bacteria that do not contain plasmids are less likely to survive.

Bacteria can lose plasmids when they divide because they're not essential to the life of bacteria and the cells do not try to keep them. But bacterial cells recognize how useful plasmids are and have the ability to take in plasmid DNA from their environment. The process is called **TRANSFORMATION**.

Scientists make use of this transformation process by making their own plasmid DNA sequences and tricking bacteria into taking them in. Because bacteria divide very quickly, scientists gain many millions of copies of their unique plasmids in a short amount of time.

To increase the likelihood that bacteria take in plasmids, scientists induce a **STATE OF COMPETENCE** in bacteria where cells are treated to make them temporarily permeable to DNA. Because plasmids often contain antibiotic resistance, scientists can filter out the bacteria by growing the plasmids on antibiotics.

> **STATE OF COMPETENCE**
> A state in which bacteria are more likely to take up plasmids.

CHECK YOUR KNOWLEDGE

1. What is gene expression?

2. What is genetic engineering?

3. How has genetic engineering helped plants and animals?

4. What can be a negative consequence of genetic engineering?

5. What techniques are involved in genetic engineering?

6. How do restriction enzymes work?

7. What are plasmids?

8. How are plasmids different from chromosomal DNA?

9. What is transformation?

10. How do scientists make bacteria competent?

ANSWERS

CHECK YOUR ANSWERS

1. The use of a gene to create a product

2. The process of manipulating DNA to produce different behaviors in an organism

3. Genetic engineering has helped plants and animals be more disease resistant and grow faster.

4. Genetic engineering could negatively impact the survival of an organism and the environment that it lives in.

5. Techniques that remove and add DNA in cells

6. Restriction enzymes cut DNA strands at specific places, leaving "sticky ends" behind that fragments can be added to.

7. Circular DNA molecules that contain genes that help bacteria stay alive

8. Plasmids can duplicate themselves even if the bacteria cell is not dividing.

9. How bacteria take in plasmid DNA from the environment

10. Scientists treat the bacteria to induce competence.

Unit 11

Life on Earth

Chapter 47

EVOLUTION

THEORY OF EVOLUTION

EVOLUTION is the change and
development of an organism's
heritable traits that occurs over the
span of many generations. Evolution
is responsible for the appearance of
many new species on Earth.

> **EVOLUTION**
> Changes and
> developments in
> an organism's heritable
> traits over time.

Evolution is influenced mainly by
the environment, which changes
over time. For example, if the
environment becomes hotter,
then organisms that cannot
survive the increased

temperatures will either move to a new environment or die.

These changes occur through mutations, or random genetic
changes. Not all mutations are helpful, only those mutations
that result in traits that can be passed down to new

offspring can lead to evolution. These offspring have **EVOLVED**, meaning that they are genetically different from, but still closely related to, their parents.

Evolution is only one way that new species are made. Humans have engineered new species themselves through a process called *selective breeding*. In this process, two breeds are bred together to produce a new breed with more desirable traits.

Labrador + Poodle = Labradoodle

EVIDENCE OF EVOLUTION: STRUCTURAL CLUES

Scientists have taken a long time to understand evolution because the evidence that supports evolution is either very difficult to find or requires studying many different species. For example, animals have body structures that perform similar functions—like the way the wings of a bird propel it into the air in the same manner that a fish's fins propel it through the water. Or the similarities between the legs of a dog and the legs of a cat. These similarities, considered examples of evolution, are called **HOMOLOGOUS STRUCTURES**.

Examples of evolution can also come from **VESTIGIAL STRUCTURES**. In humans, the tailbone is a vestigial structure; we have no tails, but the bone that would control a tail is still there.

left over

> **VESTIGIAL STRUCTURE**
> A structure that performs no function within an organism.

DON'T WORRY, YOUR TAIL BONE DOESN'T SHOW.

> **Homologous structures:** structures similar in related organisms; inherited from a common ancestor.
>
> **Analogous structures:** structures that are similar in unrelated organisms, but evolved independently in two different organisms. Not inherited from a common ancestor.

Embryology

One field that has provided scientists with evidence of evolution is **EMBRYOLOGY**. Embryology involves the study of embryos, organisms that are in their earliest stages of development. By looking at the embryos of various species, scientists can see that many species share characteristics in their early development.

The embryonic similarities helped scientists create the theory of a **COMMON ANCESTOR**. A common ancestor demonstrates that no organism is completely different from another—an important factor in the study of evolution.

454

Embryonic similarities:

EMBRYOS OF

FISH   SALAMANDER   TORTOISE   CHICKEN   PIG   COW   RABBIT   HUMAN

Fossils

FOSSILS are the most well-known evidence of evolution.
Fossils are preserved imprints or remains of prehistoric
organisms, left behind long after the organisms have died. Fossils
preserve the structure of an organism, giving scientists a good
idea of what certain organisms looked like throughout Earth's
history. They also provide scientists with a way to track the
behaviors of similar species of the past, and then compare how
similarly these ancient species behaved to the species of today.

Fossils form over millions of years as rocks, mud, and water
are carried over the remains of dead animals and harden.
Over time, the animals' remains are buried
deeper into the Earth as more silt, dirt, and
mud create new land on top of them. As the
remains decompose, the organisms leave
behind their traces, bones, or impressions.

Only a tiny percentage of organisms become fossilized. Usually, other organisms consume and decompose the body of a dead organism, returning its nutrients to the soil. When an organism is buried quickly or has hard parts like bone, teeth, or shells, it is more likely to be preserved. Scientists have tools that allow them to see the age of these fossils, which not only show when an organism lived but also how they are related to organisms that exist today.

Various Ways Organisms Become Fossilized

WHOLE REMAINS	Animals get trapped in tar, ice, or **AMBER** (a hardened tree resin) and die. Their bodies or parts of their bodies remain fully intact.
TRACE FOSSILS	Animals step in mud or tar. As the moisture evaporates, the footprint gets solidified into rock. 

MINERAL FOSSILS	The minerals in the bones, teeth, or shells have small pockets of air between them. 
	As animals get buried in the ground, minerals within the ground fill the small pockets of air and turn the animal parts to stone.
CARBON FILMS	An organism gets pressed into the hard ground over millions of years and heated by the deepest layers of the Earth.
	The organism loses all the liquids and gases in its decaying body and leaves behind a film of carbon, the element that makes up the solids of an organism's body.
MOLDS AND CASTS	Over time, an organism gets pressed into the ground and begins to dissolve. The mud and sediment hardens around the dissolving body. The space left in the rock is an impression of the organism called a **MOLD**. If mud and minerals make their way into that space and harden, it forms a **CAST**.

Sometimes, the remains have pressurized and heated so much that the residue provides no information about the species that existed and is just pure liquid or solid carbon. This is called a FOSSIL FUEL, because we use the energy within the remains to fuel many devices. Coal and natural gas are examples of fossil fuels.

PRE-DARWINIAN EVOLUTIONARY THEORY

CHARLES DARWIN is famous for the evolutionary theory that we know today, but earlier scientists had considered evolution through their own studies. Some of them have even used the formation of fossils to support their own theories.

PERSON	DESCRIPTION
Carolus Linnaeus (Early 1700s)	■ The biologist who created the system of classifying organisms that we use today. ■ Believed that the creation of new species was possible.
Comte de Buffon (Mid-1700s)	■ A mathematician who believed that living things change due to both the environment and random chance.

PERSON	DESCRIPTION
	Suggested that humans and apes were related.
Erasmus Darwin (Late 1700s)	Charles Darwin's grandfather and a poet. He was the first to believe that evolution takes place and that it even occurred before humans were on the planet, but he could not explain how it happened.
Baron Georges Cuvier (Late 1700s)	A natural historian who noticed that bones of fossilized animals were very different from bones of modern animals. Using elephant remains, he noticed that an ancient species of elephant was completely different from living elephants and concluded that ancient species must have adapted to changes on Earth between the two times.

459

PERSON	DESCRIPTION
Jean-Baptiste de Monet de Lamarck (Early 1800s)	■ A botanist and student of Comte de Buffon. ■ He studied various animals and noticed their similarities, leading him to believe that the species that existed at that time were not the only species that will ever exist. ■ He was also the first to connect the animals' ability to adapt with the changes that adaptation could have on their bodies. ■ Lamarck believed that simpler organisms become more complex as they adapt to their environment. ■ He used giraffes to explain his theory, saying that giraffes' necks began to grow because they needed to use their necks to feed on higher and higher branches. Over many generations, the offspring inherited longer necks.

DARWIN'S THEORY OF EVOLUTION

In 1859, CHARLES DARWIN built his theory of evolution on the theories of his predecessors. These earlier scientists had not been able to confirm their theories by studying living species. Charles Darwin would be the first to confirm his theories during a trip to the Galápagos Islands in 1835.

As Darwin studied the life on the Galápagos, he came across several different types of finch, a small bird. Many of the finches had different beak shapes, each of which was useful for finding different kinds of food. For example, an insect-eating finch had a long, thin beak shape that could reach into the small spaces in trees or the ground where insects lived, while another type of finch had a broad beak for crushing seeds. Darwin believed that the various environmental needs of these finches pressured their evolution from a common finch ancestor.

Darwin followed this thought and developed his theory of **NATURAL SELECTION**. The theory stated that species that were best adapted to their environments would pass their traits on to offspring. Species that could not adapt as quickly, however, would not pass on their traits.

Before his trip to the Galápagos, Darwin studied fossils, noticing that there were many species that died out

> **NATURAL SELECTION**
> The process where organisms born with physical traits best adapted to their environments survive and pass on their traits to offspring.

naturally, not due to any changes in climate or the introduction of new predators. His studies confirmed that animals that could not adapt to their environment died out.

> The expression "survival of the fittest," which is commonly used to explain natural selection, did not come from Charles Darwin. The phrase was said by sociologist and philosopher **HERBERT SPENCER** after reading Darwin's work.

Main Points of Natural Selection

- Organisms from the same species have different traits.

- Organisms compete with one another for survival.

- Individuals with traits that help them survive reproduce more successfully and pass on these traits to their offspring.

In time, organisms with the improved variation may become a separate species.

When a species isn't fit for its environment, either because the environment has changed or because competition for survival has increased, the species might become **EXTINCT** —all members of the species die.

EXTINCT? NEVER!

One of the most important mechanisms that can lead to different traits in individuals from the same species are mutations, or random genetic changes. Sometimes, these genetic changes don't lead to any benefit and are barely noticeable. When the mutation does lead to a positive physical change, it can increase the ability of an organism to survive.

One example of a mutation is **CAMOUFLAGE**. This physical adaptation allows organisms to blend into their environment. An organism's wings, feathers, leaves, fur, or hair can contribute to camouflage. An organism without camouflage might be more easily seen by either predator or prey, which might prevent them from avoiding hunters or catching food.

PRIMATE EVOLUTION

Primates form a group of mammals that include, monkeys, apes, and lemurs. Humans are the most numerous of the ape species, outnumbering all the other primates by a factor of thousands to one. Primates have shared characteristics that differentiate them from other mammals, which suggests that they have a common ancestor. Characteristics of primates include:

- opposable thumbs, which allow you to grasp objects

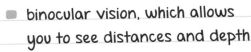

- binocular vision, which allows you to see distances and depth

- rotating shoulders, which allow you to swing your arms above your head

- relatively large brains, which allow you to process visual information and manage social interactions

HEY THERE!

When mutations happen in egg or sperm cells, they can be passed on from parent to offspring. An individual that is born with a new trait, a product of a mutation that allows for better camouflage, might be better suited for survival and thus will leave more descendants. This leads to a situation where animals that don't have camouflage are replaced by animals that do.

Humanlike primates that walked on two legs, called HOMINIDS, first appeared 6 million years ago. One of the oldest hominid fossils, nicknamed Lucy, was found in Africa. Hominid fossils from 1.5 to 2 million years ago show more humanlike characteristics.

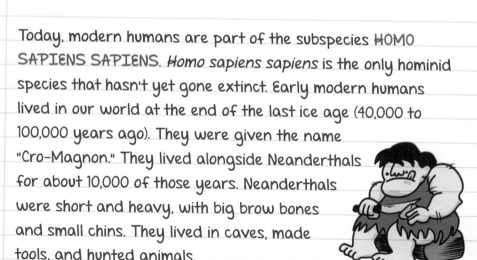

Today, modern humans are part of the subspecies HOMO SAPIENS SAPIENS. *Homo sapiens sapiens* is the only hominid species that hasn't yet gone extinct. Early modern humans lived in our world at the end of the last ice age (40,000 to 100,000 years ago). They were given the name "Cro-Magnon." They lived alongside Neanderthals for about 10,000 of those years. Neanderthals were short and heavy, with big brow bones and small chins. They lived in caves, made tools, and hunted animals.

As early humans migrated out of Africa, they interacted and mated with Neanderthals, who lived in Europe and Asia.

CHECK YOUR KNOWLEDGE

1. What is evolution?

2. What is a fossil?

3. What are three types of fossils?

4. Which scientist was among the first to believe that humans and apes are related?

5. Who was the first known scientist to believe that evolution happened?

6. When did scientists first consider that adaptations to an environment could have an impact on organisms' bodies?

7. Where did Charles Darwin confirm his theories of evolution?

8. What caused the evolution of the finch?

9. What is natural selection?

10. What evidence helped Darwin confirm that organisms that were not able to adapt to their environment wouldn't survive?

1. The change in an organism's traits that occurs over the span of many generations

2. A fossil is a bone or impression of an ancient organism preserved in rock or mud.

3. Whole remains, trace fossils, mineral fossils, carbon films, molds, and casts

4. Comte de Buffon

5. Erasmus Darwin

6. The mid-1700s

7. The Galápagos Islands

8. The environmental needs of the finches

9. Natural selection is the process where organisms with physical traits best adapted to their environments survive and pass on their traits to offspring.

10. Fossils

Chapter 48

THE HISTORY OF LIFE

Homo sapiens evolved from ancient mammal ancestors only about 300,000 years ago. However, by that time Earth was already 4.5 billion years old and had supported many more species than just those that exist now. This understanding comes from the presence of fossils within the multiple layers of Earth's **MANTLE**.

> **MANTLE**
> The region between Earth's crust and its core.

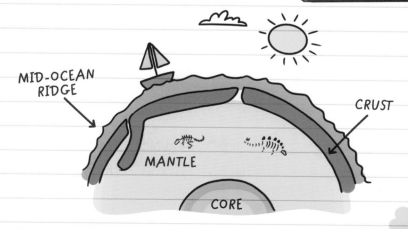

MID-OCEAN RIDGE

CRUST

MANTLE

CORE

GEOLOGICAL TIME SCALE

Many fossils are buried within the same layer of Earth's mantle, which means that many of these organisms may have lived in the same period of time. A GEOLOGICAL TIME SCALE was created to organize fossils and provide scientists with a way to study specific time periods.

> *Geology* comes from the Greek word *gē*, which means "earth," and the Greek suffix *-logia*, meaning "the study of." Geology is the study of Earth, and the geological time scale is the study of Earth based on time.

The geological time scale is a way for scientists to date fossils according to the layer of Earth that they were found in. Each time frame also corresponds to a major event, such as continents breaking apart, large shifts in the climate, or the appearance of new organisms.

The geological time scale is divided into several categories, based on the detail of knowledge that scientists have of the time.

The largest category is the **EON**, of which there are four: the HADEAN, ARCHEAN, PROTEROZOIC, and PHANEROZOIC.

Eons are divided into many smaller **ERAS**, which are divided into even smaller **PERIODS**. In the Cenozoic era, the most recent era, periods are further divided into **EPOCHS**, due to the large amount of fossil evidence we have for organisms of the time.

GEOLOGICAL TIME SCALE	
EON	**ERA**
Hadean	
Archean	Eoarchean
	Paleoarchean
	Mesoarchean
	Neoarchean
Proterozoic	Paleoproterozoic
	Mesoproterozoic
	Neoproterozoic

EON	ERA	PERIODS
Phanerozoic	Paleozoic	Cambrian
		Ordovician
		Silurian
		Devonian
		Mississippian
		Pennsylvanian
		Permian
	Mesozoic	Triassic
		Jurassic
		Cretaceous
	Cenozoic	Tertiary
		Quaternary

Use these mnemonics to help you remember the order of the eons:

Harmless Alligators Protect People

Hungry Ants Populate Plants

Hadean, Archean, Proterozoic, Phanerozoic

HADEAN EON: (Length: 600 million years)
4.6 billion years ago to 4 billion years ago

In the HADEAN EON, Earth was filled with molten lava.
It's believed that any water on the planet would have boiled away due to the incredible heat.

The Hadean is considered an informal eon, originally used to explain the period of time between the formation of Earth and the earliest known rocks. It is named after the Greek god of the underworld, Hades.

ARCHEAN EON: (Length: 1.5 million years)
4 billion years ago to 2.5 billion years ago

Eras: Eoarchean, Paleoarchean, Mesoarchean, Neoarchean

The ARCHEAN EON is marked by the cooling of Earth, allowing for the formation of land and bodies of water. Millions of years after oceans formed, the first **MICROBES**, microscopic, single-celled organisms, began to develop.

PROTEROZOIC EON: (Length: 2 billion years)
2.5 billion years ago to 500 million years ago

Eras: Paleoproterozoic, Mesoproterozoic, Neoproterozoic

The PROTEROZOIC EON is marked by the appearance of complex, eukaryotic life-forms allowed by the accumulation of oxygen in the atmosphere. Eukaryotic cells have specialized cell structures that were bound by membranes.

Multicellular organisms would eventually evolve from these eukaryotic microbes, including algae and other organisms of the Protista kingdom.

PHANEROZOIC EON: (Length: 500+ million years)
500 million years ago to Present Time

Eras: Paleozoic, Mesozoic, Cenozoic

The first complex organisms began to appear during the PHANEROZOIC EON. A majority of fossilized organisms found today are from this period.

PALEOZOIC ERA

The beginning of ocean life as we know it today.
The descendants of those species continue to live today.

During this time, the transition
of life from oceans to land
with simple invertebrates,
like worms, and more complex
vertebrates, like amphibians,
began.

- Cambrian Period
  The Cambrian period marked a boom in evolution in
  an event known as the Cambrian explosion, in which
  the largest number of organisms evolved in any single
  period of the history of Earth. Invertebrates like
  sponges, jellyfish, and worms appear.

- Ordovician Period
  Invertebrates and early vertebrates, like jawless
  fish, appear.

- Silurian Period
  Fish with jaws and vertebrates with early lungs
  appear.

  The first land plants appear.

- Devonian Period
  The first amphibians and large forests appear.

- Mississippian Period
  Amphibians and forests become dominant on land.

- Pennsylvanian Period
  Insects and early reptiles appear.

- Permian Period
  Insects and reptiles begin to spread across the land.

MESOZOIC ERA

The Mesozoic is also known as the AGE OF THE REPTILES, because reptiles dominated the land. As the largest and most dangerous predators, dinosaurs prevented the growth of other types of life-forms like amphibians or mammals.

- Triassic Period
  First dinosaurs and the earliest mammals appeared.

- Jurassic Period
  Dinosaurs dominate the land.

  Primitive mammals, which could hide or burrow underground, survive.

- Cretaceous Period
  Dinosaurs continued to dominate the land.

  Flowering plants and seed and cone plants begin
  to grow.

  Meteors collided with Earth's
  surface, kicking up dust into
  the atmosphere and blocking
  the sun. This changed Earth's
  climate, first killing plants
  and then killing plant eaters.
  Dinosaurs would eventually
  also die due to the lack of food.

CENOZOIC ERA

The Cenozoic is the most modern era, which began after
the mass extinction of several species 65 million years ago.
Mammals were able to thrive because the dinosaurs had
died. The Cenozoic is known as the AGE OF THE MAMMALS
AND BIRDS.

- Tertiary Period
  Marked by a large shift in the climate. Glaciers in
  the northern hemisphere began to form and large
  landmasses began to break apart.

All epochs of this period are defined by the evolution of surviving mammals into primates and the flourishing of primates into the earliest humans.

- Quaternary Period
The Quaternary period is marked by Earth's ice ages—periods of freezing and warming of the planet. These cycles changed the kind of life-forms that live on the planet over time.

Humanity dominates this period, with the earliest humans showing up 2.8 million years ago and *Homo sapiens* (like us) appearing 300,000 years ago.

THE ORIGINS OF LIFE

Scientists still debate how life began. All scientists view the cell, the structure that all living things have, as a key. Cells are organic structures, meaning that they are composed primarily of the element carbon. Therefore, most hypotheses on how life began start with carbon.

Miller-Urey Experiment

The most well-known hypothesis is that the first organic molecules came from a mixture of gases in Earth's early atmosphere and energy in the form of heat and lightning.

In 1952, STANLEY MILLER and HAROLD UREY re-created Earth's conditions using water vapor, methane, ammonia, and hydrogen as the gases, a pool of water to represent Earth's early ocean, and fire and electricity to represent the heat and lightning.

After the gases had been exposed to energy (heat and lightning), the scientists cooled them, causing the gases to condense into a liquid that they could observe. The result of Miller and Urey's experiment was the presence of water and several basic organic amino acids, including a few that are necessary for life to exist today. This supported the theory that the first life-forms appeared naturally and spontaneously as a result of chemical reactions and the conditions of Earth's early atmosphere.

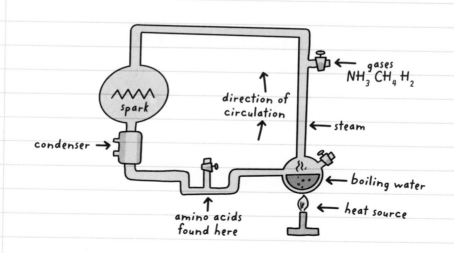

spark

direction of circulation

condenser →

← gases
NH_3 CH_4 H_2

← steam

← boiling water

← heat source

↑
amino acids
found here

Protocells

Even if organic molecules could come together in one area, like they were able to in the Miller-Urey experiment, they would have had to organize into the shape of a prokaryotic cell. The theory of the **protocell** addresses this concern. Protocells are composed of a collection of organic compounds enclosed in a lipid membrane. This could be, for example, an oil bubble that contains molecules like water, carbon, sodium, and potassium. Although this theory makes sense, scientists are still stumped on how protocells first came together and evolved into prokaryotic life-forms.

RNA World

Another hypothesis is that life is based on the creation of organic molecules that store genes as DNA or RNA. RNA is considered simpler than DNA because it is a single-stranded molecule, while DNA is a double-stranded molecule. The simpler structure of RNA, along with its ability to store genetic information, leads some scientists to consider the theory that life began with RNA.

However, unlike the Miller-Urey experiment, there is no real ability to test this.

CHECK YOUR KNOWLEDGE

1. What physical evidence helps us understand the past species on Earth?

2. What do scientists use to date fossils?

3. Why might there not have been any water during the Hadean eon?

4. What do scientists theorize caused the growth of eukaryotic organisms?

5. In which era did organisms begin to transition from oceans to land?

6. What period marked the end of the age of reptiles?

7. When did Earth's ice ages begin?

8. Why is there no evidence of mammals during the Mesozoic era?

9. Why did the dinosaurs eventually die?

10. What inspired Miller and Urey to use the substances that they did in their experiment?

ANSWERS   481

CHECK YOUR ANSWERS

1. Fossils

2. The geological time scale

3. All water would have boiled away due to the Earth's heat.

4. They believe that the addition of oxygen to the atmosphere contributed to the growth of eukaryotic organisms.

5. The Paleozoic era

6. The Cretaceous period

7. The Quaternary period

8. The Mesozoic era was the time of the dinosaurs. The mammals would not have been able to survive against such predators.

9. When Earth's climate changed, most of their food died. The dinosaurs starved.

10. The substances that they used were based on the substances that might have been present in the Earth's early atmosphere.

Unit 12

Ecosystems and Habitats

Chapter 49

THE ECOSYSTEM

BIOTIC AND ABIOTIC FACTORS

ECOLOGY is the study of how organisms interact with their environment. Ecologists call the combination of living organisms and their environment

← biologists who study ecology

an **ECOSYSTEM**. Ecologists pay close attention to populations of various species and the **COMMUNITIES** of those species within an ecosystem.

> **COMMUNITY**
> A group of different species occupying the same environment.

An ecosystem contains:

- **biotic factors:** all living organisms in that environment

- **abiotic factors:** all nonliving substances in that environment

Biotic factors in ecosystems sometimes create some of the abiotic factors that nourish the organisms within the ecosystems. For example, dead plants and animals are broken down into basic organic materials that become part of the soil. Plants need that organic material to thrive in the soil.

FACTORS	EXAMPLES	
Abiotic	Air	Light
	Water	Soil
	Temperature	

FACTORS	EXAMPLES		
Biotic	Bacteria		
	Protists		
	Fungi		
	Plants		
	Animals		

CLIMATE

CLIMATE is the combination of weather conditions that an environment experiences. This includes temperature, air pressure, rain, and the presence of clouds and wind. Different areas on Earth have different climates. For example, the equator is hotter than the North and South Poles because it is closer to the sun.

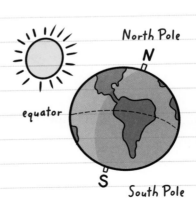

North Pole

N

equator

S

South Pole

Climate plays a role in the growth of biotic factors and is one of the main reasons for life on Earth. Over the course of Earth's history, climate has been influenced by the **GREENHOUSE EFFECT**. In the greenhouse effect, gases such as carbon dioxide trap heat from the sun's radiation.

Normally, as the sun provides the Earth with light and heat, extra heat is released from the Earth back into space. **GREENHOUSE GASES** in the atmosphere interrupt this process by capturing the heat from the Earth and releasing it back toward the planet.

> **GREENHOUSE GAS**
> Any gas that contributes to trapping heat within the Earth's atmosphere.

Carbon dioxide is a greenhouse gas. As humans have increased their use of carbon dioxide–producing fuels, more and more carbon dioxide has been released into the atmosphere, trapping more and more heat. Because temperature impacts other abiotic factors, increased temperature can have negative consequences, like wildfires, floods, tornadoes, and hurricanes.

LEVELS OF ORGANIZATION IN AN ECOSYSTEM

Ecosystems can be broken down into levels from the smallest to the largest: organism, population, community, ecosystem, biome, and biosphere.

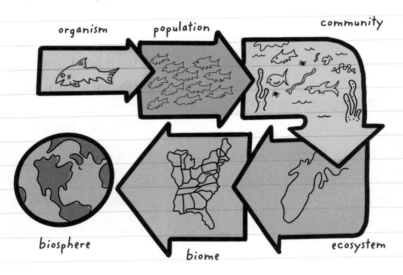

The Biosphere

Ecologists call the collection of all living things on Earth the **BIOSPHERE**.

The types of life in the biosphere and their environments are very closely connected. Populations either compete with, prey on, or help one another. Those that help one another often do so in symbiotic relationships, where two or more organisms act in ways that benefit all organisms involved. However, if the environment or climate can't support normally symbiotic organisms, they will compete with one another

sym = together; bio = life; symbiosis is the interaction of two different life-forms

for resources, sometimes even preying on one another to increase their chances of survival.

Biome

Ecologists divide the biosphere based on climates and the life within them to make it easier to study organisms in their environments. These divisions are called **BIOMES**. Biomes have similar ecosystems, climates, vegetation, and wildlife.

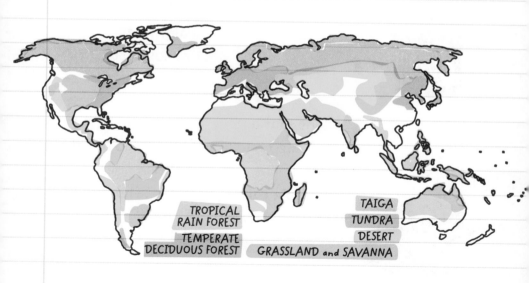

TROPICAL RAIN FOREST

TEMPERATE DECIDUOUS FOREST

GRASSLAND and SAVANNA

TAIGA

TUNDRA

DESERT

TYPES OF BIOMES

BIOME	DESCRIPTION	ORGANISMS
Temperate Forest	Forests where there are four distinct seasons.	Organisms that can migrate from or adapt in response to the changing seasons. Shrubs, Trees, Birds, Bears, Foxes
Tropical Rain Forest	Forests where rain falls all throughout the year.	Organisms that need high moisture and warm temperatures. Palm Trees, Orchids, Frogs, Crabs
Grassland	Plains that are dominated by grasses. There is very little rain, which can cause fires.	Plants that grow and spread quickly that don't need water often. Grasses, Grazing animals, predators. Bison, Badgers, Coyotes

BIOME	DESCRIPTION	ORGANISMS
Taiga	Frigid forest lands that have a cold and a warm season.	Plants that can stay strong underneath snow and ice and retain water. Evergreen trees, Animals with thick fur. Bears, Moose, Bobcats
Tundra	Harsh, cold plains with frozen soils.	Plants that have short roots. Mosses, Shrubs Animals that migrate or hibernate during colder months. Polar Bears, Caribou, Ground Squirrels
Desert	Two main seasons: a hot and dry season and a harsh cold season.	Organisms that can retain water. Cacti, Camels

BIOME	DESCRIPTION	ORGANISMS
Aquatic	The largest biome on Earth. Salty seas and fresh water.	Organisms that can live in water. Algae, Fish, Amphibians, Crustaceans, Marine mammals

(WHEE!)

Nutrient Cycles

All biomes sustain themselves by recycling the nutrients that they receive. These **NUTRIENT CYCLES** are important for sustaining the world's climate.

Water Cycle

Water evaporates from lakes, rivers, and oceans and transpires from plants.

is released

- Water vapor condenses into clouds.

- Rain falls from clouds, feeding the lakes, rivers, oceans, and plants.

Oxygen Cycle

- Plants create oxygen by using photosynthesis.

- Animals and plants breathe and use that oxygen to create glucose (releasing CO_2 as a byproduct).

Carbon Cycle

- Burning fossil fuels, such as gas and coal, and exhaling animals send carbon dioxide into the atmosphere.

- Plants absorb carbon dioxide to use for photosynthesis.

- Animals eat the plants, along with the carbon dioxide stored in the plants.

- Plants and animals die, releasing carbon dioxide into the atmosphere; some plants and animals become fossil fuels over millions of years.

ECOLOGICAL PYRAMID

Many nutrient cycles rely on the production of energy by organisms within their ecosystem. Water, oxygen, and carbon are all important cycles because they are key nutrients for the production of any organism's energy.

When ecologists separate organisms based on their methods of energy production, they find that those organisms that produce energy using abiotic factors are more numerous than those that produce energy by eating other organisms. This separation is called a **FOOD CHAIN**.

Food chains are represented like this:

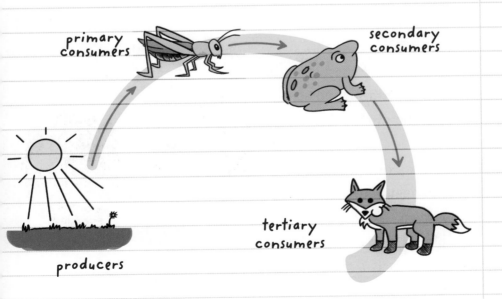

PRODUCERS

- Those that create energy using abiotic factors such as light and carbon dioxide in the Earth's atmosphere.

- There are more producers than any other type of organism in the ecological pyramid.

YUM!

PRIMARY CONSUMERS

Those that gain their energy by eating producers.

YUM!

SECONDARY CONSUMERS

Those consumers that gain their energy by eating primary consumers.

TERTIARY CONSUMERS

Tertiary consumers, also known as APEX PREDATORS, are those that eat the secondary consumers.

Tertiary consumers are at the top of the food chain and have no predators that eat them. Sometimes apex predators can fight and kill one another over prey.

CHECK YOUR KNOWLEDGE

1. What is the community of living organisms and their environment called?

2. What two factors make up any ecosystem?

3. What is a climate?

4. What effect has greatly influenced Earth's climate over the planet's history?

5. How do greenhouse gases cause the greenhouse effect?

6. The collection of all organisms on Earth is the _____.

7. What helps animals that live in taiga biomes survive?

8. What sustains the world's climate?

9. What are producers?

10. Where do apex predators lie in the food chain?

CHECK YOUR ANSWERS

1. An ecosystem

2. Abiotic and biotic factors

3. A climate is the total weather conditions that any environment experiences.

4. The greenhouse effect

5. Greenhouse gases block excess heat from being released into space. The gases reflect the excess heat back onto the planet.

6. Biosphere

7. Thick fur

8. The recycling of nutrients/nutrient cycles

9. Producers are organisms that create their energy using the light and carbon dioxide in the Earth's atmosphere.

10. Apex predators are at the top of the food chain.

Chapter 50

POPULATIONS

LIMITING FACTORS

LIMITING FACTORS are resources within an environment that can slow or stop its population growth. The availability of nutrients is one of the most important limiting factors.

> **LIMITING FACTOR**
> A condition within an environment that prevents population growth.

For example, if the amount of available nutrients in an ecosystem is high, then the population will grow until the nutrients are used up. If nutrients are low, then the population will begin to die out until the number of living organisms matches the amount of available nutrients. This kind of population pattern can be modeled by ecologists using a LOGISTIC GROWTH model.

This logistic growth model shows that the population size increases over time until the population reaches a **CARRYING CAPACITY**, the number of organisms that an environment can support.

The carrying capacity depends on the limiting factor. For example, if there was an infinite amount of nutrients, there would be no carrying capacity for the limiting factor of nutrition. In this case, the logistic growth model turns into an **EXPONENTIAL GROWTH** model, where population grows infinitely.

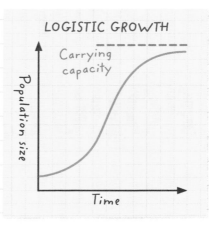

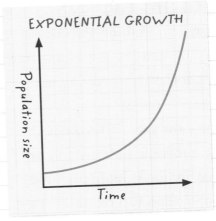

There are several limiting factors that can impact an ecosystem:

COMPETITION: All species within an ecosystem need space and food. Organisms will compete for these two things, limiting the amount that each gets.

PREDATION: Predators threaten the populations of prey, keeping their numbers low.

DISEASE: Diseases can spread along entire ecosystems and cause the deaths of many species.

NATURAL DISASTERS: Fires, earthquakes, hurricanes, and floods all disturb the homes of various animals, making the ecosystem uninhabitable, except to those that can survive.

ABNORMAL WEATHER: Animals rely on their ability to adapt to survive. Weather that is unpredictable and changes too quickly can prevent animals from adapting, threatening their lives.

The effects of the changes in climate can cause abnormal weather patterns, such as global warming, where the temperature of the Earth slowly increases each year.

HUMAN ACTION: Humans make active decisions that can threaten the lives of species and their ecosystems. Examples include burning fossil fuels, cutting down forests, and hunting animals.

THE MEGHALAYAN

The **MEGHALAYAN** is the current geological age. It is the age in which humanity has a dominant influence on the climate and environment. It was marked by the beginning of a 200-year drought that caused the disruption of many civilizations, including those in Egypt, Greece, and Mesopotamia.

CIVILIZATIONS are units of organization for human social and cultural development. Before humans settled, our species moved from place to place in search of food.

Before civilizations, food could either be hunted or gathered. Humans went wherever animals migrated to or wherever fruits, nuts, and vegetables grew. However, with the growth of **AGRICULTURE**, humans were able to settle and their populations were able to grow.

> **AGRICULTURE**
> The process of producing food and cultivating animals.

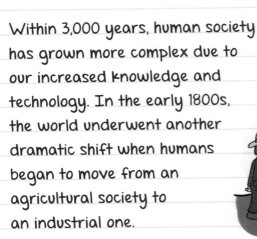

Within 3,000 years, human society has grown more complex due to our increased knowledge and technology. In the early 1800s, the world underwent another dramatic shift when humans began to move from an agricultural society to an industrial one.

Factories were created to organize workers so that they could create products that would be sold. This caused society to transition from one where people produced their own goods and traded them for money to one where people received money to produce goods. Because of this change, land that was dedicated to agriculture began to be taken up by factories. This period is known as the INDUSTRIAL REVOLUTION.

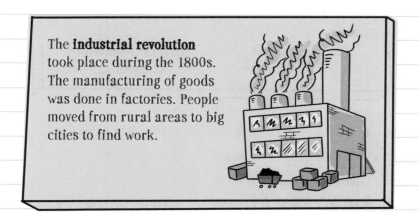

The **industrial revolution** took place during the 1800s. The manufacturing of goods was done in factories. People moved from rural areas to big cities to find work.

Conditions during the industrial revolution were poor. Many of the workers in the factories were children, who were often injured because of the dangerous machines they had to work with. Also, because factories took up a lot of land, people began to live in more densely populated cities, making it easy for diseases to be transferred from person to person. In the late 1800s, countries began to develop laws and standards for sanitation, prevention of child labor, and protection of the environment.

THE FUTURE OF HUMANITY

Biodiversity

Like any organism, humans rely on their ecosystem to maintain themselves. Our civilizations thrive on resources from our environment. So, when resources run out, civilizations can face catastrophe.

> Climate change, which causes temperature effects like global warming, brings an increase in droughts, floods, wildfires, and blizzards. These natural disasters can destroy the resources that humans use.

Because ecosystems include multiple species, a lack of resources can impact the livelihoods of plants and animals as well. This results in a decrease in population, which affects **BIODIVERSITY**—the variety of species in an ecosystem. Biodiversity is necessary for organisms to thrive in an ecosystem. When one set of organisms begins to die out, all of them face consequences.

Natural Resources

Natural resources that can be recycled or replaced by nature quickly (within 100 years or so) are called **RENEWABLE RESOURCES**. Renewable resources include sunlight, wind, and water, but also trees and other oxygen-producing plants, which can be used for many things and replanted.

504

NONRENEWABLE RESOURCES

can take up to millions of years to replace. Nonrenewable resources come in the form of fossil fuels such as coal and natural gas, minerals, and metal. To maintain biodiversity, resources must be used efficiently.

Most nonrenewable resources reside in Earth's mantle, formed over millions and millions of years.

Renewable Resources–	Nonrenewable Resources–
sunlight	metals, minerals (e.g.,
trees	diamonds), and fossil
water	fuels (e.g., coal, crude oil,
wind	natural gas)

Humans have used nonrenewable resources to build cities and countries. However, there is a limited supply of these resources. Eventually, these resources will no longer be available and humanity will have to find alternate resources that are more **SUSTAINABLE**, or renewable.

Improving Biodiversity

When humans act in ways that change the **HABITAT**, or the home, of other organisms, it can endanger biodiversity. **DEFORESTATION** (the removal of forests), pollution, and climate change are all human-caused threats to biodiversity. Even though humans can negatively impact biodiversity, they can also improve it.

WAYS TO IMPROVE BIODIVERSITY

METHOD	DESCRIPTION
Conservation of Species	As species begin to die out due to changes in their environment, humans can take care of them and establish regulations that will help their populations recover.
Transition from Nonrenewable to Renewable Resources	In discontinuing the use of nonrenewable resources, humans can reduce the destruction of the environment.
Creation of National Parks and Reserved Land	National parks ensure that animals live in their ecosystems naturally with minimal human interference.
Reduce, Reuse, Recycle	Reduction and reuse of nonrenewable resources and recycling renewable resources ensure that resources are not wasted.
Science Communication	Ecologists must communicate their research findings to the public so that they can understand how their actions impact the environment.

CHECK YOUR KNOWLEDGE

1. Why can only a certain number of organisms in a species exist in any ecosystem?

2. Explain the concept of carrying capacity.

3. How do natural disasters limit a species?

4. What is the Meghalayan age?

5. What did humans do to get food before they settled in agricultural societies?

6. What happened when humans shifted from agriculture to industry?

7. What is biodiversity?

8. What are renewable resources?

9. What are examples of human activities that threaten biodiversity?

10. How does the conservation of species help populations?

ANSWERS

CHECK YOUR ANSWERS

1. Limiting factors prevent the population of a species from increasing above a certain point.

2. The number of organisms an environment can support, determined by the limiting factor

3. Natural disasters destroy ecosystems, making them less habitable.

4. The Meghalayan age is our current geological age, where humans influence the climate and environment.

5. Humans hunted or gathered for food.

6. Land that was dedicated to agriculture was replaced by factories; people moved to cities to find work.

7. Biodiversity is the variety of species in an ecosystem.

8. Natural resources that can be recycled or replaced by nature quickly

9. Deforestation, pollution, and climate change

10. Conservation helps prevent populations from dying out.

☆INDEX☆

hearts, 299, 317, 371–372, 375–376
helical structure, 155
helicase, 433, 437
helper T cells, 395, 397
hemoglobin, 375–376
hemophilia, 442
herbivorous invertebrates, 279
herbivorous reptiles, 312–313
heredity, 414
hermaphrodites, 276
heterotrophic bacteria, 148–149
heterotrophs, 22, 99, 268
heterozygous genotype, 415, 418
hinge joints, 349
histamines, 391
histones, 431–432
holdfasts, 195
homeostasis, 25, 271, 328–330
Hominidae (great apes), 37–38
hominids, 465
Homo (genus), 37–39
Homo erectus, 38
Homo habilis, 38
Homo sapiens, 38–39, 469, 478
Homo sapiens sapiens, 465
homologous chromosomes, 133–134, 136–137
homologous structures, 453, 454
homozygous genotype, 415, 418
hookworms, 279–280
hormones, 362–364, 405, 408
hornworts, 237
horsetails, 237
hosts, 153–154
Human Genome Project, 432
humanity, future of, 504–506
humans
    actions of, 501
    body systems of, 326–330
    development of, 408–409
    water and, 65–66
humoral immune response, 394–396
hydrocarbon, 70
hydrocarbon chains, 70
hydrogen bonding, 62–64, 429
hydrogen ions, 113–114

hyphae, 210–211
hypodermis, 337
hypothalamus, 358, 361, 362, 364
hypotheses, 13

I
ice ages, 478
Ichthyostegalia, 307
immune response, 390
immune system, 170–171, 328, 389–398
immunological memory, 394
in vitro fertilization, 403
independent variables, 13
industrial revolution, 503
infancy, 408
infection, 155
influenza, 172
inner membrane, 110, 113
insects
    classification of, 287
    fungi and, 219–220, 224
    overview of, 289–290
    plants and, 244
insulin, 363
integumentary system, 327, 334–338
intermembrane, 110, 113
internal environments, 271
interphase, 121, 126, 128, 135
intersex, 409
inversion of chromosomes, 441
invertebrates, 34, 226, 275–282, 475
involuntary muscles, 343, 361
ions, 113–114
isotopes, 51

J
jawless fish, 35, 298, 305
joints, 348–349
Jurassic period, 472, 476

K
keratin, 313, 315, 335, 337–338
key viral proteins, 156
kidneys, 386
killer cells, 397

kingdoms, 29–31, 32–33
Krebs, Hans, 112
Krebs cycle, 112–115

L
lactic acid, 111, 116
lagging strand, 433–436
Lagomorpha, 321
Lamarck, Jean-Baptiste de Monet de, 460
lancelets, 296
large intestines, 381, 384–385
larva stage, 290
laryngopharynx, 369
larynx, 368–369
leading strand, 433–436
leaf-cutting ants, 224
leaves, 233–234
leeches, 280
Leeuwenhoek, Antonie van, 143
leukocytes, 391, 396
life
    characteristics of, 19–26
    history of, 469–479
life cycle, 2, 3
life functions, 20–26
ligaments, 350
ligands, 156
limiting factors, 499–501
Linnaeus, Carolus, 40, 458
lipids, 71–72
liquids, 57–58
liver, 384
liverworts, 237
locomotion, 271
locus, 133–134
logistic growth model, 499–500
Lucy (hominid), 465
lumbar vertebrae, 359
lungs, 367–368, 370–371
lycopene, 235
lymph, 393
lymph nodes, 393–394
lymphatic system, 328, 393
lymphocytes, 391, 394
lysosomes, 89

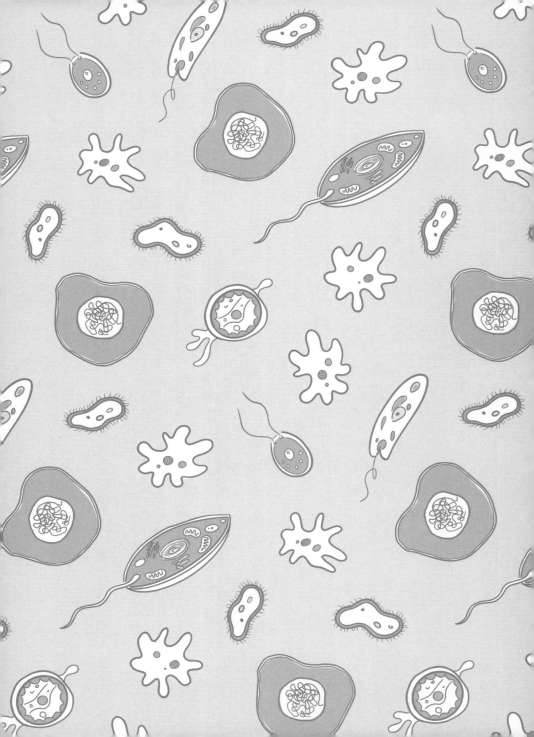